Modern France

Modern France

Angelo Codevilla

Open Court • La Salle, Illinois

Copyright © 1974 by Open Court Publishers

All rights reserved. Printed in the United States of America. No part of
this publication may be reproduced, stored in a retrieval system, or
transmitted, in any form or by any means, electronic, mechanical, pho-
tocopying, recording, or otherwise, without the prior written permis-
sion of the publisher, the Open Court Publishing Company, Box 599,
La Salle, Illinois 61301.

Library of Congress Cataloging in Publication Data
Codevilla, Angelo, 1943-
    Modern France.

    Bibliography: p.
    1. France.   I. Title.
DC412. C565   321. 8'042'0944   74-56
ISBN 0-87548-150-7

Contents

Modern France

Preface

How do institutions interact with society to form democratic France? What relationship exists between society, state and government? How do Frenchmen actually take part in the political life of their country? By what are they moved to do so? By what ties does French democracy bind its children to itself? What political forces characterize French democracy and what do they represent? What does the French democratic polity do with its energy, and what are the most likely prospects for its future tasks? How can the growing power of the state be reconciled with the apparently growing desires of particular individuals? How can the state be strong and weak at the same time? How can a democratic people be called politicized and depoliticized at the same time? These are some of the questions I deal with on these pages. They cover areas beyond the obviously political.

I attempt to answer these questions by trying to show what it is like to live political life in France on the several levels where it takes place. The purpose of my answers is to clarify the democratic origins of the paradoxes mentioned above.

I will explore institutions, parties, ideas, arrangements, for modern politics consists of these in large part; but I try to do so insofar as I am able from the point of view of the citizen of French democracy or, as the modern expression would have it, from the consumer's viewpoint. I am interested in how public life actually takes place on each level and in what it is all about.

Finally, although I cite data from public opinion polls, my understanding of the attitudes characteristic of French democracy hereafter set forth derives far more heavily from my own experience in France. The events, the pseudo-events, the proposals, the plans, the deals, the ideals which form such a large part of national politics can be followed nearly as well from afar, but one must mingle with the mass of "consumers" to understand the values placed on the several items in the political marketplace. Based for seven months in a small rural village on the rim of a valley overlooking the city of Strasbourg, I studied French democracy, looked at politics on the national and local levels, while at the same time taking the sociopolitical pulse of my neighbors in city, village and country. I have no way of knowing how representative the people with whom I came into contact were; my impression is that I was able to gather the attitudes of persons reasonably typical of their fellows. In fact, my experiences have coincided quite well with published polls.

My purpose, however, was not primarily to report public opinion but to investigate the relations between the character of French political life today and the democratic logos which animates it.

Angelo Codevilla
January, 1974

Chapter 1
The Subject

Democracy is but the political manifestation of modernity.[1] There are few peoples on the face of the earth today not governed by men who, usually quite sincerely, are attempting to conduct political lives according to their understanding of democracy. These, of course, differ. The differences between political life in, say, India, Soviet Russia, Argentina, England and the United States, are due to disparities in the locally prevailing notion of democracy as well as to characteristics of land and people peculiar to each country. Whether in China, in France or in America, discussion of democracy today overflows the bounds of the strictly political, and bears directly on the quality of life in the modern world, for differing qualities of life are inherent in the different democratic phenomena.

Despite their differences, democratic countries appear to be faced with similar difficult tasks, perplexing choices, arising directly from the logic of the idea to which they are committed. What is the logic of democracy, and in what manner should we, living in the world's oldest democracy, take it into account as we face the choices which its development puts before us?

The very disparate nature of the democratic phenomenon's manifestations suggests that the answer to these questions might most profitably be sought in examination of another nation at least as committed as ours to a democratic way of life, and, if possible, having even more fully realized it.

France is such a country. Great Britain and the Scandinavian countries are also old democracies which are commonly said to have surpassed the United States in wholehearted devotion to the principles of social equality, individual liberty, social security, etc. But, unlike the United States and France, these nations are monarchies. To be sure, their kings do not govern, but they personify the existence of the state, over, above, and independently of democratic principles. For purposes of comparison, our study must deal with another unmixed democracy. Our concern then, is modern democracy, and our subject is France.

Problems

Democracy in France, as for that matter in the United States and elsewhere, has in recent years been faced with difficulties apparently related to paradoxes which lie close to the mainsprings of democracy itself.

Democracy is that form of government which requires the most from its citizens for, according to classic democratic theory, they must not only obey laws but also decide which ones should be made, not only make sacrifices but also convince themselves it is just and necessary to make them. Democracies cannot as easily as other polities live with political indifference, much less dissent, yet such dissent, accompanied or not by indifference, has always been noted as a corollary of democracy. Thus, when the prospect of democracy arose in Europe in the early nineteenth century, the question of whether it carried the congenital disease of social dissolution was of the greatest interest. The most prominent Frenchman of the time to speak authoritatively on the question, Alexis de Tocqueville, showed by his description of American democratic republicanism that the disease need not run its course. Properly designed laws and carefully nurtured cultural patterns did much to foster the mutual cooperation, the moral scruples, in short the conditions which made the United States of America into a showplace of civic virtue the likes of which had not been seen since the passing of antiquity.

Democratic statesmen, especially in France, have always paid attention to the level of popular participation as a gauge of the system's health. Democrats fought the fiercest political battles of the nineteenth century to remove all political barriers to the right of suffrage, and to place the public power under control of the people's elected representatives, while the battles of the first half of the twentieth century were fought to level the social and economic obstacles to equal participation in democratic society. Today in France, as in the rest of the Western world, the reigning dogma of popular sovereignty in which all citizens equally share is buttressed by laws under which no citizen legally entitled to the vote may be prevented from using it; by government and opposition leaders urging that everyone turn out for every election; and, especially in France, by welfare-state measures whose rationale is—or used to be—that no one can freely exercise his portion of sovereignty if he has to worry about economic survival. Over and above welfare measures, the West is more prosperous than it has ever been. Yet despite most favorable conditions for political participation, it has now become a commonplace in France as in America that people are losing interest in public affairs, that there is widespread disaffection, widespread feeling that government is somebody else's business.

Although democracy proceeds from the doctrine of natural rights according to which government exists only to better protect each individual's private sphere, democratic states have seen the spectacular growth of state power. The government of France, more than some other democratic governments, is served by a very large administrative apparatus and possesses the legal authority to use it for whatever purpose the people's representatives think proper. Yet alongside the image of a state that controls a large portion of the national income, employs directly or indirectly over a third of the active population, and commands administrators charged with the daily conduct of business, agriculture, local government, medical care, and so on; along with the image of the powerful modern state, we must place another. Although they have had these vast powers for almost a century, French democratic politicians have not, it appears, been able to achieve what they want. Reform follows reform in a process without a clearly evident end, organized pressure groups from every sector of society are forces to be reckoned with daily and, most of all, political leaders tread very carefully when they deal with matters which might possibly involve requesting sacrifices from the people, for fear of being disavowed. Thus, defense is the least discussed subject in France, and while as recently as the nineteen fifties the ways and means of assuring France an adequate supply of energy was a prime topic of political discourse, today when its supply of fuel oil is more directly threatened than ever, politicians frankly admit to being afraid to discuss the matter in public. Alongside the image of the state's omnipotence, we must then lay that of a state weak, uncertain of its support, and radically eager to please.

The paradox of simultaneous power and powerlessness appears to affect not only the governments, but the citizens of democracies as well. On the one hand, we see throughout the Western world what can only be called a reduction of authoritative guidance of moral life, a reduction in what might be called the state's activities *"in loco parentis."* Censorship practices on political as well as pornographic materials, until recently quite common, have almost ceased. In France as well as in America, demonstrations against governments even in times of war are treated with a degree of tolerance which amazes those who lived before World War II. The French bureaucracy is today by all accounts far less haughty towards the people it administers than ever before, especially the representatives of interest groups; and in the private sector superiors treat subordinates with courtesy which would have shamed both a generation ago. In the realm of high politics, the French have forced the retirement from politics of the most powerful of their statesmen in this century, Charles de Gaulle. Yet not only in those hothouses of revolutionary behavior that are French universities does one hear complaints that people are powerless, have lost all independence *vis-à-vis* a "system" which is now in the process of reducing everyone to subhuman status. Not only does one hear nostalgia from those groups who until the nineteen fifties deprecated the old and eagerly awaited the new, but throughout society, one hears the same refrain about powerlessness over one's own life, both the quality and the quantity of which are being determined elsewhere. The people, all equally powerful sovereigns in theory, and perhaps better treated by the administrative hierarchy than ever before in modern times, feel managed.

1968

These paradoxes, as well as the very practical consequences to which they can give rise, were illustrated by the events of May, 1968. At that time what began as the revolt of a few hundred revolutionary-minded students in Paris turned into a crisis which within about two weeks convinced most of political France—which it caught by surprise—that at least the Fifth Republic and possibly much more of French society would be swept away.

What caused it? The most common explanations, that French society was reacting to a sort of political drought imposed on it by the authoritarian Fifth Republic, and that the events were the culmination of a long-building resentment of leaders and economic conditions, simply will not stand up to even the most cursory analysis. In fact, the years since 1965 had seen one presidential and one legislative election, and as much political activity as France had seen in any comparable three year period.[2] The economy was performing well, if not spectacularly, and this was widely realized. The prestige of government leaders was high and rising.[3] In any case, nothing was happening in France of the sort that would lead one to believe society was about to be shaken to its foundations, and, in fact, no one did believe it, including those whose business it is to know: the professional revolutionaries of the Communist Party who were taken by surprise along with everyone else.

What happened? By Friday, May 3, 1968, a group of about two hundred self-styled revolutionary students had sufficiently intimidated the chief of the Faculty of Letters at the Nanterre branch of the university[4] that he ordered a halt to classes. That day, the leaders called for a rally in the courtyard of the Sorbonne in downtown Paris. The confrontation with the police there set off a chain of riots, each involving a greater number of young people, which culminated Friday night the 17th with the building of barricades in the Latin Quarter and some vigorous repression on the part of the police. What were the student leaders fighting for? They made it very clear that they were out to do what they could against present-day society in general. Why did other students follow them? There are many reasons: unhappiness with what the university had to offer, disillusionment with career openings, the desire perhaps to make exams a bit easier, no doubt a general ideological predisposition to go along with anything anti-present-day society, and certainly the opportunity to do something at once very exciting and basically quite safe. But this sort of thing happened at many universities around the world without further consequences.

By Saturday, May 11, the university crisis had become a social crisis. The nation's two largest labor confederations, the Communist CGT and the Socialist CFDT called a general strike for Monday the 13th, while the Prime Minister, M. Pompidou, went on television to ask for calm and to offer the reopening of the university, amnesty, and so on. The next two weeks saw the social crisis develop: the nation's most prestigious aircraft factory, *Sud-Aviation,* and its largest automobile plant, *Renault,* were among the many that were occupied by striking workers who in so doing defied their own labor unions. These in the meanwhile, together with the several employers' councils and the government, meeting in what has since been called a "social summit," negotiated national across-the-board wage increases. On May 27 these contracts, later called the Grenelle agreements, were rejected by the workers occupying major plants. The affair had become very serious. But why? Although the workers' movement was led by young laborers, the curious phenomenon occurred throughout France of people at various levels in various social hierarchies telling the person at the next higher level that the time had come to pay back all the slights they had ever received. Slogans painted on placards and factory walls said things like "We want to run our own lives" and "Enough of patrons." The strikes were not, to say the least, primarily in support of the rioting students, or even for economic purposes. Those who took the revolutionary side in May, 1968, did so, they say, because they felt others, be these owners, managers, or in the case of nationalized industries, the state, had too much power and they too little. The students' uproar provided the opening by putting the government in a difficult position. The opportunity was there to be exploited, and economic demands were among the logical ones to make. For those not involved, they were even more important: a poll taken at the time of the rejection of the Grenelle agreements showed that a majority of Parisians, most of whom were not involved in the strikes, had high hopes of reaping some benefits from them, e.g., higher salaries, a lowering of the retirement age, improved social security provisions; in short, *progress.*[5] The very same people also feared the crisis would bring anarchy and economic chaos.

The crisis in fact had long since become political. The government had been involved from the very first, and the Prime Minister had laid its prestige on the line when he attempted to stop the affair with concessions. On May 24 the President of the Republic threw in the latter's prestige by announcing a referendum on participation to take place on June 16. By so doing he hoped to shift the focus of the crisis from the street to his referendum proposals. Neither he nor the government wanted to risk a fight with the Communist Party's apparatus, which by now had mounted the runaway horse and was rather enjoying the bumpy ride. The opposition parties, as surprised by events as the government, had also acted to take advantage of the opening, each with its particular concerns and fears. The Communists had to gain control of a movement which had started without them, but could not go so far as to provoke the entry of the army into the crisis. The socialist Left was all for aggravating the crisis to the utmost, but feared a coalition government with the Communists under the circumstances. Nevertheless, M. Mitterand declared that the public powers had been vacated, and M. Mendès-France said that he was ready to take control of a united leftist government. By May 29 General de Gaulle, besieged by members of his own party begging him to resign, and with evidence that France, but chiefly Paris, was slipping into a sort of holiday from the law, decided to change tactics. Before he did so he felt obliged to ask the prestigious General Jacques Massu and other commanders of elite troops based in Germany—quite outside the chain of command—for their support. On May 30 he dissolved the National Assembly and scheduled new elections, thus forcing the leftist parties to decide immediately whether to contest his power on the electoral plane, which would require them to help re-establish order, or to try their hand at civil war. They chose the former, and the crisis of May, 1968, ended faster than it began. Its immediate legacy was the unprecedented victory of the Gaullist party at the polls, and an instantaneous rise in the rate of inflation to "cover" the wage increases and social benefits accorded to virtually every employee in France.

Whether or not France was really close to social disintegration, it thought it was. Why? May, 1968, did not, unlike May, 1940, see ten Panzer divisions spearheading the attack, but rather less than two thousand ill-disciplined youths. They were not covered by Goering's Luftwaffe, but by the words of politicians who are not themselves the subject of enthusiasm. The openings were not exploited by fifty determined infantry divisions, but by people, most of whom thought of their discontent in the measure that opportunities for safely showing it appeared. It was not a movement directed at any positive goals nor even against any specific grievances. Its character, and there lies its significance and its danger, was that of a chain reaction: each group which successively entered the crisis did so because it then seemed that its quarry, everyone's quarry, the state, had been laid low enough for it to act. When society's head faltered, its members turned against it. Disarticulation made it possible, and further disarticulation was the result. Enough of a structure remained, however, so that when the various groups' leaders stopped propelling the movement, suddenly everything seemed to snap back into place. But 1968 is not forgotten.

The events of May, 1968, in France were watched around the world by men interested in democracy and eager to draw lessons for their own country. Certainly few direct lessons can be drawn, for so much of what happened in France resulted from institutions, persons, habits peculiar to that country. For example, in the United States, despite the centralization of power in the federal government during the last forty years, wages cannot be raised or retirements set by federal fiat, pressure groups have less to hope for from the bureaucracy, and no single nerve center exists, the capture of which might give one power over the nation. Nevertheless, the French experiences of 1968 and the political culture which made them possible are of great interest to students of democracy the world over.

French Politics Today

Anyone out to study democracy in this, the country whose name is as synonymous with it in the modern world as that of Greece was in the ancient, must necessarily be struck by the difficulty of finding his subject. The National Assembly is there, as it has been except for relatively brief periods since 1789,[6] and it is elected by universal suffrage, to the accompaniment of discordant and usually lively cries of political parties whose very names—socialist, radical, centrist, etc.—represent for students of politics the world over the letters of which the language of democratic politics is made up. At first glance, then, the subject is evident: the French people elect their parliament on whose approval a government depends, which in turn directs a highly centralized administrative bureaucracy. The advent of the Fifth Republic changed this somewhat, for now every discussion of French politics must include an analysis of the President of the Republic's relation to the Prime Minister, the government, the National Assembly, and the electorate. Excellent books such as Dorothy Pickles' *The Fifth French Republic*,[7] Macridis and Brown's *The De Gaulle Republic*[8] and M. Duverger's *Cinquième Republique*[9] generally follow a line of analysis which parallels that of the Fifth Republic's constitution. However great the value of such studies from the viewpoint of public law, the student of democracy is soon on his guard against the temptation of following in their footsteps: Maurras' now famous distinction between *pays réel and pays légal* (the real living France with its national, territorial, cultural and economic diversity vs. the France of governments and politics, the France run by uniform rules from Paris), now nearly a century old, is a warning as relevant today is it was at a time when the politicans of the young Third Republic were imposing their ways on a France where monarchial preferences and local particularisms still largely dominated. De Tocqueville in his well-known *L'Ancien Régime et la Révolution* also draws an unforgettable distinction between political life in the late Bourbon monarchy and life in 18th century France. Today, a whole host of popular opinions from the villages and cities of France constantly warn one not to take politics at face value—a warning not wholly lost on Anglo-Saxon writers for whom it is commonplace to describe the French as radically individualistic and practically ungovernable,[10] and to point to the 180 degree switches in public opinion which, for example, enthroned and dethroned Napoleon III, Pétain, and, less violently, de Gaulle. On the other hand, France, as everyone knows, is the home of rational centralized administration *par excellence,* where everything and everyone from Lille to Marseilles, from Bordeaux to Strasbourg, proceeds in an orderly official manner approved from Paris. Furthermore, just as frequent as the popular warning that politics is nothing that good *sérieux*[11] people would have anything to do with is another warning, that everything in the country is run by politics and politicians: "why, you know, they even control the price of bread." In fact, in America, France is often described as a socialist country. What is one to make of this? Surely it cannot simultaneously be true that politics, the democratic machinery and the bureaucratic institutions are ubiquitous and largely irrelevant. Surely not all those in authority are taken lightly. Then are these contrasting warnings to be thrown away? And how are we to consider the role of formal politics in French democracy?

Since popular opinion is the stuff of which politics, especially democratic politics, is made, it cannot be dismissed, but rather must be considered indicative of important truths to be discovered by careful analysis. What then are the most basic reactions of Frenchmen to the political community in which they live from which we can gain insight into its real structure? It appears to us that the most basic is some version of the old proverb that Frenchmen are divided into two groups: those who sit behind desks and those who must line up in front of them. Indeed in modern France, life outside the family does seem to lead from one *guichet* to another: the number of official agencies of the state (*l'Etat*) is great but non-official agencies from laundries to banks, it seems, try very hard to carry on in an officious manner. Authority, it appears, is both very important to Frenchmen and resented by them. We are not of course speaking of two classes of people, for the same young salesgirl in the pharmacy who takes such note of the slights to her dignity suffered at the bank where she asked for an auto loan and at the *préfecture* where she had to register her car will more than likely display a haughty attitude to a customer unaware of some requirement for purchasing medicine. Speculation as to the motives behind this mutual haughtiness-com-bined-with-sullen-obedience, whether it has anything to do with affirmation of threatened personal dignity, is beyond our scope; it suffices for us to note that these attitudes are the first *datum* which greets the student of French politics. This ambi-valent attitude toward authority, though not an exclusively political phenomenon, finds its most evident manifestation in the realm of politics. For if there can be no mistaking how the French regard authority, there is even less room for doubt-ing what they believe the source of all authority in society to be: *L'Etat*, the state.

"The State" in French usage is something quite distinct from Parliament, the government, the politicians and politics. It is from it that local officials—even elected ones—are thought to derive their powers, even as do the countless civil servants with whom one must deal. It is almost synonymous with the administration, but the whole is greater than its parts. The state delivers the mail, installs telephones, is thought to assure pensions. Furthermore, people in all sorts of authority, whether they be landlords who collect rent, physicians, or employers, are thought secure in their place because of, and therefore to derive their authority from, the state. It is also often referred to as *Le Pouvoir* (The Power). And the armed forces, are they at its service too? Yes, the answer normally goes, but reluc-tantly, for unlike the gendarmes, the armed forces and those who are called to serve "under the flags," belong to something far more glorious if less substantial: *La Patrie.* The state is something very much *sérieux* which one obeys because it is very much the thing to do, even if it entails sacrifices, but *La Patrie,* well, *that* one cheers and weeps and sings for.

The government[12] is also sometimes called *Le Pouvoir,* but is clearly seen as something different from the state. Govern-ments come and fall less often than before, it's true, but the state has not fallen in living memory. While the government has much to do with the power of the state, and therefore is believed to be something pretty *sérieux,* it also partakes of the realm of politics which hardly has any of that precious quality.

The Parliament is not "of the state." Even when far more powerful than under the Fifth Republic, it was seldom capable of concerted long-term action. It is composed of a Senate, where sit representatives of local governments, and a National Assembly composed of *députés* elected by universal suffrage. Both senators and deputies are generally seen by those who elect them as their own *chargés d'affaires* at the seat of power, whose job is to try to affect the acts of the state so that they will cause as little harm as possible to the interests of the constituency, as well as to act as advocates for special claims. Members of Parliament don't have to be trusted: they can be voted out of office, whereas the government, to say nothing of the state, cannot be so controlled.

Everything else in the public realm: political parties and personalities, election campaigns, policies and reforms, all come under the heading of politics, and to that, unless one is directly concerned, the typical attitude is one of *méfiance* (distrust). There are only two exceptions: foreign policy, which history has painfully shown to be *trés sérieuse,* having provided almost every Frenchman with grief, and not a few with occasion for generous feelings toward *La Patrie,* is paid attention to now and again; and local government which, involving personal acquaintances as well as one's own pocketbook, and in which one's vote obviously makes a difference, cannot be ignored.

In a very real sense, then, but contrary to traditional democratic notions, the administration in France appears closer to the people than the men seeking their support; in fact, from close-up, the traditional democratic order appears upside down. Our analysis of French politics today then follows the lines of popular concern: first things first.

Notes to Chapter 1

[1]Democracy was not unknown prior to modern times. Plato and Aristotle, to mention only the best known writers of antiquity, discussed it extensively. Readers of Roman history are also familiar with the democratic elements of

the later Roman Republic. The democratic phenomenon was also dealt with at some length by Machiavelli, Hobbes, Locke, Montesquieu, Rousseau and the American Federalists. At the beginning of the modern era they redefined democracy in the context of the widespread assumption of ideas either little known or widely condemned in pre-modern times. Among these are the equal, radical, sovereign individuality of all human beings and the possibility of harmonizing by artful engineering beings which are by nature at war with each other. Also, modern democracy is distinguished from democracy in earlier forms because today in one way or another it has been almost universally accepted, whereas once it had been considered one of many (by no means among the most recommended) forms of government.

It might be objected that Communist governments are quite beyond the pale of democracy. We contend that the Communists' own protestations to the contrary are not entirely cynical. See below chapters 5 and 6.

[2]Jacques Chapsal. *La Vie Politique en France Depuis 1940,* 1969, Chapters 6 and 7.

[3]See the review of the French Opinion Institute (IFOP), *SONDAGES,* 1968, No. 2.

[4]There is only one state university with many campuses. See below, Chapter II. There is also a Catholic university. Compared with *The University* it has a tiny fraction of the students and less influence.

[5]*SONDAGES,* 1968, No. 2, p. 80.

[6]These are: The First and Second Empires, during which the Assembly continued to exist, but as an adjunct to the Emporor's government; the Bourbon Restoration which soon restored some popular representation, and the World War II captive Vichy government.

[7]London, 1960.

[8]Illinois, 1960.

[9]Paris, 1960.

[10]For example, Crane Brinton, *The Americans and the French,* Harvard University Press. This book can be taken as the "writ large" version of Churchill's famous remark about the difficulties of governing a people that produces 250 kinds of cheese.

[11]This word, translated as "serious," means that and much more in French: it conveys the notion of propriety, hard work, morality, stick-to-itiveness, about all the qualities one looks for in a son-in-law. It is perhaps the greatest compliment one Frenchman can pay to another—or to his government.

Unless otherwise stated all translation of non-English materials herein are the author's.

[12]In France as in the rest of Europe, "The Government" means that committee of parliament, responsible before it, composed of the heads of the great administrative departments who jointly and under the presidency of a prime minister elaborate and oversee the execution of national policies.

Chapter 2
The State

When a woman in labor checks into a hospital or clinic, she turns in the *Livret de Famille* (family booklet) given the couple at the time of marriage and her husband's social security number. The birth, paid for by the state, will be registered, and the family will begin receiving a milk allowance for the baby from the state which, before the baby is two weeks old, will send a team of nurses on an official visit to his home to check whether he is being properly cared for. The care *must* be acceptable to the state. When he enters school, no matter where he lives in France, the child will follow a curriculum prescribed by the Ministry of Education—which also provides the books and sets the criteria for advancement from grade to grade. After school, when he is not busy with all the homework needed to satisfy state requirements, the child can participate in activities, from games to dancing, at his local state-sponsored youth house through which he may even arrange for a vacation trip abroad. As he progresses in his studies he will have to pass the difficult State Baccalaureate (secondary school) exam if he wants to enter *the* university (just as in California, the state has only one) or try for one of the very prestigious *Grandes Ecoles* (state technical institutes) which alone certify one able to exercise all professions but medicine and law. If he is preparing himself for a trade he knows that to get a good job he will have to get a state certificate of proficiency whether his field be carpentry, auto mechanics or cooking. Of course, every young man, unless he is obviously unfit, serves in the armed forces or its equivalent. French wage earners, when asked what they do for a living, reply using one of the several officially recognized categories, worker, employee or cadre. Each category is further broken down into "steps," either laborers (O.S.) or professional workers (O.P.1, O.P.2, O.P.3), and technicians (T.1, T.2, T.3), and everyone knows that the amount of money people in his category will be programmed to earn over the next five years is now being debated in the offices of the Commissariat of the Plan. The state had better, he thinks, make sure his salary goes up enough. If one is in any position of authority and, prior to the troubles of May, 1968, did not believe that his retaining his position depends on the existence of a stable, strong state, he probably does now.

When he sits down before his television set, the Frenchman knows he pays a yearly tax of from twenty to about eighty dollars to the state for the privilege of receiving his three TV channels, owned and operated by the state. If he likes the evening's fare, he knows whom to praise; if not, whom to blame. Normally feelings about the state are neutral. If, however, one happens to be a small businessman or a small farmer, he knows very well he is one of those who has been judged by the state as standing in the way of France's economic rationalization, and sees himself hanging on to his livelihood despite the power's best efforts which, in the case of the small businessman, consist of raising the price of his permit to do business so high that he simply won't be able to compete with the supermarkets, and for the small farmer, all the inducements he is being given to merge or sell out. If one is an owner or manager in a large business, he knows he is at the center of perhaps the state's major concern: modernization and expansion of industry. As such he is obliged to spend a good portion of his day with representatives from the concerned ministries, the planning commissariat, and from the *préfecture.* Finally, should a French citizen be elected by his fellows to the very prestigious job of mayor of his town, he immediately discovers he has become an official of the government in Paris and is under the immediate supervision of the sub-prefect of his *arrondissement,* then of the prefect of the *département* who, among other things, will tell him how much to spend, how much to tax, and every month will send him a checklist of things to do.

Of course, when a French citizen dies, the state regulates the modalities of his burial and the price of his funeral, while adding the TVA (value added tax) to the latter.

These are but some examples—certainly not an exhaustive list of the state's role in the life of French citizens. But the state, such as it is, has been a long time maturing. At about the time the English barons were extracting the Magna Carta from King John, which effectively guaranteed theirs and their fiefs' existence in the realm independently of the political sovereign's will, Philip the Fair, Capetian king of France, was sending out war parties followed by tax collectors to subdue the nobles; and as the British Parliament was carrying out the Glorious Revolution of 1688, across the channel Louis XIV, Richelieu behind him, was confidently declaring the identity of himself and the state. The Bourbon kings improved on the Capetians' submission of the ancient French regions, completely depriving the nobility of responsibility for their subjects, reducing them to men who quarreled over the prize of attending the king's toilet, while sending out to the provinces not only tax collectors but full-fledged royal governors called *Intendants* whose job was to make sure everything from roads to vineyards was cared for according to instructions from the center. The most famous *Intendant* was the economist *philosophe,* Turgot. It is a commonplace of French historiography that the institution of the royal *Intendant* merely underwent a change in name at the time of the revolution, thereafter being known as the prefectoral system. This is not quite correct: the powers of the prefect from the beginning, and even more as time passed, have been with some exceptions—notably in the matter of requisitioning labor—far greater than the *Intendant's* ever had been.

This is not to suggest that a straight line joins the French state as it exists in the Fifth Republic with the practices of Napoleon, Richelieu and Hugh Capet, for surely changing circumstances have seen the state preoccupied with different matters: during the Napoleonic period, for example, the emphasis was on organizing the nation to make it an efficient, responsive weapon in the hands of its Emperor; under Louis XV (18th century), it was to make the king's private garden fruitful; while under the Third Republic it was to shape a new, secular, republican and democratic France. The extent of the state's powers also varied according to the structure of the regime: the prefect under the Third Republic, although his legal powers over local governments were not inferior to those of his colleague under the Fifth, had in many cases far less real authority. This was due to the paramount fact of political life at the time—the power of parliament and the very important role played in it by mayors. For example, while Edouard Herriot, mayor of Lyon for half a century, was president of the National Assembly or president of the Council of Ministries during the Third Republic, the prefect of the Rhône found the real level of his authority below the legal limit. Today while the role of mayors in parliament is no smaller, the effacement of the latter's powers has left the prefects far freer to follow instructions from Paris. The nature of the state in the Fifth Republic is, as one might imagine, the product of a long history, of the requirements of the French people, and of the emphasis given it by the Republic's founders, General de Gaulle and his followers.

The State in the Vth Republic

"The identity of France and the state. . ." was the theme of a talk delivered by Georges Pompidou, President of the Republic, to the state's leading functionaries come to pledge their allegiance for the new year.[1] France, he reminded them, had been *created* by the state (referring no doubt to the defeat and annexation of Brittany, Burgundy, Aquitaine, Savoy, etc., by kings of all houses) and remains one nation primarily by virtue of state action:

> History shows us that our people, by nature party to divisions and to the most extreme individualism, has been able through the centuries to constitute the French nation only by means of the action of the state . . . protector of our unity, of our independence, and of our liberty.[2]

Furthermore, the President added, like other modern states the French *Etat* is charged with guaranteeing the economic security of its citizens. The speech, far from being treated as just a pep talk to civil servants, was taken by the influential Paris daily *Le Monde* as confirmation that the hallmark of the Vth Republic is the development, growth and prestige of the state.

That this emphasis does not depart from the intentions of the Vth Republic's architects, principally de Gaulle and former Prime Minister Michel Debré, is evident from even a hasty perusal of the public record.[3] De Gaulle's speech at Bayeux[4] begins with a hymn to the state, which he had saved, taken abroad in all its dignity in 1940, and brought back home to the nation, victorious and ready to re-assume its historic role. The body of the speech is the thesis that the political volatility, the history of internal conflict and the vulnerability of its territory at home and overseas require that France be provided with institutions capable of assuring the stability and authority of the state. By the same token the final pages of the final volume of his memoirs covering the period of his presidency of the Republic are filled with the accomplishments of the state he directed. Michel Debré for his part calls the following the first of the five commandments of Gaullism: ". . . There is no France without the state and there is no state without a [strong and stable] government."[5] By "the state" de Gaulle and Debré mean more than that organization which provides a great number of services like the post, social security, or criminal justice, and they certainly do not identify it with the administrative corps, which is its physical embodiment; it is even more than the means of articulating France for common action: it is the *sine qua non* of France. It is a reality which must be imposed on many who would just as soon have none of it but who, once harnessed, lend it the majestic force by which it lives. Though its majesty and power attract adherents to its cause, the state cannot establish itself without victory. The second set of the general's memoirs begins with a simple statement of how legitimacy is won and lost in France: by success and failure in war. The state, which needs for its existence the adherence of the people, is thus not *fundamentally* democratic.[6]

The general's preoccupations with the state's strength, majesty and staying power are no doubt traceable to his experience toward the end of the IIIrd Republic when it seemed to him no one was speaking and acting authoritatively on behalf of France with none but her interests at heart. He saw the army, then personified by Marshal Pétain and General Weygand, prove itself no different from other individuals and institutions in its concern for its own particular interests. Even the government, even the President of the Republic, hesitated to speak in France's name.[7] The civil administration worked quite efficiently for the collaborator regime of Vichy. In fact, the general's writings are replete with accounts of instances when he had to bypass one institution here, one elite there, in order to lead France ("I had to seek support among the people rather than from the elites that tried to interpose themselves between the people and myself.").[8] These instances were not limited to wartime: for example, in 1962 he did not shrink from humiliating the most prestigious of state bodies, the Council of State, which had interposed itself in the name of due process in a judicial matter in which the general had special interest. Thus his refusal to identify the state with any institution, a priori suspect of caring above all for its particular interests, and his tendency to make a mystical entity of it. But beyond his extraordinary emphasis on success in vital struggles and his Bergsonian stress on existence, the content of his notion of the state is simple and fairly appealing to those whose contacts with the state are of a more pedestrian order: it is the familiar positivist motto of "Order and Progress."[9] These then are the rough outlines of the state as it has been presented to the French citizens. Before we can discuss its relationship with them, it behooves us to examine its character more closely.

The Corps Constitués: The State as a Meritocratic Army

Whatever the general and his co-workers may have wanted the state to mean, to most people the state is the clerk at the *préfecture,* the school teacher, the TV producer and so on. The character of the French state, however, although shaped by the desires of the highest political authorities and by the very practical character of the services it has been designated to perform, has a structure and an ethos largely independent of both, and which itself exercises a powerful influence.

American visitors to France soon come into contact with the term *corps.* Americans know the Marine Corps, the U. S. Army Corps of Engineers; and when they say "medical corps," they refer to the medical personnel of the armed forces. The expression diplomatic corps, designating all foreign diplomats in a given capital, is probably the only non-military use of the term with which they are familiar. Thus they are surprised to hear, for example, that in France public school teachers, that is, the overwhelming majority of teachers from elementary school through the university, are part of the "teachers' corps," and that the career of everyone depends on the Ministry of Education just as those of army officers depend on the Ministry of Defense. Then there is the judicial corps: all French judges are employees of the Ministry of Justice. When Frenchmen speak of the medical corps, they mean all medical doctors trained by the state, 95 per cent of whom, although free to practice privately, have contracts of cooperation with the state's Social Security administration, through which they receive a large portion of their fees. In a similar way, engineers are said to make up the "Corps of Engineers," although less than half of all engineers work for the state. All teachers, judges, doctors, engineers are trained in state institutions. Superficially then, the impression one receives is of a nation which, conscious of the variety of tasks which must be performed in society, has, leaving nothing to chance, organized itself into—here one must fall back on military terminology—details, or working parties, or yes, corps.

One is tempted to ask whether someone was afraid that if all this social articulation were not provided for officially, it wouldn't exist. A glance back into history provides the answer: France really *has* been organized along military lines. Essentially this dates from the Revolution. The various currents of opposition to the Old Regime, as De Tocqueville tells us in *L'Ancien Régime et la Révolution,* were agreed on at least two points. First, the obstacle to progress, the affront to equality to be eliminated, was the network of social and economic arrangements and privileges upheld by the monarchy, but deeply rooted in society—the revolutionaries did not have to worry about *political* "intermediary bodies," the Bourbon monarchy having long suppressed these. Second, the means to be employed would have to be despotic, for one does not arrive at that happy moment of liberty when the last nobleman expires, strangled in the entrails of the last priest, to borrow J. Meslier's words, by sweet persuasion.[10] Even the very agents of Bourbon centralism, the civil servants, were in agreement with the revolutionaries. Steeped in rationalist doctrine—Turgot remains one of the finest examples of any age of the technocrat in public service—they were eager to see the disappearance of aristocratic and local privileges that they counted as so many irrational barriers to progress. Even before the Revolution, so it now seems, there could be no question of anything but a very powerful state succeeding the monarchy. But in order for the organ of coercion *par excellence* to become the highest expression of liberty, it had to conceive of itself as omniscient concerning the needs of citizens,[11] and to organize itself to wage war on society as it then existed.

When the wars, both internal and external, which followed the Revolution brought to supreme power a man whose name is synonymous with military genius, the French state received its pseudo-Roman (e.g., prefects, legions) military form enabling it to rule over society efficiently, to draw forth from it all the enormous human and material resources required for modern people-to-people war and, most of all, to provide itself with new leaders by educating the best of society's young, qualifying them for their tasks—administration, health, education, building, and so on—and employing them. Behind the legions lay the real army—the nation—and since a good army is a healthy army, a Ministry of Health was established, as well as one of education so that everyone might read, that no talent be wasted, no strength lost to France. A Ministry of the Interior was needed to make sure the nation produced well, and that the emperor could count on its support. It had, for example, to bring order to the French countryside: towns and streets had to be regularized, houses numbered so that people and goods might be kept track of, mail delivered and a conscription system operated efficiently, and so on.

In order to tie all these corps together, a military man would require a general staff. This is precisely what the *Grands Corps* were designed to be and that is what they still are. The Council of State, Court of Accounts, Inspectorate of Finance, the Prefectoral Corps, the Diplomatic Corps are the pillars of the administrative structures and the essence of *L'État.* We will now very briefly look at the most significant corps of this general staff: the Council of State, Court of Accounts, and Inspectorate of Finance. Then, after a few remarks on the reason for their permanence, we will examine in some detail the way in which the state, through its corps, controls the activities of local government and private associations, education, and economic activity.

The Council of State

Article 52 of the Constitution of 22 *Frimaire,* year VIII (13 December 1799) reads: "Under the direction of the Consuls a Council of State is charged with editing drafts of laws and decrees of public administration and to resolve the difficulties which arise in administrative matters." Itself a successor of the King's Council, from which one of the ranks of its officials inherits its title *(Maître des Requêtes),* it has performed two distinct functions since its inception: that of the chief of state's legal advisor (in practice, the government's) and that of highest administrative tribunal. Its 242 members are divided into five sections. The first four: Interior, Finances, Public Works, and Social Services examine proposed laws, decrees and administrative directives in their respective areas for legality, administrative feasibility, consequences, consistency and due process, while the fifth section acts as the tribunal. In addition, the council forms special high-level committees to examine especially important acts such as referenda proposals.

It is, however, as administrative judge that the council has made its greatest mark on French life. It sits at the head of a hierarchy of administrative tribunals which can declare illegal or arbitrary *(excès de pouvoir),* and therefore null and void, acts of any part of the civil administration. It also resolves jurisdictional disputes, thereby breaking up bureaucratic logjams. Historically its decisions formed a working civil service code long before one was enacted in 1946. It has acquired the reputation as the defender of citizens against arbitrariness, as defender of administrators against political pressures, and as defender of the prerogatives of the state. Perhaps its greatest contribution has been in resolving conflicts between local governments and the central administration, especially in the area of separation of church and state.[12]

The Fifth Republic has not broken with a long tradition of respect for the apex of the state:[13] Article 39 of the 1958 Constitution requires that laws be discussed by the Council of Ministers and sent to Parliament only after the advice of the Council of State has been considered. The council's members, however, as civil servants know their effectiveness depends entirely on the trust placed on them by the government, which if it desires can bypass the council. Such was the case twice in 1962 when General de Gaulle rebuffed its opposition to two of his acts. The first was the general's proposed referendum to amend the Constitution of 1958 to allow for direct election of the President of the Republic. Since the Constitution provides in Article 89 for a means of constitutional amendment via Parliament, making no mention of referenda proposed by the President, the council solemnly ruled de Gaulle's proposal unconstitutional. His reasoning— that Article 11's provision that the President can set before the electorate referenda on the organization of the public powers—is less important than his attitude toward the council:

> Now this body of officials who hold their jobs by government decrees and not at all by virtue of election, is qualified to give the executive the judicial advice it asks for, but not in the slightest to intervene in a political matter, and even less into the constitutional domain.[14]

He went on to accuse its members of base political motivation and told them he would ignore them. When, a few days later, the council "struck down" the Special Court of Military Justice (established by de Gaulle because the regular military courts were not punishing with sufficient severity officers involved in the insurrection against his Algerian policy), calling it "not conformant to the general principles of law," his anger was greater and his speech more revealing. Chief of state, he owes his legitimacy both to history and to the people's vote. His mission is thus not justiciable, and the council is, therefore, in rebellion against "that which is the law." Some matters (Algerian affairs) the sovereign people have simply chosen to confide to their chief for speedy disposal.[15] Furthermore is it not a scandal that the council brings this matter up just a week before the referendum on direct election and furthermore takes a position in favor of such heinous criminals?

Clearly the Council of State's role is circumscribed by a certain conception of the law. The Fifth Republic's claim that direct communication with the sovereign people places an agency, heretofore Parliament, now the President, above the mere law, is not new in French history. In democracy, it appears, quite as much as in any army, the boss' word *is* the law, and laws must be conceived of as tools for carrying into effect the people's will. A body whose authority lies in legal interpretation can therefore only offer suggestions or technical modifications. The council has also proved useful by providing its members, some of whom are appointed from outside the civil service, a comprehensive view of state activity and a sort of training in public affairs which is of particularly great importance in a country where the state plays the role it does in France. In fact, several major figures in recent French history have spent lengthy tours on the Council of State or began their careers there: among them Leon Blum (of 1936 Popular Front fame), Michel Debré, first Prime Minister of the Fifth Republic, and Georges Pompidou, its current President.

The Court of Accounts

The Napoleonic Law of 16 September 1807 gave France a central organ of control over state finances. Today, as then, centralized control of public expenditures at all levels of the state—including the municipalities' larger expenses—is deemed necessary both for technical and political reasons. By centralizing the authority for even relatively small expenditures, one effectively achieves otherwise unobtainable detailed control over the activities of widespread public agencies. In addition, central control assures that the standards of financial management laid down by the budget are adhered to. The Court of Accounts, however, is only the highest organ in this process in which the Inspectorate of Finance, whose role we will examine next, also participates. The court has the authority to require adherence to the inspectorate's views and generally supports the latter's financial controllers, located in the various ministries. Its 207 members assess "not only the regularity of activities, but also the standards of management. Each year [the court] submits a report to the President of the Republic containing observations based on inspections and rich in often picturesque examples of waste or abuse."[16] Like all the *Grands Corps,* the Court of Accounts lends out about a fourth of its officials for temporary service in high, often very high posts in the several ministries, thereby giving them the benefit of detailed knowledge of administrative fields and experience in actual leadership.

Thus do the French by administrative means carry out many of the controlling and coordinating functions which Anglo-Saxons, especially Americans, normally believe are the prerogatives of committees of elected representatives. But considering the vast size of the state, its many and growing responsibilities and perennial demands that it carry out fundamental reforms—be it church-state relations, economics, education—is it not better, argue some Frenchmen, that the job be done in a workmanlike way with a minimum of waste, by people of undeniably high quality bound in *corps* that have not only vast knowledge but also a long memory of past errors? To the objection that members of the *Grands Corps* are not responsible to the country the answer is readily made that their vast responsibilities were given them by men the people elected, and anyway they lend an element of authority and *sérieux* indispensable to a democracy where by definition everything is "up for grabs" all the time.

The Inspectorate of Finance

Created in 1816, this smallest of the *Grands Corps* (103 members) is the elite of the Ministry of Finance whose budget division plays far more than a technical role in partitioning the budget among the several ministries. Inspectors of finance act as expert intermediaries between the latter, the former and the Court of Accounts.

> Each ministry also contains finance officers whose job is to control expenditure; they see that the budget is respected by issuing visas of approval to all departmental decisions involving expenditure. When a particular item strikes them as doubtful these officials consult the budget division. Similarly, when requests for payment relating to local expenditure reach the appropriate minister, the controlling official examines the grounds, which are compulsorily stated; if in his opinion there is inadequate justification, no visa is forthcoming. Auditing is kept separate from the accounting side; audit work is carried out by a special category of officials, with personal financial responsibility, supervised directly by the Court of Accounts.[17]

The inspectorate is at once the bogeyman of the state—every one handling or proposing to spend money being on guard against its reportedly sharp-penciled, insensitive inspectors—as well as a combination of public whipping boy and silent partner of public men on the local as well as national level. These can promise, propose and reap political fruits at will, fully knowing the inspectorate's financial veto will keep their indiscretions from producing embarrassing offspring.

Like the other *Grands Corps,* the inspectorate is an excellent place to learn the ropes of French government. Valéry Giscard D'Estaing, currently finance minister and one of the men most frequently named in connection with future occupancy of the prime ministership and the presidency, is an alumnus of the inspectorate, as is former Prime Minister Couve de Murville.

Summary

The undeniable prestige of the *Grands Corps,* both in and out of the state, owes no greater debt than to the method by which their members are selected: competitive examination. In fact, this method of selection used throughout the French state to hire practically everyone from janitors to career diplomats, has long served to dampen feelings of outrage on the part of citizens and subordinates toward those above them: after all, those above have proved by not inconsiderable trials of mental dexterity that they belong where they are—or at least do so more than anybody else. We will look at somewhat greater length at the pervasive French institution of the competitive examination when we discuss education.

Excluding the small "outside quota" appointments of distinguished, mature citizens which the President of the Republic can make from time to time, access to all the upper echelons of the state is limited to young men graduating from the *Ecole Nationale de L'Administration* (ENA)—access to which is by competitive examination.[18] The ENA, one of the newest of the *Grandes Ecoles,* was founded by General de Gaulle's post-war provisional government in 1945, and by 1967 had trained about 1,500 civil servants. Most of these are still in government service, although about 100 have left either for political life (12 ENA graduates were among the "class" of 1967 in the Chamber of Deputies) or for very high positions in private industry. The latter phenomenon (called *pantouflage* after *pantoufles,* slippers, to denote the comfort of the arrangement) is a sign of the close ties between the state and French big business, as well as of the esteem in which the flower of the meritocracy is held.

It would not be a gross exaggeration to term the *Grands Corps* a sort of republican service aristocracy, whose titles of nobility are the exams they have passed and the power they have wielded. The latter has not been limited to formal functions, for high civil servants, heirs of the best education France can give, have, with discretion, participated in political life: the influential Club Jean Moulin[19] is largely composed of high civil servants, and most every ministry has managed to build up a distinct political character which governments have chosen to respect, not unlike aristocratic apanages. One would not, for example, any more name an ardent Catholic to head the Ministry of Education than one would a socialist to the Ministry of Finance. Most importantly for France, this disciplined meritocracy has served some of the functions of a real aristocracy, incorporating reasonably high standards in its conduct and being obeyed at least as well as military superiors are obeyed by their soldiers. The foundations of the *Grands Corps'* influence do not, however, appear without flaws. No doubt the size and complexity of state action are growing, and there can be no doubt also as to the Fifth Republic's commitment to more closely coordinated state action in order to effect the greatest reorganization of French society since the Revolution. But this very commitment causes it to suffer ill any independence on the part of the state. The President of the Republic, heretofore only the symbolic head of state, is now the real leader of the government as well. But perhaps more importantly, the cultural tradition and the educational system of which the state's high officials have been the epitome are under attack. The system's very cornerstone, the competitive examination, is, as we shall see, blamed precisely because of the results it achieves: the formation of something akin to aristocracy. Pierre Avril's view on the subject is typical: "The selection of the most talented is justified only as long as it is open to all and ensures a constant turnover of elites."[20] The argument is simply that although open to all and charging no tuition, institutions like the ENA fail to meet the other criteria of democracy. Since only an infinitesimal number of working class students ever enter, there is no circulation of elites. Thus although the system of hierarchy and standardization appears in no danger at all, the process by which these are imbued with standards may well be.

Having looked at the top of the structure, we now turn our attention to the means by which it is anchored in and acts upon the body politic.

Prefects and Centralization

It can be argued that no act of Napoleon's has had greater significance for the development of democracy in France than his establishment of the pattern of territorial centralization which still obtains in modern France. In fact no two topics in political science have been quite so closely linked as those of democracy and local government.[21] Most French textbooks[22] respect what had become the standard characterization of local government as the indispensable elementary school of democracy, while others[23] find correlated in history the trends of authoritarianism with centralization on the one hand, and of liberalism with decentralization on the other. As for the precise effects of French centralization, it is not difficult to find strongly held opinions ranging from "why, if it weren't for centralization, France would have blown apart at the seams some time ago, and in any case, could never have withstood the shocks of the last 150 years" to the view which attributes all of France's social weakness to centralization and pictures France as a field of the liveliest flowers uniformly kept from their natural growth by the oppressive blanket of the state. The controversy is not just verbal: whenever governments have tried to modernize French democracy, they have somehow modified the status of its basis: local government.[24] Our purpose here is not to give a history of this relationship but to describe its elements as they exist now.

A glance at the French countryside quickly reveals why the matter is of enduring importance: as far as the eye can see, the clock towers of churches spring up a few miles apart, each with the group of houses which appear huddled around it, forming a village, separated from others like it by a lovely countryside and century-old habits. As of the 1962 census France had 38,000 towns, 36,930 of which have fewer than 1,500 inhabitants. About one third of Frenchmen live in these very small villages, while less than a fifth live in the thirty-two cities of 100,000 inhabitants or more. The rest—half the nation

—lives in roughly a thousand intermediate–sized towns averaging 25,000 persons. Clearly, insofar as democracy depends on personal participation of citizens in the conduct of public affairs, France is physically well arranged for it. On the other hand, insofar as it is essential to democracy that the will of the whole community prevail over that of any part, the division of France into thousands of collectivities, most of which preexisted the present constitution, poses some difficulties. The architects of the French state have tried over the years to reconcile these conflicting requirements of democracy. Let us see how they have gone about it.

The Préfect

"Why if it weren't for the prefect, you would see statues of Stalin decorating the town halls of the Paris suburbs—they're controlled by the Communists you know." This remark by a sophisticated gentleman expresses the most powerful argument today for maintaining central tutelage over even the smallest acts of freely elected town governments. Were it not there, might inertia suffice to maintain the system? Or might perhaps the widespread desire for personal economic security and for economic development by their own power strengthen the state at the towns' expense? The fact that one cannot be sure is an indication of what fundamentally sustains centralization.[25] Seventy-five years ago the same gentleman might have said "If it weren't for the prefect, the village priests of the Vendée would wreck the public school system, then where would our secular state be?" He would, of course, have been right in his fears, as was Napoleon one hundred years before that when he saw peasants in the same region raising the royal flag while beyond France's borders emigres under that same flag were joining France's traditional enemies. Napoleon's answer, the prefect, was then a measure of war taken to ensure the state's monopoly on politics (symbolically, prefects still wear the uniform of their corps).

Prefects have always been unique among the *Grands Corps*

because they have never been protected by normal civil service guarantees: if the prefect is the servant of the suprapolitical state, he is also the agent *par excellence* of the government's politics in the *département* to which he is assigned. As we have mentioned, his degree of independence has varied through the years, but whether justifiably or not, the prefect and his staff are widely believed to be the agents not only of the state but of the party in power. Even in the promotion of economic activity and of compliance to the national economic plan—the facet of his role which has been most emphasized over the past few years—he is not considered impartial, and it is widely believed by local authorities that a mayor belonging to the Gaullist party will get a better deal. The idea of technocratic prefects is not being taken at face value in France, especially by those who believe themselves adversely affected by their decisions. However, the undeniable trend ever since Vichy has been the prefect's growth from representative of the Ministry of the Interior to actual chief of all branches of government activity in his area. This is giving him more to think about than ward-heeling, but much more powerful tools with which to do that sort of thing if ever he has to.

When a prefect arrives on the job, he does so as a man toward the end of his career, sure of his pension and of his knowledge of what the ministry expects of him. The only things of which he is ignorant are the particular character and needs of the area he is to rule. His first months are spent getting acquainted with each *arrondissement,* where his visit is treated by the local mayors and other notables much as once were those of a prince of the royal house come to see his domain: the newspapers give the visit much coverage, he is received with honors at each town hall, visits the local points of interest, and finally receives the local notables—as often as possible in the sub-prefecture—and listens to the recitation of their problems. On one such visit recently these ranged from insufficient sanding of roads during snowstorms to the necessity that the state take over financial responsibility for a certain intermediate school since it now bears heavily on the town's scarce resources. After each point has been answered by a member of his cabinet, the prefect makes a statement of his personal policies. Not all prefectoral visits are so non-political though. The stormy sessions in areas which have recently had a conflict with the state, or in areas with Communist mayors, recall the early days when prefects were sent to hold essentially unfriendly territory.

The Département

The prefect's domain, the *département,* (there are 95 of them in metropolitan France) is not a completely arbitrary unit despite the arbitrary nature of its founding in 1790. Not only does it roughly follow natural topographic and historical demographic-economic divisions, but by now its nearly two-hundred years of history have given it a place in French habits. *Départements,* recognized as legal persons since 1838, own, buy, sell, hire, bring suit and are sued. Most central services such as education, road building, police and social security have their offices in the *département* seat, usually in the *préfecture,* which is a building whose location everyone is likely to know. Administratively, the *département* is geographically divided into *arrondissements,* each presided over by a sub-prefect, a junior member of the prefectoral corps. *Arrondissements* serve as constituencies for the election of the *département's* assembly, called the General Council, and approximately as constituencies for the election of deputies to the National Assembly.

The prefect and sub-prefect's tasks of political control, administration of *département* business, liaison between the state, the communes and the people, and economic direction are complicated by a corollary one: everything, insofar as possible, must be performed in conjunction with the people. This is difficult to achieve because most actions at the *département* level are executions of decisions made in Paris. The best example is the budget, which although it may contain

a few items placed there by the General Council, primarily
consists, on the expense side, of precisely the amounts the
various ministries and the prefect have decided should be
spent for certain departmental services (roads, schools, fire
protection, etc.) and on the revenue side carries precisely the
amount of taxation to be imposed on the citizenry to cover
the expenses. The budget must be voted by the General Council. If the council fails to vote it, things don't change much:
the expenses and taxes take effect anyway. But the prefect,
who most likely will "lose points" with his superiors for having
exhibited such poor powers of persuasion, having failed to
associate the people with the life of the state and having given
the latter a bad name by acting on such an important matter
without an expression of popular consent, would surely be
angry and might threaten to dissolve the council and call for
new elections. This would probably not please the councilors,
for even if it produced a new council no less determined than
the old, probably nothing would change for the better. Besides,
important matters on which the council does have a say, such
as the buying and selling of its property, would have to be
left pending and individual councilors would lose what access
and influence they have with the prefect and his staff. Moreover, this is not how the game is played. As a councilor
explains it: "We and the prefect can both get something we
want by bargaining. Naturally he gets nearly all and we only
a little, but then he is in charge. No, the *département* General
Council is not the place for confrontation, but for us to declare
to the state what our needs are. For confrontation the commune
level is the place to go; there you can sometimes see *Monsieur
Le Maire* and *Monsieur Le Sous-Préfet* going at each other like
cats and dogs." In fact, there is only one example in French
history of the dissolution of a General Council (in 1874),
whereas on the town level it is far more common.

Alongside this one sees General Councils voting not only
budgets but development programs unanimously, while almost
every member condemns the approved text as insufficient or

misguided or unfair. Such, for example, was the result of the deliberation by the General Council of the *Département* of the Lower Rhine on its share of the VIth National Economic Plan of 21 February 1972. No one but the prefect spoke up in its favor, while the tone of the council president (who was also the number two man in the Ministry of the Interior) was apologetic. The general tenor of the remarks was that the state is giving too little in the way of subsidies for roads, pipe lines, etc., while forcing the *département* and the town councils to come up with most of the money (60 per cent) required to carry out the plan. Although it was pointed out that the region was allocated 2.7 per cent of the plan's subsidies while its population is 2.8 per cent of the national total, everyone was vociferously unsatisfied as he voted yes.

The General Council is theoretically the legislative organ of the *département* while the prefect is the executive officer, but while the former derives its authority directly from the people, the latter gets his from the state.[26] Perhaps nothing shows the real character of the General Council quite so well as the manner in which its members spend the greatest part of their official time: sitting on consultative committees made up of state officials and representatives of industrial, professional, or civic groups. A typical meeting would include two or three councilors, a representative from the Ministry of Agriculture, a man from the prefect's cabinet, ten of the *département's* biggest growers of sugar beets, and someone from the local sugar refinery. Or, one might see council members accompanying the chief of the *département's* sanitation bureau and one or two of the area's *députés* (representatives) to Paris in search of funds to build a new sewage treatment plant.

The council members include mayors and other persons who can afford to take time off for the two yearly sessions and committee work. They are elected for six years in contests which more often than not resemble less party battles than polls on the question of who are the most solid citizens in the area. The office is sought after less for the very little power it carries, than for the prestige and, what is more important, the access it gives to state officials. On the other hand, high state officials or *députés* often seek posts as general councilors if they do not already have another anchor in local life, such as the mayoralty in their native village. For example, Monsieur Bord, once the number two man in the Ministry of the Interior, is president of the General Council of the Lower Rhine. Pierre Avril writes that "In the [National] Assembly elected in 1967, of 470 metropolitan deputies, there were no less than 264 mayors and 245 were members of General Councils [sic]. (Not always the same men, although the two posts are often held simultaneously). Of the 50 General Councils functioning at the time, 18 were chaired by deputies, 26 by senators, and 13 by former members of Parliament."[27] The council's varied composition, then, readily permits personal communication between men at all levels of public life who are somehow concerned with the *département*'s business. But just as this gives the council far more influence than its legal powers would indicate, so do the sources of the influence appear to be not the fact of popular election, but rather the personal standing and the bargaining ability of the councilors in the congenial company of other educated Frenchmen. Popular participation at this level of government is evidently not great. But, paradoxically, from the point of view of traditional democratic notions, the more the business of government has become nonpolitical in nature, the more it has concentrated on economic development, the more persons are being drawn into the process of consultation via institutions such as the General Council. How satisfactorily this sort of consultation of notables on non-political matters substitutes for the more traditional sort of political participation is another question, but the fact remains that this is how business is done in France. Because of this, it would be vain to try to diagram the process by which a French *département* might get its place in the economic plan changed or a town would go about getting the state to take over financial support of a secondary school.

The Town

If the *département* looks to most Frenchmen like a scaled down version of the state—far away and approachable only by notables—the *commune,* as the town government has been known since the revolution, is very close at hand; its councilors, the teachers, the few office workers and the *garde champêtre* (local policeman, not a part of the national gendarmerie) are next door neighbors, while the mayor's *(maire)* face is a familiar one. And if people do not often discuss the goings on at the *préfecture,* they usually know and care about what is happening at the town hall *(mairie).* The commune has the peculiar quality in French law of being both part of the state and simultaneously an independent corporation. The councilors (numbering 11 to 37 depending on the size of the town), elected by universal suffrage according to different formulas (proportional representation or single-member districts, again depending on the town's size) choose the mayor from among themselves. From the moment of his election, however, *Monsieur le Maire* finds that he is not only an elected executive, but also an official of the state. This double status, in force in all French cities but the largest since the law of April 5, 1884, is a compromise between two views of the office, each of which represents a period in French history: under Napoleon, as well as under the restoration, both the mayor and the council had been appointed by the prefect or the government, while under the Second Republic the mayor had been appointed by the prefect or government from among a council elected by universal suffrage. The notion that the mayor is a state official has not been abandoned, only wedded to that of his dependence upon the people. What the system really does is to give towns the chance to choose who will apply the state's laws in the community as well as who will represent the town to the state. Incidentally, the man elected mayor will also take care of purely town business. In the same way the council, though not formally an organ of the state, is expected to function as such; for example, when it votes its budget containing a high percentage of state-mandated items, when it submits its decisions for prefectoral approval, or when it finds itself dissolved by prefectoral action. Individual members too can be removed by the prefect for, among other reasons, missing three meetings in a row.[28]

Most important for our purposes is the fact that when the town is allowed to act not as an agent of the state but as an independent corporation, it is for strictly non-political purposes such as the buying or selling of land. Political acts are forbidden. But what, outside of taking a position on a national candidate or law, is a political act? The answers one receives are not clear. Certainly the very fact that people can run for office at the local level under national party labels gives the whole affair a political character. In fact, political parties in France very carefully count the number of *mairies* they hold around the country, considering them valuable bastions of strength.[29]

The very fact that national politicians prize the job of mayor of their home town, even if their job in Paris forces them to leave its actual performance in the hands of an assistant, and that mayors of large cities are willy-nilly national figures, gives elections a political character. Two examples suffice to illustrate this. M. Gaston Defferre, the popular Socialist mayor of Marseilles, became a very convincing candidate for the presidency in the 1965 elections without the presidency of his party and with only his post in Marseille as a base. More significantly, while Prime Minister of France, M. Jacques Chaban-Delmas was also the mayor of Bordeaux, as well as deputy to the National Assembly from the second district of the Gironde, of which Bordeaux is a part, although he had no time for the former and holding the latter is legally incompatible with a government job. He resolved the first difficulty by letting his assistants do the job and the second by resigning after each election in favor of a substitute. This not unusual situation was the setting in 1970 of a battle between Chaban-Delmas and Jean Jacques Servan-Schreiber, president of the Radical

Party and himself deputy from the city of Nancy, who tried
to take from him not so much his position as deputy (for
Servan-Schreiber could no more hold two seats than Chaban-
Delmas could one) but his position as Bordeaux's favorite son.
Had the Prime Minister lost that election, he might well have
resigned. Of course he did not lose: the challenger managed
only 16 percent of the vote.

Evidently if town officials are prohibited from officially having political opinions, politicians are very much aware that
both officials and populations of specific localities have characteristic political preferences, and the above-mentioned contest's position as front-page news all over France for six weeks
is testimony to the political importance attached to local feeling.[30] In this context what can the prohibitions against political
acts by local government mean? In practice there is no doubt:
it means the mayor and council cannot make statements or
resolutions which the prefect (if he is supported by the administrative courts and the Council of State) would find an affront
to the authority of the state. But fear lest its monopoly on
politics be broken is eloquent testimony on the state's part to
the strength of local feeling in France.

What is the basis of local feeling? Perhaps it is the knowledge
on the part of most (until very recently nearly all) people born
in one place that they could expect to live the rest of their
lives among their neighbors. But living together no more
ensures good relations in civic than in marital affairs.[31] But
perhaps the question is badly put; rather we should ask what
local feeling consists of. It has little resemblance to the communal barn-raising spirit taught to young Americans as the
civic ideal, for it is not uncommon for Frenchmen not to have
any more than a nodding acquaintance with their neighbors
unless they had been friends in childhood. In fact, unless
unusual circumstances are involved, moving into a French
neighborhood is a far warmer experience for a foreigner, considered both as a curiosity and as no threat to anyone's status,
than for a Frenchman. This distance does not, of course, keep

anyone from satisfying his usually lively curiosity on everything from the financial status to the sexual potency of his
neighbors. One can find out the life history of an amazing
number of people from someone who professes to know only
a few by sight! But it is evident that in a country where
personal dignity is both highly prized and considered to be
indissolubly bound up with the distance between persons,
civic feeling is not likely to be based on a history of common
barn raisings. Friendship, or at least social contact, among
adults is more likely to take place among business and professional colleagues than among neighbors.[32]

Private associations of nearly all kinds are not lacking on
the town level. Even very small towns like Saint Pierre often
have an orchestra society, which might give two concerts a
year or play on a special occasion such as the funeral of the
town's oldest person, or a club whose principal task is to
organize the yearly carnival festivities on Mardi Gras. In most
towns young men near the age of military service organize
by class (birth year) for the purpose of having a good time.
In Bambach they went on a weekend trip to the headwaters
of the Rhine. More likely than not, a town will have a football
(soccer) club. The town of Ottrott, population 950, even boasts
a cultural society. These groups most often would meet in the
mairie (town hall), there usually not being a more adequate
building, and would usually have the mayor either as a
member or as a guest of honor at the yearly banquet. If the
town is large enough, it might build a special building for
sports or feasts and might charge each organization a portion
of the mortgage. These are sound rules of thumb: if there is
any hunting or fishing in the area, there will be a hunting
or fishing club, which will hold meetings and send letters or
delegations to Paris, to the prefect or to the mayor to press
for its point of view on everything from pollution control to
how the problem of foxes infected with rabies should be
handled. It will also publicize rules and might be charged by
the mayor with selling licenses. If there is agriculture in the

area, there will be one or usually more agricultural associations, with each farmer possibly belonging to one for each of his products. There is, of course, no area of France without its winegrowers' cooperative, which might handle one or more of the following: oenological information, grape pressing, filtering and bottling, marketing or market promotion and information. Recently, for example, the Federation of Alsatian Vintners' Clubs sent a delegation to explore the American market. It returned filled with hope.

As the size of towns grows, new organizations make their appearance. Some, like the National Small Merchant's Association, though it has members in even the smallest towns, has chapters only in the largest ones (10,000 inhabitants is, in France, a large town). But as one moves from small to larger towns, one notices an interesting phenomenon: a smaller proportion of people seem to be involved; the musical association draws only the best as does the football club and church choir. Of course, the mayor still addresses the annual banquet of the chamber of commerce, but instead of a small restaurant filled with one's next door neighbors, it is the hotel ballroom filled with business leaders and delegates from agricultural associations, or labor unions.

But each town, large or small, will have its association of ex-combatants, while chapters of associations of former members of certain army divisions or naval ships, or of war prisoners in certain camps are not unknown in larger towns. Recently a chapter of the association of the former crew members of the battleship *Jean-Bart* held a meeting in the town hall of Illkirch for which occasion a group of nuns embroidered a flag—such mixing of the private, the national and the religious is far from uncommon at the local level. Most town councils simply subsidize private organizations such as ski clubs, choral societies, social clubs for the blind and social clubs for firemen. Clemenceau, Jules Ferry and Waldeck-Rousseau, architects of the separation of church and state in France at the turn of the century, would be aghast at the sight of the church congregation of St. Nabor carrying on bingo games in the *mairie* or receiving religious instruction there. Sub-prefects have long since stopped trying to stand in the way of that sort of thing.

In sum, whether one's interest is karate, the theater, music, sugar beets, wine, cheese, commerce or what not, one is likely to find a club or association which suits one's fancy, although if one's interest lies more in serving the community, little besides the Rotary Club would be available. If one is interested in doing good, one would have little choice beyond the Salvation Army.[33]

As for the church, it is in a category all by itself. On the one hand France's official laicism is strong and widespread enough for devout Christians to stand out and be known as such in club, school, or neighborhood—especially if they happen to be men—while on the other, common church attendance even in a small town does not seem to result directly in even the sort of social intercourse that comes from a fishing society. Yet one gets the feeling, which we will discuss in Chapter 5, that the church plays a bigger part in the community than the evidence suggests. In any case, it is one of the largest institutions in any town, both in terms of the building and of people, and the regularity of its functions, the importance of its holidays and the solemnity of the births, deaths and marriages which it celebrates loom large even in the lives of unbelievers. And, if church and state are separated, God, town, family and *La Patrie* are united in the church vestibule where the familiar names of the shockingly numerous war dead (10 for World War II and 42 for World War I in a town of 950!) are solemnly inscribed. In France, in fact, the expression for local or parochial contains (even as in English) reference to the church, specifically to its steeple *(clocher)*. And Frenchmen, religious or not, like to describe themselves as attached to their *clocher.*

Although at first sight Frenchmen would appear to be "joiners" second to none, a second glance shows that most organizations on the local level exist either for the fun or the profit of their participants. How Americans can join the local Democratic Club or the Young Republicans in the same spirit in which they join the church choir or the Rotary is difficult to explain. In France political parties, although they have dues-paying members outside of Paris, are not (Communists excepted) well organized on the local level. One looks in vain in local or regional newspapers for activities of the local organizations of national political parties, and one only occasionally finds very small blurbs announcing, to give one example, that the Alsatian Regional Committee of the French Socialist Party would urge its members to abstain on the upcoming national referendum on the enlargement of the Common Market. Politics does get to the local level, but not via associations.[34] In France one does not participate in something of a political nature lightly, although there appears to be not the slightest hesitation in joining a group whose purpose is the particular advancement of its members. The former is at best *peu sérieux,* not very serious, and at worst, somewhat dangerous, while the latter is not only *sérieux,* but something above reproach. When one asks why the distinction is made, why is it all right to join the one and not the other, one usually gets the following answer or a variation thereon: "Someone might have something to say against you if you got mixed up in politics; they *(on)* could say you wanted to tell people what to do, occupy yourself with business that is not your own. But how can anyone say anything bad of anyone who tries to make sure the state respects his interests? It's the most natural thing in the world." Once again we see here the division between the state and politics. But also we begin to understand how the two touch at the local level.

What *is* the nature of local feeling? France is, as we have said, the nation of small towns *par excellence,* so much so that even the city dwellers are influenced by the small town perspective. Thus, in a country where it is very important to know and be known, yet difficult to establish familiar relations after childhood, where equality in politeness and political expression does not hide a very strong desire to know the social rank of those around one, where a strong sense of personal dignity is coupled with an equally strong fear of embarrassment, home towns offer a true island of social security. The differences between localities, perhaps more imagined than real, are also not to be taken lightly as the mere residue of a time gone by, hanging on in the minds of persons on the fringe of society. In northern Alsace, for example, persons from a young radiologist to an old librarian agreed that life is much different in the south—an area only 20 miles away. People there are too open and jolly, so goes the common view, which attributes the difference to the fact that down there people grow and drink more wine! Everywhere in France one hears characterizations of the inhabitants of other regions that sound much like discussions of foreign lands: "Bretons? Oh, they're dreamers; Celtics, you know." How much more comfortable it is where one knows just how to act, to get along! The residents of St. George, Utah[35] might find the people of Villé cold and their organizations stiff and selfish, but the latter, though they might not hesitate to describe themselves in the same terms, feel very much at home in their town, much more comfortable, in any case, than they would feel anywhere else.[36] In one's own town, one does not have to answer questions as to who one is or to be embarrassed by an equality which leaves no excuse for not being socially higher than one is.

But no account of what one's home town—or neighborhood—means to Frenchmen would be complete without mention of just about the only period they leave it eagerly: vacation time. This is about double in France what it is in the United States and absorbs a far greater proportion of a family's resources. When a Frenchman goes on vacation (unless he wants to go "back home"), he wants to go someplace he is utterly unknown, where his status will be limited only by his budget, and where he can enjoy himself without the normal social constraints. Everyone understands that there is a difference between what is permissible at home and on vacation: a dress or a shirt may be bought for vacation time which a "serious" person would not dare to wear on familiar streets.

Frenchmen feel strongly about their home town. But if this feeling is quite unpolitical, somewhat romantic, like the attachment of believer and unbeliever alike to the town steeple, it is not devoid of political consequences. When people know each other well, from club or café, and when every imaginable special interest group has an organization to present its case, one does not need an opinion polling service or even debates before the whole community to learn who thinks what and how strongly. Conversely, people value the informal channels based on chains of acquaintances through which they can make themselves heard to get the help they need.

The mixture of the private and the political realms, which is the hallmark of democracy, takes place nowhere so well in France as on the local level. But this is due not only to the sort of internal nonpolitical cohesiveness which we have just described, but also owes something to the one thing the town must do as a unit: face the state. Since it does so for most purposes in the person of its mayor, it is by looking at his role more closely that we continue our description of the town.

The mayors of large cities like Marseille, Bordeaux, Lille, Strasbourg, especially those who also sit in Parliament, are not like the mayor of St. Nabor (population 235), available to all at the *mairie* two evenings a week and at home all the time, and their large staffs, modeled after the state bureaucracy, are almost as permanent and as impersonal. Still, even in the cities, citizens in common conversation and newspapers in normal reporting speak of *la mairie* without the hint of awe used when the state is the subject, and most of all without using the pronoun *ils* (they). The mayor, it is commonly thought, is one of *us.* He may, as in the big cities, be somewhat distant—though never as distant as the government or the state, for he can be voted out—but he usually does his best to cultivate the feeling that he is one of *us,* out there handling the necessary and difficult job of dealing with *Le Pouvoir* for the good of the city. He is certainly not thought of as a bureaucrat: in fact when, girded with the tricolor sash, he gives his fourteenth of July address or lays a wreath to the war dead, he seems to personify *La Patrie* almost as much as a general. In fact, French mayors of cities large and small spend remarkably long periods in office—Edouard Herriot's half century in Lyon was not that unusual—without benefit of what Americans know as political machines and usually without much criticism. The latter is not because French mayors are above reproach, but because it is commonly believed that the mayor does not do harm of his own free will. If local taxes are raised, it is presumed—usually correctly—that the mayor resisted as much as possible and presented the council with the least painful choice possible. For example, when during the spring of 1972 towns all over France raised the tax on commercial establishments *(Patente)*, the protest posters which sprang up in practically every store window in the country were aimed not at the mayors who had proposed or the councils which had voted the tax, but at the government in Paris asking *it* for relief. This position was in fact well founded. But in towns big and small *Monsieur Le Maire's* importance lies in his ability to act as the citizen's guide and protector when dealing with state officials, helping to formulate requests and grievances. The smaller the town, the less important one has to be to take one's cares to the mayor. These are most often simple requests for information concerning the state, its benefits, career opportunities and regulations. For example, a young man approaching military age and wondering whether he qualifies for an exemption as a supporter of his family or whether he must serve while his family receives compensation for his absence must seek his answer at the *mairie,* which registered his birth, registered him for the draft, will effectively decide (for its recommendation is normally taken) if the young man is to serve, and will pay his family compensation in case he does. In the same way someone wanting to open a grocery store would see the mayor as his first step.

On the state's behalf the mayor also registers births and deaths, performs marriages, runs hospitals (if any) and cemeteries, assures public order and street cleanliness, regulates markets and inspects food on sale for wholesomeness. If he falters in his public record-keeping, he is personally liable for damages (mayors therefore take out liability insurance), while if he fails, for example in the maintenance of order, the whole town can be sued for damages. This is what happened to Cherbourg, which was condemned by the Council of State to pay 120,586 francs ($24,000) to a worker who had been injured in 1968 by strikers as he was going to work. The mayor did not do his job, said the court, and now the town must raise taxes a bit and pay damages. The mayor must also execute all state laws and carry out the instructions of the prefect, whose office every month sends out a bulletin to all mayors reminding them of deadlines, asking for statistical information of all sorts (e.g., how many meat animals were killed in your town last month?), directing that certain policies be followed (e.g., "Poison for foxes will be set out this month in all areas known to harbor them"), or certain laws to be enforced with particular energy, and informing them of prefectoral decisions such as the rate at which towns must contribute to departmental road or fire expenses or that certain towns have been chosen to be fused with others, whether they like it or not (see below Chapter 6). In one such recent bulletin in the *département* of the Lower Rhine, the prefect notified the town of La Broque where it would henceforth hold its school council meetings.

There is, of course, no debate proper in the town council on mandated items in the budget. Councilmen vie in their declamations that the state is going to bankrupt all.[37] It would not be far from the truth to say that the common stand unanimously taken against the items on which the town has no choice has provided many a council with the cohesiveness needed to deal with matters on which they do have a choice.

These are many. The most important ones, which arouse the greatest interest in towns large and small, are the so-called *"équipements collectifs"*: schools, public buildings of all kinds, swimming pools, road improvements, etc. But even here the town is not alone. Theoretically towns can decide to build something and, if the prefect does not object, hire an architect, a builder, and be on the way; but things are not done like that. The prefect's is only the first clearance: the engineering services of the state are consulted: if it is a school, the representative of the Ministry of Education; if a pool, the man from Sports and Youth, etc. In practice, they must agree on the project. Usually, though, it is not so simple, for a *maire* would be foolish to overlook the possible availability of state subsidies for at least part of the project's cost. But subsidies must first be obtained, and therefore more bases are touched, more editions of the proposal made. Perhaps the most welcome part of the Reform Law of 31 December 1970 is the provision *anti remontée,* which theoretically gives the various ministries' agents at the department or regional level the power to decide such questions without the dossier making even one trip to Paris.[38] However, both deeply ingrained habits and some recent developments make town officials—especially in the larger towns—skeptical.

We refer to the state's assumption, especially under the Fifth Republic, of the role of initiator in the development of everything and anything connected with economic and social development within the framework of the plan.[39] It is much more likely nowadays for a mayor to be told by his sub-prefect, usually in a conference with his colleagues from adjoining towns, that he needs some *équipement collectif* than the other way around. The problem then will be to make sure it is built. For a small town this can be a serious problem. An example both extreme and characteristic is that of Créon, a town near Bordeaux, which was condemned by the Council of State on 2 July 1971 to pay a fine of 40,000 francs ($8,000) for having failed to provide itself with a sewage treatment plant and consequently having polluted a river. The mayor explained his case as follows: "For a long time we have asked to be enabled to build a treatment plant. But the state refused us its subsidy. Without this help the *département* cannot intervene and the loans either are not available or carry exorbitant interest rates. . . ."[40] Besides, he went on to argue, the town as a corporation did not pollute, but citizens individually . . . , etc. He lost, and the town paid.

Larger towns have an easier time conforming to the requirements of the plan because of the greater prestige of their mayors and because the government has decided to encourage smaller towns to join for the purpose of more efficiently playing their part in the scheme for national development. The units that can manage to set up a committee for cooperation with the plan can expect that it will be consulted by the authorities making up the Regional Program of Development and Equipment (PRDE), that is, the region's role in the plan. The PRDE is written by committees theoretically sitting in the prefecture, but inevitably each must work closely with the various ministries in Paris. In fact, such consultation is the essence of the plan's method. Practically, each territorial unit concentrates on pressing upon the planners the limits of its resources so that realistic targets will be established and a maximum of aid will be forthcoming for reaching them. Units of local government are under no legal compulsion to fulfill the plan, but the pressure to try very hard is great. For in these matters the state comes to the local level with, first of all, great authority, with some ideas, and most importantly with only part of the money. Monsieur Pierre Pflimlin, former prime minister under the Fourth Republic, minister of state under Charles de Gaulle, while *maire* of Strasbourg and president of the Strasbourg Urban Community comprising twenty-seven of the city's suburbs, once explained to the City Council as he presented them with their role in the PRDE how the figures before them had been arrived at: the local committee under his presidency working with the prefect and experts from the ministeries had decided what was needed to fulfill the plan, and then had to bargain with the ministries for the amount the state and the communes each would pay. Out of a request for 800 million francs, Strasbourg was promised 484 million. M. Pflimlin added:

> The local units — urban community and communes, will in principle have to furnish 650 millions. Clearly, the investment package will be supported at the rate of 43 percent by the state and 57 percent by the local units. One must further note that out of the 484 million pledged to our area, at least 150 millions are destined to finance projects of departmental, regional, or even national interests: I cite at random the National School for Handicapped Children, the new rectory buildings, the National School for Architecture, the Cité Hôtelière, the technical building college, and finally the new House of Detention whose clients perforce are not all from Strasbourg. Insufficient with regard to the needs of our expanding urban complex, the investments written into the PRDE require from our units a level of participation far beyond their means, that is to say, of the resources they can mobilize while maintaining their fiscal pressures within bearable limits.[41]

We now come to the subject of local revenue. Towns, of course, are big property owners, and nothing prevents a wise mayor from turning the *forêt domainiale* into a tree farm, or the vacant field under the cliff into a lucrative campground. Towns are very much in the real estate business and sometimes in the hotel and tourist business too. Of course, they charge fees for the use of hospitals, swimming pools, party halls, etc. The more money they make this way, the less taxes they will have to impose. So, mayors are expected to be good businessmen. But management of its "private domain" yields only a small part of what is needed, as do fees for services such as garbage collection, marriages, etc. So taxes must be heavy. They are of two basic kinds, a payroll tax and the *"Centimes additionels."*[42] The first is collected by the state as a supplement to the income tax and redistributed to the towns in proportion to their financial need. The second, the major source of revenue and ill feeling in French towns, can only be explained historically. Up to 1917, French taxes consisted of the "four old ones" (*les quatre vieilles*), taxes on built-up real estate, non-built-up real estate, residential occupancy (*mobilière*) and on business establishments (*patente*). Communes and *départements* were allowed to impose upon their citizens a small surtax on the total collected by the state within their jurisdiction. Or, as they put it, collect some additional *centimes* (cents) on each franc of taxes. When the state decided to switch its fiscal base to income and other taxes, it left local governments with the old system, only instead of collecting their additional *centimes* on real taxes, they now took them on assessed valuation — what they termed *principaux fictifs* (fictitious principles). Thus if the total value of the "four old ones" in a given town in a given year is calculated to be 100,000 francs, an additional centime is worth 1,000 francs (200 dollars). As time passed, inflation reduced the value of the franc, and the tasks of local governments grew, the number of these centimes imposed soared so that now the "four old ones" are being collected at many times their value. The communal council of Molsheim, population 9,000, for example, adopted an altogether normal budget which set the tax rate at 23,760 additional centimes plus an extra 800 centimes on the business establishment "tax." The extra emphasis in the *patente* seems to be due as much to a preference for indirect (or hidden) taxes as to state policy with regard to small businessmen, for business taxes are merely passed on to the large number of consumers in higher prices and generate much opposition only from a relatively small number of businessmen involved. In fact, the much-talked-about final solution to the hectic local fiscal situation involves sharing of the TVA (tax on value added), the very latest word in indirect taxation, between the state and localities.

There is no doubt, though, that these taxes, especially the *patente,* are shaping French towns. Already hard-pressed by the competition of shopping centers, French merchants find in the tax yet another obstacle to their survival. One of their posters reads: "What would this town look like without us?" But this is only one of the questions to which citizens must look for answers not among themselves but in Paris.

However, local, but especially town, institutions do represent their citizens, if not for the purpose of recognizably political action, then surely for the purpose of achieving good relations with the state. In France one does not fight against City Hall, but with it; not perhaps out of love, but of necessity.[43]

From the state's point of view, town institutions serve very well indeed; they afford it with a most effective agent on the scene, the *maire,* who has great authority to act on its behalf and none at all to go against it, even if he sometimes is recalcitrant. Moreover, the elected status of town officials, the latitude they have in transacting the town's private business, and the mediating role they play between citizens, interests, and the state makes them not only effective in persuading the people to accept administrative decisions, but also gives Frenchmen a feeling of participation available nowhere else in their democracy. For this reason local officials are excellent interlocutors for the state as it works to modernize the country and stimulate its economy.

But because local institutions have served well, it is believed they can be reformed to serve even better in the future as intermediaries in planned modernization. Thus, the "reform of local institutions" is one of the prime topics of discussion in political France today. As the various proposals proceed primarily from Gaullism and are an integral part of it, we will treat them at some length in that context. It will suffice for us now to mention them. First, since French towns are thought to be too small in population and financial resources to support and utilize the *équipements collectifs* needed for a modern way of life, they must be combined. Second, since efficiency demands that decisions on development be made away from Paris, closer to the job site, but the 95 *départements* are too small to be units of planning on a grand scale, they, too, will be grouped into regions (resembling the old royal provinces).

But care must be taken, so the reformers continue, to avoid twin dangers: the new units must not be political; that is, they must not, either because of the powers they have or the manner of their officials' election, be in a position to challenge the state's monopoly on politics; on the other hand, they must effectively represent the people and interest them in what is going to happen in their area, so as to "associate the people with the reforms." In the long run, if they succeed, the reforms might also engender some of the civic spirit the French state so badly needs.

In other words, the object of the reforms is to re-create the present relationship of the state and its most peculiar institution on a more efficient, more fruitful scale. Whether or not they succeed, given the delicacy, importance, and complexity of local feelings, is a big question.

But if control of territory is the most immediate condition for the survival of the state, surely the kind of person which grows up in it is no less important in the long run. In fact, no achievement of the French state has been as widely acclaimed as the French educational system.

Education

One Frenchman in 100 is a teacher employed by the Ministry of Education which, in all, employs 800,000 people: one Frenchman in sixty-three.

But even when education was smaller numerically, it was always among the chief concerns of the French state. For the *philosophes* who inspired the Revolution it was the means by which people would be lifted out of the ignorance which, more than the king's army, kept them from living a life worthy of men; for Condorcet it was the antidote to the poison of religion, for Voltaire the path to virtue and for Rousseau a natural right. For Napoleon it was a military necessity to provide his cohorts with enough skilled personnel and the home-front with administrators. For the Third Republic, author of the French public school system much as we see it today, it was as well a dictate of conscience (for, it was believed, men are fully men only when they can exercise the peculiarly human faculty of reason), a doctrinal imperative (for democratic doctrine demands a citizenry wedded to the Republic by knowledge of its legitimacy, and able to choose intelligently those who will best care for its interests), and a measure of political war against the power of the Catholic Church, which had a large hand in education and, until the eve of World War I, was loudly supporting a restoration of the monarchy. In this tradition, French educators have, until recently, tended to see themselves in the triple role of defenders of the Republic, mainstay of the *Patrie's* defense, and ambassadors from the realm of culture. They operated a system of primary education that was universal, compulsory and secular, followed by an equally secular but highly selective secondary system leading to the Baccalaureate exam, the passport to either the university (seat of culture and training ground for teachers, doctors and lawyers), or the specialized, prestigious *Grandes Ecoles,* from which come the higher technical cadres for state, army and economy. Even as France was divided into 90 (now 95) *départements* for political administration, it was divided into 23 *académies* for the purpose of academic administration.

The French state cares about education. We, for our part, would fail to convey how much were we to proceed with our examination of the school system without mentioning that every couple married in France from 29 April to 31 December 1972 received from their *maire* as a wedding gift from the Ministry of Education, a package of six classics of French literature personally chosen by *Monsieur le Ministre:* works by Voltaire, Stendahl, Balzac, Victor Hugo, Chateaubriand, and Flaubert. In his announcement, the minister, M. Guichard, reminded Frenchmen that they are among the poorest readers in Europe and pledged that he will follow up on M. Pompidou's longstanding effort to remedy that. We could find no one who thought this expenditure of 6.5 million francs a bad idea, only skepticism as to how soon after the wedding the gifts would be made use of.

The elementary school system has changed less in its curriculum than in the concept which animates it and in the personnel which staffs it. Up to the 1950s the elementary school had been designed to give everyone, but above all to the overwhelming majority (95 percent in 1900) who would receive no other formal schooling, a self-contained package of instruction enabling all to express themselves adequately in spoken and written French, to do the arithmetic necessary for normal personal business, a basic understanding of the world of science around them, and the proper opinions about their country. Teachers knew how much time they had, and long experience had taught them how to make the most of it. Today Americans do not cease to wonder at the breadth of knowledge displayed in ordinary conversation by adult Frenchmen who never went beyond the fifth grade. But if Monsieur Boudin's knowledge of Victor Hugo was probably not gained in the fourth grade twenty-two years ago, it is certain that it was there he gained both the ability and the desire to gain it on his own. Today, while the emphasis on reading, writing, arithmetic, and French history has not greatly diminished, everyone knows that since schooling to age sixteen is now mandatory, the five elementary grades are for all children only part of their schooling. But the loss of urgency and unity in the elementary school is less the consequence of the increase in the length of obligatory schooling than of the dilution of the teacher corps, doubled in size in the past fifteen years and now no longer composed of carefully chosen "missionaries," but of young people of uneven preparation and dedication.[44] Among the practical consequences of this is a two-fold increase in fifteen years of the proportion of children who must repeat at least one elementary class. This now stands at 80 percent. On the whole though, standards remain high and parents delight in the amount of their children's homework, sure sign that they are not wasting their time.

The changes which have taken place in secondary education are more significant. The symbol of these changes is the demise of the famous *Examen d'entrée en 6eme*, the entrance exam for secondary education, accomplished over a fifteen year period long before the official date of its passing on March 16, 1972. Taken after the fifth grade and designed to select those best fitted for academic pursuits, it used to be the first of a long series of exams which young Frenchmen aspiring to high stations in life had to pass. Like the others they would face, such as the "Bac"[45] to enter a *Grande Ecole*, or to take a sought-after job, it was difficult and absolutely impersonal: the examiners would be brought in from another part of the *académie* to ensure anonymity, synonymous with equality of opportunity. Now all this is changed. As a twin measure of democratization and of increase in educational opportunity — for disproportionately few children from workers' or farmers' families were passing the exam — the exam was abolished. The sixth grade was opened to practically all and an admissions committee including educators, administrators, psychologists, and parents has been established in each *département*. The committee decides on the basis of a child's individual *dossier*, taking into account besides grades and academic evaluations, the family's socioeconomic situation. But more significant than the rarity of exclusions is the very personal basis upon which decisions are made and the apparent paradox this poses: heretofore democracy required equality of treatment which in turn required anonymity to ensure only professional criteria would be considered, whereas now the same principle calls for discrimination on very personal bases for which individuals are not responsible: their socioeconomic origins.[46] The explanation no doubt includes the difference between equality of opportunity, which was guaranteed by the exam system, and equality of results which is the aim of the new.

As the exam disappeared, a new secondary system emerged: the children who would have remained in the primary system, the *Primaire Supérieur* — for by 1960 the school-leaving age had been raised to sixteen — now did their last four years in new *Collèges D'Enseignement Général* (CEG, colleges of general instruction), while the growing number of those "admitted to the sixth" now found the first four years (or "first cycle") of the Lycée renamed "College of Secondary Instruction" (CES). The final step, which occurred in 1964, allowed those completing the CEG as well as those completing the CES to enter the final years of the Lycée to prepare for the "Bac" exam. Since the CES and CEG offer a variety of courses, only some of which prepare one for the "Bac," while others treat subjects of general or career interest, students are able to sample several alternatives before deciding whether to switch to a technical (trade) school, enter a technical or agricultural Lycée or to continue to pursue the prestigious "Bac." But undoubtedly what keeps an even greater percentage of young people from the Lycée (45 percent of seventeen year olds are there now) is that the "Bac" looms both as a promise and as a threat. One can take the exam in one of five series (A-E, and many sub-series) corresponding to different fields of concentration, but one knows from experience that even in the easiest series (A, literature) about 30 percent fail, while in some of the more difficult ones (D and E, mathematics and physics) the failure rate reaches 55 percent in some academies.[47] Those who fail have in effect gambled and lost three or more years, since a majority, especially since the easing of the Lycée, take more than three years to prepare for it. Moreover, failure is not taken lightly in France.

The state has done its best without resorting to compulsion to steer a majority of young people into vocational preparation: one reads from time to time of high officials declaring the nobility of technical trades; and a recent change of policy makes it possible to earn a Certificate of Professional Aptitude (CAP), heretofore available only in the technical schools, without leaving the CEG-CES system.[48] De Gaulle, for his part, often chided educators for not authoritatively guiding young people into occupations for which they were fitted and needed.[49] But the prestige of the "Bac" is great even if after it one is practically constrained by the scarcity of jobs at that level to go on with education.[50] The problem, purely one of social prestige being preferred over a secure living, is one which faces the state which, most agree, has an obligation toward those it trains. Of the four possible solutions (withdraw the state from manpower training, re-institute competitive exams for academic secondary education, institute "compulsory guid-ance," or somehow find or make jobs for all), only the last two are being talked of.

The questions of prestige, of the nobility of occupations, have overshadowed another far more important one: Is the purpose of education the formation of a certain kind of man or of a certain kind of useful social operative: citizen, engineer, etc.? As we have indicated, the republican founders of the French school system had not seen the possibility of conflict between culture and social utility. It was socially and politically useful that men be formed in a particular kind of culture. That one should attempt to give people more of that culture than they could grasp or more than they cared for was against the tenets of that same culture. The views of one old Lycée professor are typical: a man of the Left, a socialist since youth, he had devoted his life to bringing that precious liberating culture, Descartes, Rabelais, Racine, etc., to the sons of the people. Now he finds his classes crowded with youths who in his view were allowed to get there without giving sufficient proof that they want to be there, are able to handle the work, or understand where it is they are. They neglect his courses shamefully, he complains, for they believe only subjects related to success, such as spoken English and mathematics, are relevant to their futures. There may be a few in his classes who care about culture, but with so few teaching it is very difficult. At best he puts good books into their hands. Even the dreaded hurdle of the "Bac" has been lowered. "Of course over a third still fail," a young lady with four years' teaching experience in a Paris Lycée told us, "but that is only because the grading is so much easier now. Students tell me to go to hell, that they will study for two weeks before the exam and pass. Since the ministry's quota has remained firm, two-thirds of them are right by definition." Educators in general sympathize with these professors' views, while invariably adding one or more caveats about the academy's role as a state institution and the consequent necessity to serve changing social needs and bend to changing demands. But how to harmonize needs, especially changing ones, and quality learning? Here ideas are scarce. In fact it is difficult in a democratic society concerned about its place in the modern world to conceive of educational reforms by separating vocational training and liberal education thereby restricting access to something prestigious or believed to be synonymous with social advancement. Everyone wants social mobility, but only as long as it's upward. This includes most intellectuals, few of whom, especially among those of the New Left, regret the decline of high culture and the cheapening of the "Bac." After all, one hears, the history of democratic freedom is that of the fall of one privileged class after another: the privileges of landed nobility disappeared even under the monarchy, with the revolution went those of birth, and after the first war, those of the rich. It was about time the last institution allowed to grant titles began to shake! But in fact both institution and titles have been shaken less by the few who profess hatred for them than by the many who, seeking the prestige and social position long associated with the kind of man formed by high culture and seeing culture merely as a means, are trampling it, snuffing it out in the rush.

What reveals best of all the predicament of secondary education is the wave of suicides among secondary teachers (eight in a three month period at the end of 1971) and the ever-present newspaper stories of teachers suffering nervous collapses. These occur for a variety of reasons—one much–publicized suicide case involved a Lycée mathematics teacher in deep disagreement with a ministry directive on teaching the New Math—but the very variety of causes shows the number of

stresses under which the system is now operating. Interestingly, religion, which was once *the* key problem of French
educators, is hardly mentioned anymore. The final blow to the
"issue" was delivered by the so-called Debré Law of 1959,
which offered state contracts (i.e., financial support) to private
schools (i.e., Catholic schools, primarily) if they met certain
state criteria. Since then the state has been financing "Catholic" education and no one raises a hubbub about it. The public
schools are of course firmly secular, but every pupil has
Wednesday (formerly Thursday) off, at which time churches
hold religious instruction. Even in Alsace and Lorraine, which
have preserved the German tradition of religious instruction
in school, school is out on Wednesday. The state, which once
was so adamant on the subject, simply is not any more. But
then again, neither are the churches.

The problems of French higher education, though related
to those of the Lycée, are different. Its growth has been more
spectacular than that of secondary education: in 1950 only 6
percent of Frenchmen went on beyond the "Bac," whereas in
1970 more than 20 percent did. But one part of the higher
education system, the university, has absorbed most of the new
enrollment. For it, physical overcrowding has been only a
relatively minor cause of grief.

Having momentarily pushed out of the forefront of one's
mind the hirsute vociferous minority of students, one begins
to grasp the dimensions of the trouble by glancing at the Paris
daily *Le Monde* where high level jobs are advertised: whether
it is for an engineer, a sales manager or an account executive,
the ad will carry the caption *Grandes Ecoles.* These "Great
Schools," originally a Napoleonic concept, are under the Ministry of Education, but completely independent of the university.
They have a near-monopoly on higher professional education in France. We have already mentioned the ENA (National School of Administration). Some others are: ENP (Poly-
technic), which has a history of training administrative and
technical cadres for the army and for industry (a surprising

number of generals are polytechnicians, including the first two commanders of the First Army), the ENE (electricity), and ENM (mines), ENI (civil engineers) and ENS, the *Ecole Normale Superieure,* completion of which constitutes the very highest qualification a professor in French higher education can have. Georges Pompidou, President of the Republic, alumnus of the *Ecole Normale* (and therefore called *Normalien*) is only the most obvious example of how the *Grandes Ecoles* have trained the men who now lead France in so many fields. Entrance is always by competitive examination. Courses in preparation for these exams, given by Lycées, or by the *Ecole* itself, seldom occupy less than two years of a man's life. Little wonder that once a man has successfully entered and passed one of these schools he feels that he belongs to another class of men! It is difficult to overemphasize the importance attached in France to initial qualifications. By hard work and luck in exams, one can rise from the lowest to the highest social stations. But once the exam is taken the decision is made: one belongs further up or one does not. Other means of ascent are not so open. Armand and Drancourt, in *The European Challenge* (Paris, 1968), have blamed the importance attached to exams for slow economic progress and social tension. In fact, the ties that bind alumni of British public schools are not stronger than those of *Normaliens* or *Polytechniciens.* The university, on the other hand, except for its faculties of medicine and law and for its function as a trainer of teachers, was intended simply to educate men, little thought being given as to how they might be employed. Its faculties are open to anyone with an appropriate "Bac." The university is in crisis today, while the *Grandes Ecoles* are not. An example will begin to elucidate the difference.

A young man who recently received a doctorate in electronics from the university after seven years of hard work and excellent exam grades spent a year in vain trying to find a job as an engineer at a time when France is experiencing a shortage of qualified engineers. The reason was that although his knowledge equaled or surpassed that of graduates of the ENE or the ENP, he did not have the title. Finally he gratefully accepted a position with a large company—with only token salary for the first two years—where he would work as an engineer and with luck as the years pass be considered on a par with men who have less of everything except an official title. Switching jobs will always pose problems for him of course. Why, then, does any man whose future is not already assured and who is interested in something other than medicine, law or education choose the university, knowing careers and opportunities are there in limited number? For our young man the university had been the easy choice: he had not wanted to spend years preparing for an entrance examination, compensation for which effort is far from certain, for one can easily fail. So he went to the university and there joined most of his fellows in *the* university topic of conversation: *debouchés.* What job will I be able to get?

The widespread anger in the French university can be largely attributed to the anguish about *debouchés.* That the anger is related to a lack of participation in curriculum formation, budgeting, etc., on the part of students and young professors has been cast into doubt by the overwhelming apathy with which students especially have greeted elections for delegates to the university councils established after the riots of 1968 to give students a sense of participation. After the novelty of the committees passed, only about 35 percent of the students has bothered to vote. In 1971 participation at the large universities ranged from 9 percent at Rennes to 59 percent at Nancy.[51] Nor do the political battles for which French universities are famous any longer rage. The fortunes of the national political parties have, with the exception of the Communists, long since ceased to interest the university world. As we will see when we discuss the political agenda before France today, most items are rather boring unless one happens to be directly interested:

rates of growth, social security benefits, party squabbles without consequence, not at all the sort of thing that fires up students or, for that matter, the parties themselves.[52] Only one burning political conflict exists: that of the *Groupuscules Gauchistes,* little ultra-leftist groups against the Communist Party, bourgeois society, and so on. But despite the efforts of Jean-Paul Sartre and incidents such as the death of a *Gauchiste* in a riot at the Renault factory gate, their activities interest primarily the police. But where students are unhappy and resentful largely over the lack of *debouchés,* are young and have time on their hands (less than 40 percent ever receive a diploma), even a small spark can set off a destructive, if brief, fire.

As for the general public, its concern with the university, besides the maintenance of order and the scarcity of *debouchés,* is the fact that only 6 percent of the university students come from poor families. How to get more people in (for one does not speak of ejecting those who are there now) and how to prepare for them a worthy, prestigious job afterward: those are the answers one receives to the question of what should be done about the university! There is of course little the Ministry of Education can do, given academic freedom, to gear the traditional university curricula to the needs of industry, but it is trying to set up cooperative consultation sessions between deans and businessmen for that purpose. In addition the government has been putting pressure on businessmen to stop requiring graduation from a *Grande Ecole* for high level positions.

Coordination between business and the university, however, is very strongly opposed by professors and politically active students in general. It would somehow be demeaning to the university's character to subordinate its noble concerns to the requirements of rotten capitalist society. This was one of the many stimuli agitators used to animate the 1968 revolts. One gets the feeling students feel cheated: they have spent their time on a road presumed to lead to the life of the elite, and no sooner can they see its end, than the image of that life dissolves for them.

As for increasing the proportion of proletarians in the university, the state would like nothing better, but there is very strong resistance among educators to any further tampering with the "Bac." The problem of the university is one the state must solve, for it cannot afford to continue to supply the educational system with teachers educated in an atmosphere of disappointment, concern, and politics of such a strange sort. After all, the supply of teachers trained in the old school will not last forever. This crisis is one the ministry is ill-equipped to handle: even if in the future it succeeds in "democratically" cutting the flow into the university (or more likely in making more jobs available to graduates) and although it wields great power over all faculties, conflicts between the two opposing views of education in democracy are not of the sort that can be resolved without a clear view of what education is. The men of the Third Republic, animated by a particular view of democracy, fashioned the system in one coherent manner but those who have reformed it (de Gaulle and Fouchet) did so without an opposing comprehensive view.

The State and the Economy

Some examples of the economic enterprises owned and operated by the state only begin to indicate its importance in the economic lives of Frenchmen: the entire production and distribution of coal, gas, and electricity belongs to the state as do the only two important French-owned oil companies; the entire rail and maritime transportation industries, the largest airline (Air France) as well as the telephone network; the nation's largest automobile company, Renault, representing 30 percent of all auto production, as well as the country's largest aircraft manufacturer (SNIAS), which accounts for 60 percent of the industry's production; the largest banks, including the

Credit Lyonnais and the *Caisse d'Epargne,* accounting for roughly 50 percent of deposit banking, as well as several large insurance companies, which together do about 40 percent of the industry's business. In toto, state-owned companies possess about half the total fixed corporate assets in France and account for well over half the Gross National Product.[53] Beyond ownership, the state exercises considerable control over everything from labor's wages, to the quality of products, to prices. Further, as both owner and supervisor, it has taken the lead in shaping the future lives of all Frenchmen by means of large-scale economic planning meant to change the country not only economically, but also socially and politically. But perhaps more significant than the role it actually plays is that which it is believed and expected to play, for it has become habitual for Frenchmen to look to the state for what they desire and to blame it for what they lack.

When the price of milk rose nine centimes, Madame Arin, one of the overwhelming majority for whom the rising cost of living is the number one preoccupation in life,[54] said: "They're raising prices again; how do they expect people to live," referring not to the farmers or the storekeepers, but to the only agency thought at once capable of setting prices and responsible for one's standard of living: the state. In this case Madame Arin was right: the préfecture had indeed decreed a new price for milk beginning in April, subsequent to an agreement of the Common Market countries on a new schedule of agricultural price support levels. Since the beginning of the Agricultural Common Market, agricultural prices have been set this way. This is but one way in which the state controls prices. The most direct involves simply the price policies of state-owned enterprises, but a variety of other more or less complicated ones has been in force for most of the period since the end of the Second World War. The current price control policy appears more liberal than some in the past, since it involves no direct controls on the prices of industries employing less than twenty persons, on luxury goods (defined as goods taxed at a rate superior to one-third of their value), and on products in heavy competition with imports.

As announced by the minister of finance in March, 1972, the system establishes a guideline of 3 percent for rises in industrial prices. Industrialists were invited singly or by product-sectors to negotiate with the ministry a price policy for the '72-'73 season. This policy, once embodied in signed contracts, would be adhered to by the signers within the conditions set down in them. This is not a mere prohibition against price rises greater than 3 percent per annum, because ministry officials have been instructed to take into account the company's particular situation. Companies having especially benefited from productivity increases are not to be allowed so much leeway as those, for example, having suffered from strikes. If a company refuses the invitation, it will merely have to submit all proposed price changes to prior approval by the Finance Ministry. No comparison need be made between the degree of sympathy shown non-contractors and contractors. Furthermore, all companies and persons engaged in services (barber shops, garages, etc.) must follow a price schedule laid down by the prefect in each *département,* or more precisely all engaged in services who do not explicitly notify the ministry to the contrary are presumed to have agreed to follow that schedule.

This "contractual policy" has its major significance outside the realm of prices, for these, after a generation of controls, have been rising at an annual rate of about 6 percent since 1968.[55] Labor unions as well as industries are strongly encouraged to "contract" their demands and although the former—especially the CGT—have not been signing in droves, they all have been discussing their desires with representatives of management and of the state and finding out how much support or opposition would be forthcoming from the latter were certain demands pressed. In other fields this policy has borne fruit: March, 1972, for example, saw the National Council of Employers *(Patronat)* and the major labor confederations brought to agreement by the state on a plan by which unemployed persons between 60 and 65 years of age receive, beginning July 1, 1972, early retirement benefits amounting to between 60 and 75 percent of their last salary, depending on age and number of dependents. For the state, more important than the share of the cost each agreed to have its members pay is the prospect of business and labor leaders who participated in the discussions going back and "selling" the plan to their constituents. Here was a "problem" which was agitating labor circles and to which the press was paying much attention: people over 60 who lost their jobs were having a hard time finding new ones and what was the state doing about it? Instead of bearing the criticism, or deciding on a solution unilaterally (say a placement program, or an early retirement program), and then informing both business and labor how it would be paid for, the state called for negotiations and succeeded in sharing with "representatives" of the interested parties responsibility both for the particular solution and for the pay deductions and forced contributions which would in any case have had to be imposed to finance any solution.

We placed the term "representatives" in quotation marks because, of course, employers do not elect by universal suffrage the men who bargain with the state on early retirement or on any other matter: The Employers Council is a voluntary organization of big business, somewhat comparable to the National Association of Manufacturers (NAM) in the United States and can be said to "speak for business" only in a figurative sense, while labor unions count as members only about a fourth of French wage earners. Obviously treatment of such groups by the state as veritable plenipotentiaries for a class of interests tends to deliver to them from above much authority that had not been granted them from below. The tendency of the authorities, whether at the ministry or prefecture level to seek representatives of the people in this manner is, to be sure, a great inducement for Frenchmen to join interest groups. Businessmen especially cannot afford to have competitors "represented" and able to propose obnoxious regulations while they are not there to protect themselves. Thus in certain product sectors and professional groups, membership does approach universality. This approach however causes some very practical difficulties. The case of labor unions is illustrative: already in the troubles of 1968 it was clear that thousands of workers no longer saw the unions as their agents but as a sort of labor relations division of the state or of the plant. In fact, it was the spontaneous growth of ad hoc groups characterized more by their radical pugnacity than by their radical social ideology which was so disquieting about the 1968 disturbances, which so heightened concern with participation in general, and paradoxically, convinced the government its contractual policy is the key to social peace. Commentators friendly to the government agree the remedy is to extend and decentralize the contractual process so that consultations on price or wage levels, standards, etc., will associate as many people on the grass roots level as possible.[56] But on complex matters, whose opinions are to serve as the basis of discussions? Committees are of necessity abstractions of society. On what basis are their members to be chosen? And since unanimity is inconceivable, on what basis are decisions to be made? Voting is a priori excluded, for that would politicize everything and make rational harmonization of interest impossible. These difficulties are put into proper perspective, however, if one remembers that as far as the state is concerned the purpose of cooperative consultation is not so much to make decisions, but to organize adherence to them. The flow of ideas and authority can only be from the top down, since the higher one goes the more comprehensive a view one should have of the needs of the whole and the more power one has to turn decisions into effective action. But people all the way down the line must have a feeling that their needs have been taken into account and that they have had a chance to be heard. The best way to do this, French officials have decided, is to lay down general policies and then to allow various interests to decide, under state supervision, how they will play their part in them.

Contractual policy or cooperative consultation is the basic *modus operandi* of the plan and, along with economic growth, is itself one of the things the plan is to promote.[57] First established by General de Gaulle's post-war government on January 3, 1946, to strengthen the state by stimulating and coordinating economic recovery, it has grown into a vast effort to modernize, rationalize and economically stimulate France. Covering a period of five years (as of 1972, France was in its sixth plan), the plan is not as in Communist countries a set of legally enforceable decrees formulated and promulgated by the state and heeded by its subjects, but a semi-original attempt rationally to direct all significant public and private economic activity down to the individual plant or bridge by means of discussions open to all interested parties culminating in a general understanding of needs and the responsibility to do one's part in meeting them.[58] It is the foremost current example of "soft" or "democratic" as opposed to Soviet-style "hard" planning.

The General Commissariat of the Plan is a small bureau directly under the Prime Minister with only 60 professional staff members (in 1967). Most are high level personnel on loan from the *Grands Corps* and enjoy enough personal prestige and political support to draw information and cooperation from the rest of the administration. The Commissariat's task is to draw up the plan and supervise its execution, but its activity is that of a coordinator, and the real work of the plan is done by about thirty vertical committees known as "modernization commissions," each for an area of French life affected by the plan: university, steel, culture, chemicals, schools, sports facilities, agriculture, roads, and so on. Here sit high "representatives" of the interests involved together with civil servants from the concerned ministries plus the Ministry of Finance and the Commissariat of the Plan. The following table gives a breakdown of the membership[59] of the Fourth Plan's (1960-1965) committees:

Employers (including the nationalized industries)	715
Farmers	107
Employers' Professional Associations	562
Trade Unionists	281
Civil Servants	781
Other (university teachers and independent experts)	691
Total	3,137

The civil servants, armed with the statistics of the Economic and Financial Research Service (the possible), and with the ideas of the highest political authorities (the desirable), coordinate the desires of the interested parties and with their cooperation forecast output, employment, and above all, investment. This last allows for the adjustment of borrowing pressure and the partitioning of that scarce French commodity, investment capital. Theoretically this allows simultaneously for maximum return on investments, a minimum of inflation, and attention to social priorities. In addition to the vertical, there are also "horizontal" committees, the most important of which are the regional ones whose task is to individualize the plan for a particular area in harmony with the whole. Regional committees, as we have seen, write the PRDE and see to its implementation at the regional, departmental, and communal levels.

The committees' work continues once the plan has been drawn, for revision goes along with implementation, but most of all because one of their most important functions is to give the socioeconomic sectors "represented" by their members a continuous feeling of participation. The solemn votes of approval cast by the Parliament as well as the Economic and Social Council, are intended to consummate the nation's common agreement on the plan. The plan, as General de Gaulle used to remind his countrymen, is a national moral obligation. Whereas in his war memoirs de Gaulle had considered economic power merely as one of the principal elements in a nation's greatness, in the memoirs of his presidency the tone changes. In our time, judges the author, an increase in economic well-being is essential not only to the power but to the political existence of nations. Since modern means of communication allow everyone to compare his possessions with everyone else's at all times, constant economic improvement is essential to social peace.[60] Briefly, in the Gaullist vision, politics on the "home front" is not really worthy of the name: only *Grosspolitik,* played on the largest of stages, deserves it. At home the very efficient management of things should replace the wasteful, divisive and weakening clash of persons and ideas. Only by eliminating it, by turning people's attention from what amounted to self-destruction to the task of building, could order and progress triumph within, laying the basis for grandeur without. This required a change of attitude on the part of both state and citizens: the former had to become a stimulator but the latter had to learn to enjoy what is good for them. Even the plan's economic ends are themselves supra-economic. Chief among them is a change in common attitudes toward economics.

Not that Frenchmen had ever minded wealth, but some of their attitudes had not been conducive to creating massive amounts of it. Historians usually mention the following causes: the rate of saving and capital formation had always been among the lowest in the West, family businesses predominated, fear of borrowing was widespread, the tax burden was high, the powerful state was not particularly friendly to capitalism, and while the *Grandes Ecoles* turned out some leaders enamored of technology, educated men in general were against business. For us, attempting to judge what the past must have been like by observing its remnants in the present, it seems worthy of mention that in France money is seen as a means to status, not as a substitute for it. Consequently, since the great grantor of status, the state, bestowed it on a thoroughly nonpecuniary basis—the competitive exam, and the state did not encourage capitalism, it is not surprising that more energies were not turned to the demanding, continuous task of business expansion. Not very much has changed, except the attitude of the state, and that has made a difference.

Managerial headaches, long hours and short lunches for executives and, above all, bigness and efficiency are "in." *Le Surmenage,* the lot of the overburdened executive, is today as popular as liver ailments once were. The newspapers are filled with talk of millions of francs invested here and there, the term *"Industrie de Pointe,"* industry on the leading edge of technology, is pronounced with a mixture of reverence and desire—every town wants one. Even *Le Monde,* the newspaper of the elite, now joins in the praises of the symbol of it all: *L'ordinateur,* the computer. And in November, 1970, a unique industrial association was founded: the criteria for membership are an annual growth rate of at least 17 percent and a profit of at least 10 percent per year. Its first national congress was addressed by the Prime Minister.

Evidence as to the feelings of French businessmen can be found in the public opinion polls: in 1970, the French Public Opinion Institute journal *Sondages* published a portrait of French "businessmen"—significantly using the English language term—which showed them overwhelmingly concerned about the lack of management skills in France (88.4 percent), a sure sign they are not being neglected, and about the unenterprising banking system (70.5 percent), a good indication that it is changing. They also agreed they need to take more risks, export more and do more research. Their attitude toward the state was ambivalent: three-fourths agreed taxes are too high, but 95 percent and 94 percent respectively agreed that the state should build up the country's infrastructure (roads, etc.) and that companies have social responsibilities. Finally, 91 percent agreed the state spends too much money supporting agriculture. *Le businessman* thus is thoroughly modern and trying to be more so. In favor of freedom? Yes, but he is more concerned with obtaining state aid and just as worried that others might get it. But most important of all, because of the status given him by his association with the state in exchange for his independence, he is no longer ashamed of being an entrepreneur.

What have the results been? The condition of the French economy, according to the figures, is good, even excellent. In 1970, the French GNP grew at the world's highest rate, 5.4 percent, and per capita income stood at $2,500 per year. In fact, France, at least since the mid '60s, has been improving both GNP and per capita GNP at a rate greater even than Germany's, while also surpassing the latter in investment. Just how much credit for France's economic progress should be attributed to official efforts is impossible to say, but even admitting that gross figures have only a limited meaning in a country where so many transactions are actually in-house affairs of the state, France is prospering.[61]

The state's passion for bigness, however, has had some side effects which may prove harmful. Foremost among them is a drop in the rate at which new companies are being formed. Now at .9 percent (nine new firms per year per 1000 existing ones), it is less than one-tenth that in the United States (9.8 percent) and one-third below the rate (1.35 percent) at which French firms are disappearing! Thus, at a time when the active population is growing in numbers and business is the order of the day, France is losing 9,000 businesses a year. The article in *Le Monde* which reported these figures (September 1, 1970) also spoke of concern on the part of some state planners about the lack of dynamic innovative shoestring operations in France. These, by proving the feasibility of new methods and products, often act as a leaven on larger ones. After citing examples of this in the American business world, the article mentions that in the United States 80 percent of the dollar amount of business done on new products is done on products developed outside the research programs of large companies, where four-fifths of the innovations made are never pursued. The fact that the only French firm to participate in the American moon landing is a very small, ultra high-quality optical company was cited to clinch the argument.

But the logic of the state's role in the economy is against smallness. Further, the state's choice of big businessmen as interlocutors in planning accentuates the already strong tendency of Frenchmen to regard that which has official sanction as more *sérieux* (and by implication, that which lacks it as not so *sérieux*). Consequently, the young firm's two basic needs, easy loan capital and lack of interference, are not likely to be met in France. Perhaps indicative of the state's attitude is that the bureau within the Ministry of Industry which used to be known as the "Secretariat of State for Small and Medium Enterprises" has changed its name to "Secretariat of State for Medium and Small Industry." Most small businesses in France are farms, shops or artisan's enterprises. Their relationship with the state is an interesting one, for they belong to people who are among the most fiercely independent-minded in France. They also are, as a rule, deeply worried about the future.

The source of their troubles, as they see it, is the state. The farmers are probably wrong: the 15 percent of the population engaged in farming is not decreasing faster than it is probably because of massive government price supports, but, as it is, one French farm closes every 12 minutes and 2.7 percent of the total farm population becomes dependent on the wage economy each year. But small farmers know the state considers the passing of their way of life a necessity. Small businessmen have just as much resentment, but better cause for it. The heavy local business taxes, the 20 percent tax that must be paid whenever a small business changes hands, favoritism shown big business, the fact that unlike salaried employees they do not have paid vacations—these are but a few of their complaints. Because of them 600,000 shopkeepers and 800,000 independent artisans have long considered themselves at war with the state. In 1956 they gave the Fourth Republic a major shock by electing 52 deputies to the National Assembly in what many thought was a fascist revival. In the 1960s, however, the Poujadist movement, as it was called, dissolved, its leaders, including Pierre Poujade, joining the Gaullist majority. But in 1969 the *commerçants et artisans* waged a violent campaign which political observers believe helped to defeat the referendum and caused the general's departure. In the early 1970s they remained the most vociferous group outside the Maoist Left. They demand not only an end to discriminatory taxation, but also their inclusion into the state social security system, subsidies for artisans changing to more lucrative trades, and rent control for commercial establishments. The point here is that even the most strident anti-state group asks the state to be taken under its wing. The government in fact moved to grant many of their demands in 1972, doubtless because shopkeepers and artisans are needed in its electoral fold. The "package" included a provision for state aid to their pension funds, which, however, will henceforth be run under tighter supervision and will require contributions at the same rate as salaried workers. Another measure provides for a special exit subsidy to small shopkeepers over 60 whose businesses have become unprofitable—to be financed by a tax on supermarkets. The latter provision, however, was bitterly contested by the supermarket lobby and the decree was not officially published until new financing was arranged. But perhaps farmers, artisans and shopkeepers are not perfect examples because they are the largest interest groups in France and as such depend not so much on the state as on politics. These attitudes risk appearing curious unless one keeps in mind that when the state alone is considered all-powerful, it is natural to blame it for misfortunes, while looking to it alone for relief.

Constant in the strength of its nonpolitical body, but capable of changing policy swiftly when ordered by its political head, the state is the object of reliance, but not of confidence. This makes the state's control over the French economy a fragile thing; this made it possible for the antics of a few hundred students in 1968 to become a free-for-all of demands, the satisfaction of which cost a 12.5 percent devaluation of the franc and began a period of inflation which the state has not been able to close. But if the elaborate relationship of state and economy does not avoid difficulties, political or economic, it does assure that what occurs in one area is felt in the other as well.

Summary

The things which most concern people, that seem to give the greatest personal satisfaction, such as retirements, vacations, job qualifications and security, as well as those which are the subject of the greatest worries, depend on the state.[62] The relatively high standard of living and the very symbol of modern Europe, the Common Market, are the subjects of the everyday work of administrators. The Common Market was even conceived by one: Jean Monnet who was the first *commissaire* of the plan in 1947. Politicians, the story goes, talk pompously and give you nothing but troubles. Now, thank goodness, we don't hear so much from them; we have professionals running things and we are living better. More depends on the state and less on politicians: the notion of simultaneous politicization and depoliticization is not at all paradoxical. Rather it depends on the traditional lack of distinction between the state and politics.

As we have said, perhaps the hallmark of the Fifth Republic has been its identification with the state. The state's long suit is not legitimacy (call father he who gives you bread!), nor even the elaborate set of legal or administrative guarantees that power will be fairly used. The latter are unknown to most, expensive, and anyhow applicable only to unusual cases. Rather the state's strength lies in its massive presence in areas very important to people, resulting in a sort of predictability. The state embodies legality, propriety, seriousness, internal security and the hope of a better life. The word "confidence" is too unambiguous to describe the feeling it engenders: "reliance" is better.

Significantly the most serious recent attempt in France at

analysis of the state has come from precisely the high officials who make up the leftist Club Jean Moulin. Their volume, *L'Etat et le Citoyen,* Paris, 1961, is based on the realization that life in modern France is characterized less and less by the liberties which men spoke of in the 18th century and lived in the 19th. But is each citizen not more interested in reaping the real benefits of good government decisions rather than in the exercise of his numerically infinitesimal power in national elections? The club thinks it is and regrets the passing of what was a noble illusion. Frenchmen do not seem to mind that many national decisions are taken by appointed rather than elected officials; after all, how many issues did the people ever really decide? The attitude of officials is of far more practical importance, for it really bears on how freely, smoothly and peacefully people will be allowed to enjoy their private lives.

This sort of liberty has little to do with participation in the conduct of public affairs, and is worlds away from the traditional democratic concept of deliberation and decision on the common good by the whole body of citizens or their representatives, served by persons—civil servants—who faithfully carry out their decisions. Whatever one's political opinions, in France no one thinks of the state as a servant. After all, so goes the disturbing argument made by some of the most perspicacious democrats, these private liberties were enjoyed even more ardently before the advent of democracy. The various monarchies were usually quite content to leave people alone if they paid their taxes, and they certainly took interest groups into account. Was it really worth it then to go through 150 years of anguish over democracy just to get a stronger state? Would it not have been better to leave the principle of authority alone and have reformed the state? Of course, the state today, unlike then, takes care of individual economic needs, and this is quite good, but what does this have to do with democracy?

French leaders today in fact are concerned about making up for a certain lack of popular participation in public affairs by means of administering territorial and economic units as well as other interests, e.g., the professions, education, and so on, through a system best described as cooperative consultation. This is the most salient feature of modern French democracy. The organizations consulted are perfectly free to disagree with state policy, and have every opportunity to try to convince officials to modify it, but since cooperation with the state is a legal obligation for local governments, and a practical necessity for others, the system aims at agreement more or less on state terms. The state in turn is obliged to take into account the political power and the nuisance value of each interest when it formulates its terms. But this sort of participation is not very appealing to Frenchmen. The Club Jean Moulin, whose members speak from experience, writes:

> He [the Frenchman] prefers dealing with an authority which imposes solutions upon him, which permits him not to feel responsibility for them, to remain free, to limit thus the social constraint exercised upon him.
>
> [Citizens of towns do not want to impose taxes on them-selves]...they prefer the state constrain them to pay taxes against which they can be indignant, while decrying, however, the sad state of their schools.
>
> Employers refuse to negotiate with their workers' repre-sentatives because they cannot bear that their authority be chal-lenged face to face; they prefer that these same workers by their political pressure obtain from the government measures univer-sally applicable, perhaps harsher for them because they will take less into account their particular situation, but against which they will be able to revolt, which they will resist, and perhaps succeed in evading.[63]

The state of course is not in an enviable position when its representatives try to reconcile two sides out to get what they can, give what they must, and remain free to feel bitter.

Some problems are particularly difficult to handle by coop-erative consultation: especially that of education. The two notions of equality which underlie today's battles within French education are utterly irreconcilable, as is the division between those who see the school as an institution preparing for jobs, and those who see it as an instrument for the perpetuation of culture. Then there are the conflicting demands for more places in the university and for more plentiful job opportunities for graduates: finding solutions is the state's job! Those who demand are usually not themselves engaged in private efforts to solve the problem.

As for private groups, they too, with the exception of recreational and some artistic societies, usually exist primarily to deal with the state: to protect themselves, or to get something from it. Seldom do private societies envisage doing something in common that does not involve a request to the state, and with very few exceptions (clubs like the Jean Moulin), do they advance such views on the *public* good.

The state is a very peculiar entity: unlike the *Patrie,* no one gives to it; it takes what it needs. It does not seriously try to ask favors or sacrifices because it has nothing in the name of which to ask. On the other hand, no one asks favors of it: one demands what one thinks it owes one by right! But if the state has no friends, neither does it have any organized enemies. Those interests which decry it most do so with their palm extended. But more important, looking at the political spectrum from left to right, we do not find, as in America, a great party which is thought to stand primarily for the diminution of the central government's responsibilities. In France, as we will see, the Right, even the extreme Right, because of a long-standing love affair with authority and an equally long-standing fear of popular disorder, is a firm supporter of the centralized state. The various parties on the Left, for their part following an equally old tradition, see the powerful state as the perfect instrument for transforming society according to their beliefs. Most people, however, as we have said, are neither friends nor enemies. The state just *is.*

But what if it were not so centralized, or so strong, or charged with so many responsibilities? Why there might *be* statues of Stalin in the Paris suburbs, and who would make four or five week vacations obligatory? A lot of people, so the argument runs, would need nothing else to stop functioning as they should. Then where would calm and prosperity go? President Pompidou, it seems, articulated a very widespread feeling: the state, as it is, is fundamental to the existence of France as it is. But in the same breath he warned the state can fulfill its mission only if it enjoys the people's confidence, and that it must gain this by conspicuous devotion to the welfare of each and all. But in matters of welfare the nation is necessarily composed of "each's": people cannot share a subsidy or a wage increase the way they can share a love or a hate, and even pain caused by price increases borne by all does not engender solidarity like the sufferings of war, which are certainly borne much less equally. The state's authoritative harmonization of interests is, in fact, never defended as a positive good, only as a dam against worse conditions, and the process by which it does its work does not foster the latter's growth. This is because, of itself, the state embodies no purpose beyond its own particular existence.[64] In other times *L'Etat* was seen as the instrument of the empire's greatness in which all could share, or as the bulwark against the hated Germans. That, too, tended to confuse *L'Etat* and *La Patrie.* The state in fact has always been animated by some purpose outside itself.

We therefore now turn our attention to the source of the spirit which animates the state and the goals it serves.

Notes to Chapter 2

[1]*Le Monde,* January 3, 1972.

[2]*Ibid.*

[3]General de Gaulle's major works are: *Mémoires De Guerre 1940-46* (3 vols, 1954-59), Paris, Plon. *Mémoires D'Espoir 1958-* (2 vols, 1970) Paris, Plon. *Le Fil De L'Epée, La France et Son Armée, Vers L'Armée De Métier* and several volumes of public speeches all personally written, and published principally by Plon of Paris. Michel Debre, who headed the committee which drafted the Fifth Republic's constitution has a long list of publications, expressing similar views on practical problems of government. The work which most clearly reveals his intentions with regard to the new constitution is *Refaire Une Démocratie, Un Etat, Un Pouvoir,* Paris, 1958.

[4]Pronounced just after he left the presidency of the provisional government in 1946 and outlining the design of the constitution he would give France twelve years later, this is one of the four or five most important speeches in the general's life. See the appendix to Vol. 3 of his war memoirs.

[5]Interview in *Le Figaro,* 30 November 1970. The others are briefly: 2. France should strive for the front rank in European affairs; 3. France should, by monetary soundness and economic modernization, build the basis for her power; 4. French society should be bound together by the participation of business and professional groups in state policymaking; and 5. France should bring her know-how and culture to countries in need of it. We will discuss each point in greater detail when we deal with the phenomenon of Gaullism in following chapters.

[6]*Mémoires d'Espoir,* Vol. I, *Le Renouveau,* Paris, Plon, 1970, pp. 7-8. The relationship of Gaullism to democracy will be dealt with in Chapter 6.

[7]General de Gaulle's role in the last weeks of the Third Republic is best described in the first volume of his *Mémoires de Guerre, L'Appel* (Paris, Plon, 1954). William Shirer offers some interesting contrasts in his *The Collapse of the IIIrd Republic,* New York, 1969.

[8]*Le Salut,* p. 8.

[9]See especially *Le Renouveau,* p. 8.

[10]One can profitably read on this subject Bertrand de Jouvenal's *L'Art de la Conjecture* (Monaco, 1964) as well as De Tocqueville's *L'Ancien Régime et la Révolution,* Hannah Arendt's *On Revolution* and any of the works of Turgot and Condorcet.

[11]Guido de Ruggiero, *History of European Liberalism,* Boston, 1959 p. 360.

[12]See Pierre Escoubre, *Les Grands Corps de L'Etat,* Paris, 1971.

[13]The president of the Republic and at other times the emperor or the king have been head of state, while symbolically the Council of State is headed by a vice president in expectation that its meetings be chaired by the head of state himself. The council is however the apex of the state as we have been using the term.

[14]DeGaulle, *L'Effort,* p. 46. On this incident and on the "special tribunal case" also see Pierre Avril, *Le Regime Politique de la Vème Republique,* Paris, 1964, and Philip M. Williams, *French Politicians and Elections, 1951-1969,* London, 1970.

[15]De Gaulle, *L'Effort,* pp. 76-77.

[16]Pierre Avril, *Politics in France,* Baltimore, 1969, p. 197.

[17]Pierre Avril, op. cit. pp. 184-185.

[18]Two types of ENA entrance exams are given: one for holders of certain university diplomas and another for those already in the civil service, the ratio being about seven to one. The outside quota varies from corps to corps, and in the diplomatic corps a special examination is given for entrance into the Far Eastern Corps to graduates of the School for Oriental Languages.

[19]Jean Moulin was the first president of the Council of Resistance during World War II. He was killed by the Gestapo. The club is to the French left what moderate members of the John Birch Society would have wanted to be to the American right.

[20]Pierre Avril, *op. cit.,* p. 206.

[21]The classics, in an area covered by countless works, are: Montesquieu's *L'Esprit des Lois, The Federalist Papers* and De Tocqueville's *De La Democratie en Amerique.*

[22]For example, Francois Goguel, Alfred Grosser, *La Politique en France,* Paris, 1964, especially pp. 45-46.

[23]For example, Hervé Detton, *L'Administration Regionale et locale en France,* Paris, 1953, especially pp. 8-9.

[24]The key dates and events are: 1790, a committee of the National Assembly divides France into 90 *départements* and about 40,000 *Communes* (towns) building on existing "natural" and historical divisions, giving each town an elected assembly, but subordinating all to its own emissaries. 28 *Pluviose* year VIII (1799) Napoleon formally established centralization with prefects in charge of *départements,* and mayors in charge of towns. All are appointed by the Ministry of the Interior. Even members of local deliberative bodies are appointed. Little by little the laws of 1831, 1867 and 1871 allow greater participation in the choice of local officials and to these greater freedom of action until the law of 1884 fixed the status of local officials as it has come down to us, plus or minus relatively minor arrangements and excluding the temporary changes made by the Vichy government. In 1971 the Fifth Republic legislated the principle of mandatory fusion of small towns into more economically regional units.

[25]This is not meant to downgrade the influence of tradition on political practice, for history is replete with examples of its triumph over "parchment barriers" placed in its way, e.g., Article 87 of the Constitution of 1946 provided that "local authorities will be self-administering with councils elected by universal suffrage. Their decisions will be put into practice under the supervision of the mayor or president." Despite this, the prefects continued on the job, and no council's decision took effect without going through him up the customary chain of command.

[26]The council does elect an executive committee to advise the prefect while between sessions, but this shadow executive has only moral authority.

[27]*Op. Cit.,* p. 179.

[28]See Hervé Detton, *L'Administration Régionale et Locale en France,* Paris, 1953, p. 76. Although since this book was published numerous changes in the law regulating local government have been made, most provisions of the old law are still valid.

[29]An article by Jeannine Verdès-Leroux in the 5 October 1970 issue of the *Revue Francaise des Sciences Politiques* gives us an idea of how mayors of

towns with populations above 2,000 line up politically: only 17 percent of the mayors do not consider themselves aligned with a party. The nation's two biggest parties, the Gaullists and the Communists, are relatively weak, while some old parties, like the Radicals, or even parties that no longer exist at the national level, such as the S. F. I. O. (French section of the Workers International, succeeded by the Socialist Party and the United Socialist Party) and the MRP (Popular Republican Movement, a Christian-Democratic party which has since disintegrated, its members joining either the Gaullists or the Center) hold the lion's share. This shows that in elections which involve people they know personally, Frenchmen are relatively slow to change their minds, whereas the rapid rise and fall of political parties at the national level shows they are far quicker in the judgment of larger, more impersonal matters with which they are less acquainted.

[30]Francois Goguel, in his *Géographie des Elections Francaises de 1870 à 1951,* Paris, 1951, as well as Philip A. Williams, in *French Politicians and Elections 1951-1969,* London, 1970, convincingly demonstrate how candidates and propositions of the left, right and center, regardless of the label each went under in any given election, have not shown significant geographic variation in performance over the past century. Furthermore, this relatively stable *political* map roughly coincides with the map of church attendance in France, the more conservative areas being also the ones where religion is taken most seriously and vice versa.

The sources of these attitudes, political and religious, are indeed remote. Two examples will suffice to shed some light on them. One often-cited story tells of a town in a mountainous region characterized by conservative politics and heavy churchgoing which ever since the Revolution has been voting for the most leftist candidates available while neglecting the church *en masse*. The origin, it seems, is the village priest at the time of the Revolution who, instead of fighting it, split with his colleagues and joined it. Especially when the rate of population movement is low, local memories, it seems, are long. The second is the case of the Hudson Institute, synonymous in American policy research circles with forward-looking thought, which in the course of a study on the future of Europe, found that there exist significant differences in the behavior and attitudes of Europeans regarding some of the most important things in life, from food to religion, race, politics, art, etc., differences which follow the boundaries not of the nations as we have known them for about 300 years, but of the political units of roughly the sixteenth century. How much longer the character of this town and of these regions will remain discernible in this age of easy movement is difficult to say. Nonetheless, they exist now.

[31]Edward Banfield in his *The Moral Basis of a Backward Society,* Glencoe, Ill. 1958 has given an unforgettable description of a small town in southern

Italy where a stable social and demographic situation is coupled with an almost complete lack of civic consciousness and cooperation.

[32]Laurence Wylie in his very perceptive *Village in the Vaucluse* (Harvard, 1957) describes at some length just how people in a French town, whose economy is more atypical of France as a whole than its attitudes, get along with each other.

We, for our part, have often wondered about the emphasis not just Frenchmen but Europeans in general place on maintaining a certain distance between each other, whether they belong to the same socioeconomic category or not. Clearly, answers such as: "It makes for smoother, trouble-free relations where everyone addresses everyone else formally and does not get too close for comfort," simply beg the question. Undoubtedly some of the desire for distance and for the secrecy of one's economic status is due to both embarrassment at the possibility of being discovered less well off than one's neighbor and to fear that the tax assessor will come to find one better off—reason for taxing one more heavily. But even if this explains the secrecy, it does not explain the emphasis on formality, especially if one notes that it is present in smaller doses the further away one goes from large towns, and from people who have contact with the larger society. One actually finds backward farmers and some laborers ridiculing the polite ways which are nowadays nearly universal in Europe, even as one finds in old European literature, from Rabelais to Montaigne to Boccaccio, that the polite form of address was reserved for use by members of lower classes toward those of the upper. It seems then quite as good an explanation of the phenomenon as any other that the sort of formality and distance so widespread today is a testimony to equality achieved by a sort of inflation of the social currency. The mode by which a member of the upper classes addressed one of the lower was, after all, one of the burning questions of the early 19th century. This has been quite definitively resolved, but in a manner which still strikes some old Europeans as incongruous: imagine two poor devils addressing each other as if each were a Count! In a similar vein a somewhat shaggy student reacted this way to our question on what he thought of the French manner of keeping one's distance and of reserving the familiar form for children and dogs: "These . . . bourgeois prejudices! What does it do for me if an official calls me Monsieur? He still treats me like dirt, and then s___ on me!"

[33]There is nothing in France, or for that matter in the rest of Europe, to compare with what in the U. S. have become institutions: the March of Dimes, the Cancer Fund, Heart Fund, etc., and nothing to compare to Jerry Lewis Telethons or United Fund drives. There are two basic reasons: the feeling that if there is really a need, it is the state's responsibility to take care of it, what with all the money it takes in, especially from people like myself, and a general mistrust of do-gooders. The very widespread feeling is that

people simply do not go in for that sort of thing without ulterior motives. Newspaper stories of disreputable organizations which solicit money from the public under charitable pretenses and divert it to their own gain simply reinforce common attitudes. Besides, proper *sérieux* people just do not go around to their neighbors asking for money any more than they do to try to persuade them to vote for someone, or to sell Fuller brushes, Avon products, etc. Besides, what a fearful thing to be fooled!

[34]The one notable exception to this is the subculture fostered by the Communist Party in the towns, mostly around Paris, whose councils it controls, and where the labor unions associated with the Communist-controlled General Confederation of Labor (CGT), together with their auxiliaries, are strong. There the lines between politics and society are blurred in a particular way: there it is almost normal to be involved with something public because it is the declared enemy of political society.

[35]Edward Banfield began his *The Moral Basis of a Backward Society* by comparing the evident civic articulation of St. George, Utah with the evident lack thereof in the southern Italian town.

[36]We have already hinted that our discussion about home towns does not apply to some categories of young managers, officials, army personnel, etc., who have either their profession as a home or have lost their roots, and of course to Parisians who have never experienced the life of the town like other Frenchmen, and whose life has been that of the nation. In fact, this phenomenon is spreading rapidly, although as it does the myth of home substitutes itself for reality. But insofar as the town remains important, it does so for some fairly old reasons.

[37]This is not pure bombast. Under the Fourth Republic it was common for the National Assembly to engage in a form of budget balancing on the national level which had unfortunate consequences on local governments: the Constitution, prohibiting deputies from advancing propositions which would lower revenues or raise expenditures, made it simple to legislate new expensive programs or raise the budget of old ones (welfare is only one example) while simply stating that the extra expense would be incumbent on local government, which could neither refuse the program nor escape the necessity of raising taxes.

[38]This law, amply discussed in press and Parliament (see especially *Le Monde,* November 26 and 27, 1970, and *Le Figaro,* December 17, 1970) and hailed as the Magna Carta of the towns, has two main provisions besides the delegation of power to state agents on the scene: one enables mayors to delegate more of their responsibilities to their assistants and the other states that town budgets and other permitted official acts take legal effect fifteen days after being deposited at the prefecture without need of specific approval. This last, amounting to a change from positive approval to negative veto, is both as critics claim a very small administrative change, and as proponents

declare something which can open the way for greater reforms. See Chapter 6 *infra.*

[39]See Chapter 4 *infra* for an explanation of the general concept of the plan. Here we limit ourselves to a glance at its implications for towns.

[40]*Le Monde,* July 3, 1971.

[41]*Les Dernieres Nouvelles D'Alsace,* Strasbourg, March 18, 1972.

[42]Larger cities also collect a small amount from taxes on entertainment, alcoholic beverages, etc.

[43]One searches in vain in reading and conversation for examples of *maires* subjected to demonstrations or indignities during the 1968 crises when these were the lot of so many in high places in France.

[44]The teacher qualification system is as follows: after about four years of university study, one can present himself for examination for the *Licence* in his area, and after a year or more of studies, for the *Maîtrise.* With at least the *Licence,* one can take the competitive examination for one of three teaching qualifications: CAPSES, qualifying one for a post in a CEG; CAPET, qualifying one for a post in a technical school or Lycée; and CAPES, which opens the door to higher secondary teaching. All who are admitted are guaranteed a position. Holders of these qualifications make up about 90 percent of the corps. The other 10 percent is made up of *Agrégés* who have passed the *Agrégation* exam, to take which requires a *Maîtrise* and much preparation, sometimes at the *Ecole Normale Superieure* (ENS, see below). These are the corps' elite, who enjoy superior salary and prestige throughout their entire career. While one commonly hears that during the 1960s the standards for the other certificates were lowered, and that even teachers without certificates were allowed in the classroom, the prestige of the *Agrégation* remains intact, even if every other person who speaks of it sooner or later uses the word "Mandarin" to describe it.

[45]The *Baccalaureat* exam is taken after seven years of secondary education, usually at age eighteen. It is the passport to higher education and to responsible positions in government and industry. The exam for entry into the sixth grade was dropped gradually, at first only for those with good school records.

[46]A student excluded by this committee has the right to try his luck on the exam, but since exclusions are for rare ineptitude, exams usually only confirm them. It would have been very interesting to observe the reactions of the French had the new system been adopted without a concomitant near abolition of exclusions. One can only surmise it would have been distinctly less popular than it is today. In fact where competition for scarce places remains, so do the impersonal exams.

[47]*Le Figaro* on July 15, 1971, published the results of the year's "Bac" exam for 16 out of the 23 academies: the highest success rate was 77 percent for series A in the academy of Amiens and the lowest, 43.5 percent for series E in Aix-Marseille.

[48]*Le Monde,* November 26, 1970, and March 4, 1972, respectively.

[49]*L'Effort,* p. 181.

[50]To solve this problem the ministry established two-year diploma-granting, university-level technical institutes, whose graduates, however, have had difficulty finding work. Too low to be officially designated *cadres* by the Ministry of Labor, they were too high to be *techniciens* or specialized workers.

[51]*Le Monde,* January 5, 1971. At the very small universities such as Mulhouse and Toulon the rate was much higher, 71 percent and 78 percent respectively.

[52]André Piettre in an article in *Le Figaro,* dated November 21, 1970, characterized the unpolitical politics of the university by adding to the distinction between real country and legal country that of mental country: the France of popular concern, of politics, *and* of the university. While the first two have drawn together, he noted, the third is agitated by cries echoed neither among the people nor among the parties. The Republic could stand, in years gone by, teachers committed to the political Left, but he now doubts whether it can stand teachers committed to the unpolitical Left. The *Gauchistes,* to be sure, are a small minority, but the large majority of yesteryear's leftists, disgusted with the nonpolitical quiescence of France under the Fifth Republic, look nowhere else. "A new romanticism à la Fourier fights it out with anarchism, and a neo-marxism with mysticism in a new gnosis. One lives in another world which one is incapable of defining."

[53]P. Bauchet, *Propriété et Planification,* Paris, 1962.

[54]Regardless of the polling organization or the particular political situation at the time of the poll, results in recent years have shown rising prices or the government's obligation to fight them at the head of the French people's concerns. Even during the Algerian War in 1958, the French Public Opinion Institute found that the "pecuniary question" was of more personal importance to the public than "the repercussions of the situation in Algeria" by a factor of 58 to 3 (*Sondages,* Vol. 20, 1958, No. 3, p. 4). Interestingly, though, the same public when asked what was the most important question for France, placed the Algerian situation and the economy both at the head of the list within one point of each other. (This was not without implications for the man searching for a solution to the war, as we well see when we discuss Gaullism.) In 1971 the need to fight high prices was still leading the list of worries with 61 points (*Le Figaro,* July 13, 1971).

[55]The official figures are: 1968, 4.5 percent; 1969, 6.4 percent; 1970, 5.7 percent; 1971, 6 percent; for the first quarter of 1972 it was above 7 percent. Practically everywhere one hears the real rise is much greater. Giving voice to this the largest labor federation (CGT, Communist controlled) conducted its own market-basket price survey in February, 1972, and claimed the increase for 1971 to be over 9 percent. Practically everyone claims his buying power has decreased. The state figures on wage increases belie this. Wages in the private sector rose 35.7 percent in the three year period 1969-71, while those in the public sector rose a few percent more. However, these figures are not

necessarily reflected in take-home pay, including as they do, reductions of the work week, increases in vacation time, seniority rights, social security and retirement benefits, etc. During this time also taxes, social and retirement contributions rose. It should be added that with the exception of agriculture, and there only at the products' source, controls are intended only to set ceilings on prices, not to prevent price competition, but in fact the latter is not fierce.

[56]*Les Dernières Nouvelles D'Alsace,* March 12, 1972.

[57]Here are a few sources on this unique method of economic control: J. A. M. Hackett, *Economic Planning in France,* London, 1963; M. M. Postan, *An Economic History of Western Europe, 1945-1964,* London, 1965; Regis Paronque, *Le Malaise Français,* Paris, 1967; Michel Crozier, *The Bureaucratic Phenomenon,* Paris, 1967; Vera Lutz, *French Planning,* Washington, 1965; John Ardagh, *The New French Revolution,* New York, 1968.

[58]Those familiar with the ideas of Saint Simon—the administration of things replacing the government of men—and with the economic management practices in Italy in the 1920s and '30s, in Vichy France under Jean Bichelonne, and to some degree under Albert Speer in Germany in 1942-44, will find themselves on familiar ground when studying the plan.

[59]Hackett, *op. cit.,* p. 47.

[60]*Le Renouveau,* pp. 139-145.

[61]The plan's effectiveness can not, first of all, be gauged by the proximity of its figures with actual economic performance. The two have been very close: 6.2 percent and 6.3 percent respectively for the IVth Plan and 5.7 percent for both in the Vth; but this is because the Plan's estimates undergo constant revision to keep in line with performance. Figures should not, in any case, be taken at face value. For example, the rise in GNP of 8.7 percent in 1969 represented largely the inflation forced upon France by the attempt to appease the disorders of 1968—a loss from which the economy has taken years to recover. Also, when one reads that labor costs are higher in France than in Germany by some 2.5 percent, one should not assume wages are higher there or purchasing power greater. Rather, it signifies that a greater amount of "social benefits" are assessed on the basis of man-hours worked. Neither can one take at face value the figures for the proportion of the GNP taken by taxes and "social benefits"—in 1967, 36.7 percent for France and 35.1 percent for Germany. Such figures become significant only if the efficiency of the administrative apparatuses and above all the specific purposes for which the moneys are spent are known.

One can not be certain how much the French government had to do with the awakening of economic interests in France and how much of it should be attributed to imitation of the popular idea of America, love of modernity, and the example of the *Wirtschaftswunder* next door in Germany. All three, America, modernity and Germany, especially the last, are constant themes of government officials and economists.

Finally, of course, we must mention the successful example of German economic policy designed by Ludwig Erhard. Some of the strongest remarks against planning and harmonization by a modern statesman can be found in his *The Economics of Success*, Princeton, 1963, especially pp. 157 and 265-267.

[62]Charles Frankel, in "Bureaucracy and Democracy in the New Europe" in S. Graubard, *A New Europe?*, New York, 1964, holds that throughout Europe the importance of the tasks entrusted to administrations and the successes they have achieved have greatly diminished the people's interest in representative democracy. In the case of France, we certainly agree this is the case.

[63]Club Jean Moulin, *L'Etat et le Citoyen*, Paris, 1961, p. 201.

[64]The word "particular" here is used in the same sense as in Rousseau's *Contrat Social*.

Chapter 3
The Government

France had, and to some extent still has, a parliamentary system of government, normally characterized by the separation of powers between the legislative, executive and judicial branches of government. The legislators, so democratic theory runs, are elected by the people to make the laws, which the executive carries out under the supervision of the independent judiciary. Parliamentary democracies add one more safeguard to the system: the executive (significantly known as "Le Gouvernement" in France, in Italy as "Il Governo," in Germany as "Die Regierung") not only does not make the laws it executes, but does its administering under the watchful eye of the legislative branch, the confidence of which it must retain or else resign. But this only partly explains the position of *Le Gouvernement*. One example indicates another dimension: while the outcome of the parliamentary battle over the 1946 budget for the French Armed Forces was still uncertain, the chairman of the Socialist Party, Andre Philip, declared that General de Gaulle's cabinet should not take the Assembly's vote of a sum below its request as a reason for resigning. The general's answer that he most surely would so take it was very much in the tradition of parliamentary government.[1] "The government" has not historically considered itself as anybody's executor, but rather as a unit endowed by the confidence of a democratically-elected body with the right to "run the country" with the advice but mainly with the consent of that body. Governments have historically assumed that as long as they are in office they should have a free hand, and that without it, office is not worth having. Their effective exercise of sovereign power over the state makes them the heirs of kings, but democratic constitutions, according to which their power comes via universal suffrage through one or more assemblies, have placed parliamentary governments in a peculiar position.

In Britain, where for 150 years the cabinet has exercised the old royal powers, relations between government and Parliament have been unambiguous only because of the two-party system, which virtually ensures that whoever controls the cabinet will also control a majority of the House of Commons. A presidential system such as obtains in the United States, on the other hand, resolves the question of the executive's authority both by having its head popularly elected for a fixed term and by stipulating the manner in which disagreement between it and the Congress shall be resolved without the resignation of one or the dissolution of the other. In the United States, in fact, when one speaks of "the government," one does not mean the President and his cabinet, or even the executive branch, but the entire constitutional apparatus over which authority is spread.

In France, however, as in the rest of the Continent, there has historically existed a profound enmity between on one hand the government engaged in the business of ruling, and on the other the Parliament, composed of the people's representatives, each charged by a constituency with obtaining favor and avoiding harm from the rulers. The former is sovereign in effect over the state, while the latter can affirm its theoretical sovereignty only by periodically toppling the former. The traditional extra-legal bridge between government and Parliament has of course been the political party, but in France elections did not until recently bring to Parliament a disciplined majority united by common political purpose and thus capable of acting simultaneously in government and in assembly: in the one effectively ruling and in the other legitimizing that rule by consent of the majority. Thus we hear of a historic conflict in France between the principle of sovereignty and that of representation: the government preoccupied with "running" the state and the Parliament with representing the people.[2] A far cry from the democratic dogma of government *by* the people!

In France the principle of popular representation has been united with that of governmental authority only by the Gaullist institution of the presidency of the Vth Republic: the elected head of state from which proceeds the government. But the conflict is far from resolved. As Michel Debré declared during the campaign for the new Constitution (17 August 1958), "The President of the Republic is national legitimacy; the Parliament is the expression of democratic life." This "national legitimacy" was also, to be sure, democratic then, and became more so in 1962 with the adoption of the constitutional amendment providing for popular election of the president. But the split between the sovereign state—legitimate because as necessary and inescapable a thing as death and taxes—on the one hand, and representation on the other, is evident here also. And what of *Le Gouvernement,* upon which the exercise of sovereign power rests? The authors of the Vth Republic placed it between—if not equidistant from—sovereignty and representation. They saw their enterprise as something far more fundamental than a mere "strengthening of the executive." We, for our part, are not going to examine French government from the standpoint of the traditional categories of separate legislative, executive and judicial powers, since we contend these divisions are today, in the case of France, misleading.

Leadership in the Fifth Republic
Sovereignty and Representation in the French Tradition

If the struggle between the principles of monarchy and democracy which began with the storming of the Bastille on July 14, 1789, was settled definitively about a hundred years later[3] with the former's defeat, the older question of how the principle of popular representation is to be reconciled with that of sovereignty remains. The latter, the very foundation of the modern concept of the nation-state, was first formulated by a Frenchman, Jean Bodin, in the sixteenth century.[4] Sovereignty is, among other things, absolute and indivisible. Only since this view was adopted have some in the West considered anomalous the presence of corporations, or in general of groups which claim to derive their existence from sources other than the sovereign authority of the state, be the latter a monarchy or a republic. The expression "a state within a state" has since been used to allege that an organization—a political party, an army, a church, a unit of local government or a university—by claiming the right not to be interfered with by the state or the right to perform certain functions with regard to its members (tax, promote, punish)—has arrogated to itself attributes which can only belong to one supreme agency in any given area. Thus, also, despite the works of another Frenchman, Charles Secondat, baron of Montesquieu, French political practice has eschewed a real separation of power and has tended either to diffuse the whole power to govern in Parliament or to concentrate it, whole, in the small group called *Le Gouvernement.*[5]

When the government consisted of the king's ministers, the king was sovereign and the state's legitimacy proceeded from him. The Bourbon kings had eliminated as many "states within the state" as they could and the Revolution had continued their work, so when the nineteenth-century monarchies set out to organize popular adherence to the state by mixing popular with royal legitimacy, no longer having anything like the old Parliaments or the States-General to contend with, they first appointed representative chambers and then allowed them to be elected. Their job was not to govern, but, as the early British Parliament and the old States-General had done, grant the government on behalf of the governed the right to collect taxes and discuss with the government the laws it was going to promulgate. One side wanted to make its rule more palatable and therefore more effective while the other looked to safeguard their constituents' interests.

When democracy replaced monarchy as the principle justifying the state's existence, one republican constitution after the other (Second and Third Republic) tried to establish the principle of separation of power between the legislative branch (Chamber of Deputies and Senate), now the sole representatives of the sovereign people, and the government, that committee of the chamber charged with executing laws and watching over the state administration. The system never really worked well. Before World War I, when it worked best (one cabinet headed by Waldeck-Rousseau lasted from 1898 to 1901, a record for French parliamentary governments!), the government was truly an emanation of the Parliament, the latter's committees paralleling each ministry, the committee chairman and minister often changing place. There was hardly an independent executive power, the legislative branch supervising directly the relatively few laws it passed, and laws being proposed with equal ease by any among the large number of parliamentarians more or less identified with republicanism, whether or not they happened to hold a government position at the time. Governments came and went often enough for most good republicans to get their chance in office. For most French politicians at the time the distinction between government and Parliament existed only on paper. For one purpose, however, the distinction existed in fact: the government could and often did get voted out of office by Parliament.

This condition has been described countless times: governments differing from one another only by virtue of the personalities which dominated them would be voted out, and once ministerial portfolios reshuffled, voted in again, and so on. But through the early part of the Third Republic there was real continuity of policy: the forces of monarchy were defeated, compulsory secular education established, the army's general staff purged, the Catholic orders disbanded, the church expropriated, and so on, all against heavy opposition. Why then did the Parliament, whose majority was so engaged, again and again deny its own executive committee? The clash of such strong personalities as Clemenceau, Combes and Ferry before parliamentarians who enjoyed complete independence from party discipline and, for the length of their term, even from their electors—for everyone knew Parliament would not be dissolved—certainly played a part. Certainly also the hope was always present that a change of government would bring personal advantages. But we should not underestimate the popularity of government crises, the widespread popular relief that was felt in France whenever *Le Gouvernement* fell. Parliamentarians themselves enjoyed defeating a group which "responsibility" might have rendered too haughty. For the public, the "boss" had been fired, the people had shown that they were indeed free and could not be trifled with, that they were superior to the government, that, in the end, *they* were sovereign.

The importance one still finds attached in France to the Parliament's power to cause the resignation of *Le Gouvernement*—even when that power is as circumscribed as it is in the Fifth Republic, is both great and indicative of something very important. In conversations with gentlemen of the Left one is certain to find bitterness when the subordination of Parliament to the government in the Fifth Republic is mentioned. Yet these same men recoil even more strongly at the suggestion that the Constitution be modified in "presidential" fashion, separating executive and legislative powers, confiding the latter exclusively to Parliament. An American partisan of congressional power can explain to his heart's content how in America any congressman can propose any law, how congressional committees bury, resuscitate, and metamorphose laws no matter where they come from; how Congress has the various executive departments and even bureaus—come to it hat it hand. We have found even leftist Frenchmen quite uninterested in this sort of legislative sovereignty. Their argument is simple: in a "presidential" system no matter what legislative powers the Congress has, it cannot overthrow *Le Gouvernement*. The recently deceased Vincent Auriol, former President of the Republic under the IVth and one of the "greats" of the IIIrd, put it succinctly: "When there are no more ministerial crises, there is no more liberty."[6] Even as under the kings, then, the principal task of representatives has been seen as a negative one: the limitation of the sovereign's prerogatives.[7]

In the Third Republic deputies were elected from *arrondissements,* each a single-member district electing its own "ambassador" to *Le Pouvoir* (The Power). The Senate, elected by local notables—mayors, general councilors—was similarly constituted. Once in Parliament, this "political class" was free to arrange its relations with the government as it wished. Thus, with the exception of the early years when the issues of monarchy vs. republic and church vs. state dominated the country, elections were not occasions for the French people to pronounce themselves on political matters, but to choose among personalities. Church and state, monarchy and republic, war and peace, these matters stirred Frenchmen; but when it wasn't a matter of these, most simply were not interested. Local politics, concerned as it was and is with relations with the state and with personal prominence, sent to Parliament a political class bound to seek favors for very particular interests, but otherwise quite free and detached from the rest of France. But under those conditions, parliamentary majorities were quick to form and quicker to dissipate. Two consequences ensued: Parliament had difficulty deciding on courses of action, and whatever action was decided upon was felt by Frenchmen not to engage them personally, but to be *their* business—the government's and the politicians'.

The easiest course of action in matters where parliamentarians disagreed, of course, was to confer the power of decision upon the government. This was all the easier because one could easily both go back on any decision taken *and* punish the deciders by voting the government out of office. It was also a convenient course of action given not only the controversiality of issues before Parliament, but also their growing number and "particular" character. By this we mean that the character of legislation gradually changed. After the great questions were dealt with, the state took up the burden of "running" the economy and of assuring certain material qualities of personal lives: medical care, vacations, etc. Law was no longer an expression of norms or orientations conceived as general, impersonal, and lasting, but a means of authoritatively running society from day to day. This has meant in France as elsewhere that laws dealing with labor regulations or agricultural controls had to be drafted not by generalists but by specialists in the field disposing of the requisite statistics. Since the activities of society are many, the laws must be many, and since conditions change, so must laws. Furthermore, decisions in a representative assembly became difficult to achieve, as representatives of groups concentrated more and more on the "particular" task of protecting their constituents.[8] After all, it is not unreasonable to find more attention paid to securing particular advantages when there are more particular advantages to be secured. No wonder majorities became harder to come by.

In France the practice of delegating legislative powers to governments dates to the First World War. Experience, especially the events surrounding the Dardanelles campaign, showed the conduct of operations should be left to the government. Thus Clemenceau was entrusted with broad powers which the monarchist Maurras in a bitter pun called "Monarchie" (my-archy). The problems of post-war recovery undertaken by the state were no less difficult to handle by the representative method. So once again full powers to deal with the situation were granted to the government. But if this state of affairs was exceptional in the twenties (Poincare's "dictatorship" in 1926), it became the rule in the thirties: of the six years which preceded the fall of France in 1940, about half were passed under regimes in which the representatives of the sovereign people had delegated "full powers" to governments. These, from Daladier's in '34 to Blum's in '36 to Reynaud's in '40 took over effective sovereignty on financial, social, and defense matters respectively. According to Alain, one of the most perceptive observers of political France of the time, the representatives had as their principal function "making noise in front of officials' desks," that is, smoothing administrative paths for their constituents. Of course, from time to time, the representatives would unseat the sovereigns, but having responsibility for important matters and not being able to agree on what to do, they soon would invest another effectively sovereign government.[9] Historians such as William Shirer have remarked that the Third Republic was not killed by the German invasion, but that it committed suicide: the representatives of the French people, or at least most of them, meeting in Vichy in July, 1940, without personal threat, simply voted the Republic out of existence, giving all power to Philippe Pétain. It is often overlooked that this renunciation was not at all contrary to the manner in which democracy had been adapting itself to modernity.

After World War II, debate in the Assembly which wrote the Fourth Republic's Constitution (1946) centered on how to strengthen the executive while preserving in principle the unity of sovereignty and representation. The primary means agreed on was extra-constitutional: the institution of proportional representation, it was thought, by giving the leadership of political parties control over the nomination of candidates for deputy, would provide for a responsible party system in Parliament.[10] The political party, as political scientists have long known, resolves the "problem" posed by the separation of powers by making it irrelevant, thus restoring to sovereign authority the unity which modern theory and the nature of the tasks confided to modern government demand.[11]

Proportional representation (PR) certainly succeeded in making deputies dependent on the parties, but to such an extent as to undermine the intentions and even some of the explicit provisions of the Constitution. One of these stated that the president of the Council of Ministers would be responsible for the government policy and for the choice of its ministers. With a regime dominated by parties however, the cabinet became a meeting place of ambassadors from the several parties. The only president of the council to stand on his right to choose ministers was Pierre Mendes-France in 1954, and it cost him the support of the Socialist Party, whose chairman, Guy Mollet, argued that the voters had not expressed themselves on their choice of a prime minister, but rather had confided to their party the task of representing them. He was correct: since governments consisted of coalitions which could be expected to form and disband several times in the five–year period between elections, and parliamentary dissolution was not considered likely, the voter could not help but give the party of his choice "full powers" on his behalf. Furthermore, since those who formed the government were the parties' emissaries, one could say that sovereignty was divided. At least that is the impression one gained by successively walking into ministries controlled by MRP (Christian Democrats), Socialists or Communists and seeing the pictures of the respective party presidents (and, in the case of the Communist Party prior to 1956, of Stalin), hanging on the walls!

Under the Fourth Republic, then, the conflict between sovereignty and representation moved into the very heart of government. As a result government crises were just as frequent as in the Third Republic, but they lasted longer: whereas a week was the norm in the Third, they averaged several times that in the Fourth.[12] Governments, however, insofar as they existed independently of the parties which composed them, were sovereign, at least vis-a-vis the Assembly which conferred upon them full powers to deal with situation after situation: not only Indochina in 1954 and Algeria in 1956 and 1957, but also economic and social matters. For example, in 1948, control over prices was turned over to the government, and in 1954 Parliament even authorized the government to raise certain taxes at its discretion! How anachronistic it was for the Assembly to solemnly legislate in particular cases dear to constituents while in thorny matters limiting itself to criticism and delegation of responsibility.[13] The governments, for their part, did their utmost to encourage the trend. Their weapon: the "question of confidence" itself: whereas the Constitution prescribed that an absolute majority of the Assembly would be needed to defeat a government, as we have seen, everyone agreed a relative majority would do. Governments, then, would attach "the question" to key elements of their program as a means of imposing upon the parties making up the government the choice between supporting the program or facing a crisis. In 1952, during Edgar Faure's first cabinet, "the question" was posed twenty-three times in forty days. The occasions? The place of bills on the agenda, limitation of debate, which amendments would be considered. During forty days Faure exercised sovereignty, then he fell; neither rise, exercise, nor fall being connected with a decision of the people.

If under the Third Republic the people had been strangers to the government, they had reasonably close relations with their deputy, whereas in the Fourth popular estrangement from the government was accompanied by detachment of the deputy from his constituency. France as politically represented by the Third Republic was an agglomeration of localities and interests which grudgingly consented to be governed. As politically represented by the Fourth, it was a place where a half-dozen partisan powers tried to share something each thought indivisible. Michel Debré described this condition in two books aptly entitled *These Princes Who Govern Us* and *The Death of the Republican State.*[14]

When danger threatened in the form of the May 13, 1958 revolt of the army, the civil administration and the European population of Algiers, the parties could not draw support from the population, from the state, or from each other. They could only agree, as the deputies had in 1940, to turn over full powers, including that of making up a new constitution, to one man: Charles de Gaulle.[15]

The Representative President

"Give us work, give us work," chanted a crowd of coal miners in the streets of Nancy. Their plea was addressed to Georges Pompidou, de Gaulle's successor as President of the Fifth French Republic, then on an official visit to that city. A few days later on the same tour, the newspapers spoke of a "presidential gift" to Alsace when on traversing Alsatian territory *Monsieur le Président de la République* announced that the new Paris-Strasbourg highway would be ready by 1977, two years ahead of schedule.[16] Such examples show better than any legal text where effective sovereignty is thought to reside in France, and belie characterizations of the Fifth Republic as merely something which would pass along with its founder.

The character of presidential press conferences in the Vth Republic became immediately evident to foreigners and Frenchmen alike: when de Gaulle occupied the office, these were like royal audiences. Newspapermen then remarked the formality of the setting and the haughty bearing of the general. But perhaps the attention paid to the Gaullist style directed observers away from the realities of the new presidency: when Georges Pompidou gives a press conference one can see in the absence of glitter that his office is held responsible by everyone—including himself—for just about everything that goes on in France. The standard of living, the number of cars on the road, of washing machines and television sets in the home, the number and size of apartments being constructed by the state, the number of swimming pools in the nation, all have been growing. And if no one reproaches him for taking credit for this, comments by the press and by men on the street indicate satisfaction at his shouldering the blame for poor telephone service. As the effective head of *L'Etat,* and chief not just of the executive but of *Le Gouvernement,* he does not need de Gaulle's manner to be what Michel Debré, author of the Constitution, thought a president should be: a republican monarch.[17]

But what is a republican monarchy? To answer the question we must go back to its foundation. The political institutions of France had lost legitimacy in 1940, by their self-renunciation as well as by their defeat. This, in de Gaulle's view, is won or lost on the field of battle.[18] There, more than anywhere else, are tested a power's internal cohesion and its will to live. The *Pouvoir* which had governed the Third Republic had shown itself insufficient to assure the life of the state. France had been ruled by "discordant factions which only divided it," and the state had been nothing but the scene of "clashes of mutually exclusive ideologies, of factional rivalries, of would-be actions, neither lasting nor far-reaching."[19] After the war, he declared, the re-establishment of such a regime, even if "arithmetically legal," that is, if supported by a majority, would be "without national legitimacy." Opposed to this was his government, which had won its right to govern by freeing France. More real though it might be, he noted, once compelling circumstances ceased, the majority did not seem to care about this sort of legitimacy.[20] In fact, when in 1958 *Le Pouvoir* came into his hands again, it was not placed there by a majority but by the very divided factions who were incapable of wielding it in the face of danger. Two incidents are relevant here. First, when soon after the events of 13 May 1958, the new president of the Council of Ministers, Pierre Pflimlin asked de Gaulle, then a private citizen, to help the government re-establish control over the army, the general let him know that his request was proof of his incapacity to rule and an indication that he should resign in favor of someone capable of doing so.[21] Later, after Pflimlin's resignation, the general ad-

dressed as follows the president of the Senate, André le Tro-
quer, who had objected to his taking over full powers: "Well,
if Parliament follows you, I will do no other than to let you
explain yourself to the parachutists, and to re-enter my retreat
closing myself up in sullen silence."[22] We can safely say that
the referendum of 28 September 1958, in which the French
people ratified by 17.6 million vs. 4.6 million votes the Constitution of the Fifth Republic, important as it is to the legitimacy
of its *Pouvoir,* is not its source.

Title I of the Constitution states that "national sovereignty
belongs to the people who exercise it through its representatives and by way of the referendum" (the 1946 Constitution had said "through its representatives in the National
Assembly"), while Title II begins by stating that "The President
of the Republic sees to it that the Constitution is respected.
He assures, by his arbitration, the normal functioning of the
public authorities, as well as the continuity of the state."
Besides being chief interpreter of the Constitution, he is also
guarantor of national independence (Article 5), charged with
the power to "take the measures required by circumstances"
to counteract grave threats (Article 16), the chief of the armies
(Article 15), the man who decides whether or not to consult
the people by referendum, and the man who names high civil
officials as well as the Prime Minister (Articles 13 and 8,
respectively). Finally, he is described by Michel Debré as the
keystone of the constitutional edifice. Thus, by his function,
he is the single representative of the Republic, and although
the Constitution provides for other representatives, he is "a
power . . through which the nation's will to live will be able
to express itself."[23] The President is that first of all because,
being one man, he incarnates unity more than any party or
combination of persons ever could.[24] Second, because of the
way the founder of the institution and his followers understand the role of the state and of power in modern democracy,
and third because of the specific powers attributed him by the
Constitution.

The election of the President by universal suffrage[25] provides Frenchmen with an opportunity to confide to one responsible person the task of ruling. But, just as importantly, it provides them and their other representatives (deputies, etc.) with the chance to divide into two groups: those for and those against the President. Certainly France is not a two party system, but the expression "La Majorité," which prior to 1958 denoted the unstable coalition of parties forming *Le Gouvernement,* now has another meaning. The finance minister, M. Giscard D'Estaing, gave it the commonly accepted definition: "The majority is defined by the presidential election . . . it is a team to which the country has confided the task of leadership."[26] "The team" is composed of all those politicians who supported the winner in the presidential election and now are his aides in the government and Parliament. The job for which its "coach" is responsible is effective leadership of the state, on behalf of both winners and losers. It is, in short, to represent Frenchmen insofar as they have one common interest, or as so many Frenchmen put it, to build a state out of divergent interests. Knowledge of this, partisans of the Fifth Republic believe, has increased the electorate's tendency to "responsibility" in presidential elections, whereas when electing representatives to Parliament, the people cannot help but be faced with and succumb to the divisive appeals of particular interest. Parliamentary elections draw from people the necessarily divisive preferences of each for his own ideology or interest while presidential elections and referenda, confronting them with two choices on great matters, elicit the expression of a general will regarding government.[27]

The French presidency is meant, no doubt, to be "above politics" in its stewardship of the national interests. Both de Gaulle and Debré had made this one of the major themes of their recommendations during the Fourth Republic, the latter declaring the necessity to de-politicize that which is essential to the nation and the former describing the President's job as that of national arbiter above political contingencies.[28] This

has led some commentators to conclude that the French presidency, notably under de Gaulle, did not exercise political leadership.[29] Actually, de Gaulle thought that being "above politics"
was the most political thing he could do, and that given his
powers, whether he applied himself to partisan organization
or not, something like a Tory party would grow to support him.

Since the politics of the French presidency are meant to be
the politics of state, only by abstaining from the lower kind
can the President keep his prestige intact for matters such
as the Algerian affair where he has to "overcome and, if
necessary, break the opposition of all the feelings, habits and
interests" involved. This politics aims at mastering those
painful situations which, short of war, agonize political communities. *Le Pouvoir* depends on prestige, and prestige on the
successful exercise of power.[30]

The high politics of the French presidency are meant to flow
downward. In fact, the meaning of "national arbitration" has
steadily widened: already in 1958 Debré had stated the President would not limit himself to the role of supreme judge
of political quarrels, and by the time Georges Pompidou was
elected to the job, national arbiter meant master of all French
politics. Without pausing to consider whether or not, given
that the national interest is not always self-evident, the notion
of national arbiter necessarily implies that of a master, let us
now look at how the President exercises his powers.

"The President of the Republic is the captain and the Prime
Minister is his first mate."[31] Thus M. Jacques Chaban-Delmas,
then Prime Minister of France, explained his relationship with
Georges Pompidou, himself formerly de Gaulle's first mate. He
went on to add "The Prime Minister is not on the same level
with the President of the Republic, if only because he has not
been chosen by the people, but designated by the chief of
state." He could have added that he is not on the level of the
ministers, either, for by virtue of Article 39 of the Constitution,
only he and members of Parliament—not ministers—are allowed to officially propose legislation. The Constitution estab-

lishes a very definite hierarchy of governmental power. The President names the Prime Minister and receives his resignation. It says nothing about their precise relationship, leading political scientists to wonder what it would have been like had the general chosen the post of Prime Minister.[32] Its essentials were however settled on the day the general took office as President of the Republic. Michel Debré visited the Elysée Palace, and that evening the following communiqué was published:

> At the end of the meeting General de Gaulle charged M. Debré with making some suggestions on the subject of the future composition of the government. At 7:30 p.m. M. Debré was again received at the Elysée. He submitted for the approval of General de Gaulle his ideas concerning the general politics of, and the names of the persons who could become his colleagues in, a future government. The President of the Republic named M. Debré Prime Minister and upon proposition of the Prime Minister, he named the members of the government.[33]

When several days later he submitted his cabinet for a parliamentary vote of confidence, Debré submitted not his choice nor that of a party, but that of the President; and when he resigned in 1962, it was as a result of a disagreement with the President, not as a result of parliamentary hostility.

After de Gaulle was elected for his second term, this time by universal suffrage, he did not submit the second and third Pompidou cabinets to a vote of confidence. No cabinet has since been submitted. A glance at the general's memoirs confirms that he considered cabinet ministers "his," and that he descended to the level of detail in the affairs which most interested him. Foreign affairs, Africa, defense, were declared in 1958 to be a "domain reserved" for the President. The man who declared it, Jacques Chaban-Delmas, than secretary of the UNR (Gaullist party), later confirmed this domain still exists for the general's successor.

The Government and Law

The ability of the President's government to rule depends

at least as much on the constitutional relationship between government and Parliament as it does on the attitude of the latter toward the former.[35]

Since, as we have already noted, the government does not come into existence through any act of Parliament, but can be divested of its functions by such an act, let us first look at how this negative parliamentary responsibility, outlined in Art. 49 of the Constitution, works. First of all, simple debates or questions posed by parliamentarians for members of the government cannot be followed by any vote, nor can the Assembly vote any resolution which might be construed as "political" in character; that is, expressing approval or disapproval of the government. This, of course, has deprived debates of most of what used to make them interesting both to participants and to spectators. When the Prime Minister asks the National Assembly for a vote of confidence on a declaration of policy or on his entire program, there must simply be an absolute majority against him if he is to fall, but if he "poses the question" with regard to a particular law, the procedure is different: the law is considered adopted and confidence granted if a censure motion is not put forth within twenty-four hours and subsequently passed. Very important laws have been passed this way, notably the authorization for the building of France's nuclear *Force de Frappe.*[36] The censure motion is difficult to make—10 percent of the Assembly's members must sign it (those who do are not eligible to sign another for the remainder of the session)—and difficult to adopt, an absolute majority of the membership being required. Thus, absences and abstentions count in the government's favor. Only once in the Fifth Republic has a censure motion succeeded: that was in October 1962, in protest against the general's referendum on direct election of the President. Parliament, of course, was dissolved immediately. The new elections, run on the issue of the referendum, pitted an enlarged coalition of Gaullists, campaigning for universal suffrage, versus the parties of the

Fourth Republic campaigning against it. The former saw the number of their deputies increase from 195 to 229.

The list of advantages which the Constitution offers the government is long, but perhaps the greatest is contained in the enumeration of the matters reserved to laws and therefore to Parliament (Art. 34). These are many: state revenue, civil rights, criminal statutes, civil service, etc. But more significant than length is the very fact of enumeration. French law had heretofore not been characterized by distinctions based on the objects of acts; rather in the words of Pierre Avril,

> The value of acts depends on the authority which takes them, and the hierarchy of authorities is founded on a democratic theory of sovereignty according to which the acts of the Assembly, itself the product of universal suffrage, are paramount over all other authority and constitute the keystone of law.[37]

In other words, whereas heretofore any matter which became the subject of a law had been *ipso facto* a legislative matter, now for the first time since the Revolution the notion of a restriction on the acts of the representative body has appeared. This limitation of Parliament's domain is no longer as in the case of divestitures in years gone by the result of individual acts of renunciation, which, however frequent, were necessarily limited in time and objective, but a principle of the regime. The Constitution itself now ranks above Parliament as does its guarantor, who alone may or may not ask the sovereign people's direct intervention by means of referendum.

Outside of the Parliament's domain is that of the government, which can and does take sovereign action by decree in all unenumerated areas (Art. 37), as well as the actions it deems necessary and proper pursuant to laws passed by Parliament.

But what concerns us here is the Fifth Republic's "legalization" of the government's position as chief legislator. First, the government can ask Parliament for the power (Art. 38) to temporarily treat matters by decree which the Constitution specifies are in the domain of the law (Art. 34). This regulari-

zation of an old parliamentary habit is noteworthy only because it immediately follows in the text of the Constitution
a distinction between the domain of law and that of decree,
and a stipulation that Parliament cannot intervene in the latter.
It is followed by an article which makes clear that once Parliament has delegated its powers under Article 38, it cannot take
them back until the allotted time is up.

Second, the agenda of both houses is set by the government
(Art. 48). Effectively, no subject can be discussed in Parliament
unless scheduled by the government except for one session
each week scheduled for parliamentarians' questions and the
government's answers. Such questions and answers cannot be
followed by any vote. But the questions are scheduled by the
president of each house, normally a member of the "majority."
Moreover, parliamentary sessions are short: the two regular
sessions beginning on 20 October and 2 April last eighty and
ninety days respectively. Outside these periods (and of a national emergency defined by Art. 16), Parliament may not meet
unless convoked by the President of the Republic at the request
of the Prime Minister or of a majority of the members of the
National Assembly. However, the only time a majority of the
Assembly tried to call itself into session in this manner (March
1960), President de Gaulle merely refused to issue the order.

Third, Parliament must, if the government requests it, vote
on texts of laws acceptable to the government. That is to say
that Parliament does not have an "item veto," and that its
members may submit amendments only if these are acceptable
to the government (Art. 44). Naturally a government which
aims to please, especially its own parliamentary supporters,
allows many and varied amendments in committee, using the
parliamentary process as a sort of "cooperative consultation"
or collective bargaining on the highest level. But even as in
other types of "cooperative consultation," the government has
both the first and the last word. Of course, amendments tending
to increase expenditures or decrease revenues are unconstitutional (Art. 40).

Fourth, with regard to proposals for the budget and the taxes required to finance it, if these are not acted upon within seventy days of their introduction, the government is authorized to promulgate them by decree (Art. 47).

Finally, if there is disagreement on a law between the two houses of Parliament, the government has the choice of letting the impasse stand or of asking the lower house to decide the issue.[38]

It is not surprising, therefore, to note that whereas in 1957, the last full year of the Fourth Republic, out of 198 laws adopted (852 were proposed), 71 had been proposed by non-government members of Parliament; in 1959, the first full year of the Fifth, out of a total of 52 laws adopted, only one had been proposed by a member of Parliament.[39]

The consecration of one type of representation over another does not make the Fifth Republic undemocratic. What large modern democracy, a prosperous banker asked us, not only directly elects the head of its government, but also asks the citizens themselves to decide on important national questions by way of referendum? And in what modern democracy is the economic plan elaborated by fully four thousand persons, most of them private citizens, with the application depending on the cooperation of thousands more? Besides, if there is real discontent, the Parliament can always provoke a crisis. These are strong arguments.

But what kind of crisis? Here is a very important matter. Raymond Aron, no opponent of the Fifth Republic, once remarked that perhaps the common belief in the Fifth Republic's stability should be revised. After all, he said, one crisis like that of 1968 is many times as harmful as any one of the crises under the old republics. The 1968 crisis was not parliamentary.

Cooperative consultation is designed to elicit information, agreement and cooperation, not to foster free choice by the members of the body politic. The unwritten rules are straightforward: each "cooperant" asks for as much as he thinks the government can give, and the latter allots what it feels it must in order to keep any given cooperant cooperating. The frustrations of each cannot cause the system to falter. The same is true of institutions of local government. Weighty political choice can be exercised only on the national level. As for referenda, of which General de Gaulle once said that they express "God's voice,"[40] they were designed to elicit ratification of presidential policy. On one occasion (1969), the people said "no" to the question and the President resigned. Given that it is the President who proposes them, it is difficult to imagine how these episodic questions can fail also to involve that of popular confidence in the President. Its withdrawal by a negative vote can have but one consequence in a democratic regime. The same can be said of the relations of government and Parliament: the former rules the latter unless something revolutionary happens to the country.

The regime's basis is democratic: the Constitution declares that the law is supreme and can only be made by the people's representatives or by the people themselves united in their diversity. Yet, when the law thus understood manifests its supremacy, the event can only be described as a crisis. The coincidence of two opposites, normalcy and crisis, suggests that perhaps this notion of law no longer fits with political practice. The rules by which society lives, in effect, the laws, are made by the government. Its power to make them is not limited by other laws. The very source of the power is seen as the source of law itself. This, of course, is the plenary grant of full sovereignty to the President and his chosen ministers. Laws pursuant to such a grant, as General de Gaulle reminded the Council of State in 1962 and then the general public, are not justiciable. Only a revocation of the grant, a destitution of the power, can effectively gainsay it. But any such act is bound to be, along with the wait for the next *Pouvoir,* somewhat unsettling.

This discussion would not be complete without mention of a divergent development in French constitutional law. On July 18, 1971, the Constitutional Council, a constitutional court provided for by Title VII of the Constitution of October 4, 1958, for the first time in its history, held unconstitutional a law proposed by the government and passed by Parliament. The government accepted its decision, as indeed Article 62 of the Constitution obliges it. Heretofore, its main functions had consisted of certifying the results of elections and forbidding Parliament from overstepping the bounds in which the Constitution encloses it. One of its rulings had barred as unconstitutional, because not expressly permitted, Parliament's voting of resolutions expressing "political intentions."

Its July 1971 ruling struck down a law which had been the subject of bitter controversy. It had been intended to modify the law of July 1, 1901, which established the system of state control over all private associations. The 1901 law is based on two principles: any group wanting to meet regularly must file a statement of membership, organization and purpose with the prefecture, which in turn must deliver to the organization a *recepissé,* an authorization to exist. Only after this can the organization be accused, brought to court and disbanded. The new law would have allowed the prefect to submit requests for the *recepissé* to a court which could rule the proposed organization illegal *a priori.*[41] The Ministry of Justice had simply wanted to turn *de facto, a posteriori* control into *a priori* control.

Though the matter was not of immediate practical importance, it nevertheless set a precedent. Article 5 makes the President the guardian and perforce the interpreter of the Constitution. The Constitutional Council in this case contradicted the President's government in the name of the Constitution. In so doing, it based itself on the preamble—a rather vague listing of rights which even includes the right to a job. The body of the French Constitution primarily specifies relations between the President, government, etc. Except for Articles 4 and 26 it can hardly be said to contain provisions or prohibitions on the basis of which one could hold any law unconstitutional in substance. It would therefore take many such precedents in cases of far greater practical importance before one could say with assurance that new exercises of the sovereign lawmaking power are subordinate to old laws. But a precedent is a precedent.

The New Representative Role of Parliament

Deputies and senators are not primarily lawmakers, but representatives. "We are essentially agents of communication and of expression,"[42] said Edgar Faure of himself and fellow members of Parliament. Goguel and Grosser,[43] after stating that in France, as elsewhere in the modern world, representatives are not up to the task of orienting or defining policy, specify the following functions of Parliament: First, drawing the attention of government experts to needs, and to places where government programs are not having desired effects. Parliament is the spokesman for the users of public services. Representatives can therefore be of great technical assistance in drafting and revising government policy: "A law is almost always better written than a decree." Second, Parliament is a sounding board. Government decisions do not have to be modified—it is sufficient that those in power know that they will surely be fully scrutinized for them to fully examine their ideas and work up arguments convincing both to parliamentarians and to the public at large. These functions pretty well define the French Parliament today.

Most French parliamentarians still spend most of their time "running errands" for members of their constituency. If Norman cheese, Alsatian wine, or steel from Lorraine is exhibited at a Paris fair, alongside the product will be a good number of the area's parliamentary delegation. Members of Parliament also participate *ex officio* in the working committees of the plan, and are an indispensable avenue of contact with the Paris administration—and even with the local prefect—for interests in their constituency. Their role, which absorbs their time and energy, in short, is not essentially different from that of other "representatives" of private groups engaged in cooperative consultation.

But the Parliament is inescapably political if only because

it is elected and everyone knows its support is necessary to the government. It, therefore, necessarily represents, along with France's requests, France's *mefiance* toward government.

The Political Bases of Government

Electoral System and Parliamentary Majority

If democracy is rule by the majority, then democratic France has been looking for a national ruler for the last century. The Fifth Republic, more aware of this than previous regimes, introduced two major electoral innovations to try to produce a lasting "national majority:" the election of the President by universal suffrage and a "majority system" of electing deputies. Having discussed the former, let us now briefly look at the latter.

France is divided into 487 constituencies, each entitled to one deputy. To be elected, candidates must receive more than 50 percent of the ballots cast in that constituency. If, in any given constituency, no candidate receives a majority, a runoff ballot is held the following Sunday (in France elections are always held on Sunday) between the two highest placed candidates, better placed ones having withdrawn.

The "majority" system is a return to the Third Republic's electoral scheme and an emphatic denial of the Fourth's: proportional representation. The present system still allows all parties to field their own candidates for the first ballot, but it puts a very strong premium on the formation of only two coalitions for the second. Thus, old parties have disappeared and new coalitions sprung up.[44] This is just what the Gaullists wanted. They did not institute a plurality "first past the post" system, even though it would have put greater pressure on political forces to form only two coalitions, because they felt French opinion was so divided and the Communists so strong in some areas that the chances of moderate coalitions would be improved by the requirement that the winner be able to poll at least 50 percent of the vote.

The results of the majority system have been about as expected: since the coalitions are second-ballot arrangements, they are still that, just coalitions, but they are more solid. Above all, the influence of extremist parties has been cut down. For example, whereas in the 1958 elections, the last held under P.R., the Communists, with 18.9 percent of the votes cast, received 21 percent of the seats in the Assembly; by 1968, 20 percent of the vote—on the first ballot—only gave them 7 percent of the seats. In 1973 despite a second-ballot alliance with the Socialists and Left-Radicals, 21 percent of the vote only gave them 15 percent of the seats.[45] An almost constant number of voters, to be sure, continues to express its antagonisms by voting Communist, but the majority system gives entire constituencies, which normally do not include a majority of such electors, the chance to elect but one representative. Not surprisingly, the candidates have been going where the majority of the votes is, and so have the elections.

After the 1968 elections, the majority in Parliament held about 72 percent of the seats (291 for the Gaullist UNR and 61 for its allies, the Independent Republicans, won with 43 percent and 4 percent of the first ballot vote, respectively), while after the 1973 elections it held about 56 percent of the seats gained with about 38 percent of the vote. After each election, the actual majority in Parliament turned out to be considerably greater than on paper because of the "rallying" of numerous individuals and small groups: for example, Jean Louis Tixier Vignancour's Republican Alliance for Liberties and Progress, a rightist group, after the 1968 election, and assorted centrists after March 1973. These of course are deputies elected on their own rather than on the Gaullist label's strength.

The principal aim of the system was, of course, to help establish a connection between *election* and *government* such as exists in Britain and to make it possible for a certain kind of government to exist: under a majority system of election the proportion of seats won to percentage of the vote received is higher for moderate than for extreme parties. This rule holds true most obviously for elections where the contrast between moderation and extremism is most obvious, that is to say, for elections in times of crisis, domestic or foreign, or when the ascension to power of extremist candidates is a real possibility. Thus, as we saw in the case of the Communists, it was most obvious in 1968 and somewhat less operative in 1967 and 1973. This rule obviously also holds more for the second ballot of any election, when candidates are usually elected, than on the first when preferences are expressed and questions made. But the arrival in the Assembly in the fall of 1962 of the first compact parliamentary majority in French history was due at least as much to the polarizing influence of de Gaulle and his referendum as to the electoral system.

The unity of parliamentary and presidential majorities is also made more likely by one of the most curious practices of the Vth Republic. Since 1962, despite an express constitutional prohibition of simultaneous governmental and parliamentary office holding, nearly all government ministers have stood for election for the Assembly, campaigning on the government's and the President's behalf, but each making it clear by naming a "substitute" he has no intention of occupying his seat. In this way the insertion of both the government and the President in the parliamentary campaign is doubly assured. The same "government" team of ministers and parliamentarians, of course, takes part in the presidential campaign.

Parliamentary versus Presidential Majority?

Standard journalistic speculation on French government nowadays[46] usually includes the question of what would happen were Parliament to be dominated by a majority hostile to the President of the Republic. The brief history of the Vth Republic already has provided us with the one example of such a situation. In 1962, once the Evian agreements ending the Algerian War had been signed, the power of the white Algerians' terrorist organization (OAS) broken, and the army brought under control, every political party except the Gaullists united in their determination to whittle not just de Gaulle, but the presidency of the Vth Republic, down to size. They defeated de Gaulle's chosen government, headed by Pompidou, and put their hopes on new elections. The precedent for the course of action they chose was the MacMahon crisis of 16 May 1875. The President accepted the challenge and dissolved Parliament. Had the results of the 18 November 1962 elections, like those of 1875, shown an increase in the power of forces already strong enough to deny confidence to the President's government, it is not unlikely the Vth Republic's Constitution would have evolved in the direction of that of the IIIrd's. The government's great powers vis-à-vis Parliament, which allow it to rule unless there is a consistent majority against it, would have allowed it to maintain some independence, but Prime Ministers would have had to take into account the wishes of the parties as well as those of the President. The overwhelming Gaullist victory in 1962 does not preclude the former outcome to a future battle between President and Parliament.

Such a battle is not likely for two reasons: the popular election of the President in which, as we have said, a "majority" is formed and from which the parties take their bearings regarding public opinion; and the existence of the Communist Party as it is today. The latter is a true catalyst for the Gaullist majority for the following reasons. The several parties of the Left, constantly fearful of entrapment by the powerful united Communist Party, while at the same time conscious that only by means of a united front of the whole Left can socialism be brought to France, constantly vibrate between a united front and anti-communism without ever achieving either. Since they do so independently of each other, this makes even non-communist leftist unity, let alone a center-left coalition, difficult. Such a coalition between the Socialist and Communist parties was formed for the parliamentary elections of March 1973. The fact that it lost is perhaps not quite as significant as the demonstration it gave of the above principle. As a result of their common campaign on the basis of a common program, the Socialists and Communists elected in 1973 have been cooperating far less than their predecessors.

The Communist Party, for its part, retains an organization whose strength is impressive, and a fidelity to Moscow the constancy of which does not escape French electors. Just as importantly, outside of the men who run the government, it is the only political force organized to exercise power. Its strength makes it one of the natural poles of French politics; as long as it remains thus, elections under the "majority system" will pit Communist electors doomed to both minority and isolation against a necessarily anti-Communist "conservative" majority. Those who are unwilling to vote Communist must turn to the other "serious" alternative, the President's majority, or waste their vote in support of the traditional parties. Under these circumstances, it is not likely that the presidential and parliamentary majorities will be very different.

Issues and Majorities

While he lived, Charles de Gaulle was the single largest political issue of the Vth Republic, and it is about his person that the majority formed which modernized French institutions. He was brought to power, he liked to repeat, by events. The majorities which supported him and his men in Parliament in eight elections between 1958 and 1968 did not particularly support any one of his propositions, for he made every election a choice between himself and a leap in the dark. But what, besides order, did he represent to his majorities? Were his victories due to his high politics in Algeria, Europe or against the U.S., or to the low politics he practiced against his opponents?[47] But by posing these questions, we have already left the realm of government for that of politics.

Notes to Chapter 3

[1]French "ministries" or "cabinets"—in short, governments—have resigned for a great variety of reasons. Only twice during the IVth Republic did governments resign after having lost a vote of confidence asked for by someone other than the President of the Council (Schumann, 1948 and Queuille, 1950). Out of the ten resignations following a requested vote of confidence, only four were obligatory, confidence having been denied by an absolute majority. Five resignations were not related at all to votes of confidence: the Ramadier cabinet resigned in November 1947 because of a rumor that Léon Blum was not available to serve as President of the Council, and two years later the Queuille cabinet resigned because the defection of the minister of labor promised to entail a defection of the Socialist Party on future votes of confidence.

French governments have considered even a hint of attenuation of their authority as good reason to go. This is why it is misleading to describe "the government" in a parliamentary system as an "executive" as the term is used in American politics, though not perhaps in its original sense when it was used to denote the authority of kings' ministers.

[2]This theme is found, for example, in Goguel and Grosser, *La Politique en France,* Paris, 1964, Pierre Avril, *Politics in France,* Baltimore, 1969, and in the first and third volumes of General de Gaulle's war memoirs. But although the theme is not uncommon, attempts at explaining the existence of this conflict within democracy are. Some of the best in France were made by G. Burdeau in "La Conception de Pouvoir Selon la Constitution du 4 Octobre, 1958" in *Revue Française des Sciences Politiques,* 1959, p. 87, by Georges Vedel in his report to the International Political Science Congress in Rome (1958) published in the *Revue Francaise des Sciences Politiques,* 1958, p. 758; and by Pierre Avril in *Le Régime Politique de la Ve République,* Paris, 1964, especially Part I, Chapter 1 and Part II, Chapter 1. Finally, the distinction between leadership and representation will not be unfamiliar to readers of James McGregor Burns who in American politics attributes the former to the President and the latter to Congress. See *The Deadlock of Democracy,* Englewood Cliffs, 1963, and "Excellence and Leadership in President and Congress," *Daedalus,* Fall, 1960.

[3]The dates are as follows: 1793, Louis XVI is beheaded and the Revolution conducted by the National Assembly. Its children, Robespierre first among them, devour each other. 1795, "The Terror" is replaced by a constitutional republic in which the Assembly is led by a Directorate of Consuls. 1799, General Napoleone Buonaparte becomes First Consul. 1804, he crowns himself Emperor. 1814, defeat of Napoleon and Bourbon restoration (Louis XVIII and Charles X). Chamber of Deputies appointed by the crown. 1830, "July Monarchy" of Louis-Philippe of Orléans known as *Philippe Egalité.* A constitution provided for an elected chamber and an appointed senate (total electoral body, circa 200,000). 1848, revolts and establishment of the Second Republic

with "parliamentary sovereignty," rise and fall of governments. In 1851, Napoleon III is elected President of the Republic and proclaims himself Emperor in 1852. 1870, defeat at the hands of Prussia. 1871-75 the interim republic of M. Thiers, in which monarchist majorities in both chambers search for a king. In 1875, the Third Republic establishes parliamentary sovereignty. In 1889, with the collapse of the "Boulanger" plot, the last realistic hope of the monarchy vanishes.

[4]Jean Bodin, (1530-1596) published his *Six Livres de la République* in 1576. He definitively disposed of the intricate structure of corporations—guilds, parishes, the Church, cities, nobles—which formed mediaeval society and, along with the king—heretofore *primus inter pares*—had claimed to derive their authority from its one source: the will of God. Whereas only God had been considered Sovereign before, Bodin made of sovereignty an attribute of the *Res Publica*. At least for those who had not read Machiavelli and Guicciardini, here ended the *Res Publica Christiana*—the whole of Christendom with its manifold political organization—and began the *Res Publica*—now unequivocally translatable as the state. Bodin defined the state as a number of families under one "Supreme Power" (Book I). Here for the first time since the passing of antiquity we see the notion that political power provides society with its form (Aristotle, *Politics,* Book III, Chapter 4). Louis XIV's identification of himself and the State would no more have been comprehensible prior to Bodin than the notion of social engineering. Supreme power is just that; it is not authority which compels the spirit but the ability to compel action. It is also absolute, indivisible (one) and perpetual. It will not do, however, to term it tyranny, for that does not depend on the amount of power exercised, but on the end which power serves, although the tendency for the sovereign power to substitute itself for the society it rules is inherent in the concept of sovereignty. Finally, it is interesting to compare Bodin's warning in Book I about the disintegration of the state following the sovereign's loss of power with the speech of Michel Debré before the French Council of State in 1958. Advocating the Vth Republic's constitution, Debré stated its purpose as "first and above all to try to re-constitute a power, without which there is neither State nor Democracy, . . . neither France nor Republic." (*Revue Française des Sciences Politiques,* 1958, p. 7.) Also, cf. Voegelin, *op. cit.*

[5]In Books 11-13 of *L'Esprit des Lois* (1748) Montesquieu set forth the doctrine of the separation of powers: legislative, executive and judicial, as it has come down to us. Separation is essential both to the achievement of liberty and to popular control. His paradigm was England, where, at least in years gone by, both Parliament and the judiciary had enjoyed great independence from the royal executive. At the time he wrote, however, the crown's control of Parliament and judges had united these powers to an extent which would not be equaled again until the era of modern political parties began in the second half of the nineteenth century. By then, of course, the executive could be held to account for its actions before the electorate.

[6]*Le Monde,* 24 Nov. 1959.

[7]This notion of popular participation is not the only possible one even under monarchy. The English monarchy developed a means of association during the Middle Ages by which the people's representatives cooperated in actual legislation. The king in the mediaeval scheme was merely the head of a body which existed both in form and substance independently of his will. By the early fifteenth century, Sir John Fortescue, 1385-1474, could describe in his *De Laudibus Legum Angliae* a *Dominium Politicum et Regale,* a royal and political rule which proceeded from the king *in* Parliament. The positive part taken by the people's representatives in the actual political governance of England habituated that country and its children to think of political decisions as matters of common interest and not merely as acts of a power which it is necessary to propitiate and guard against. Through representation for the purpose of doing worthy and useful things in common, the Constitution politically articulated England. For an excellent analysis of Fortescue, articulation and political existence, see Chapter II of Eric Voegelin, *The New Science of Politics,* Chicago, 1952.

[8]The growth of the omnicompetent welfare state is generally cited as the cause for the decline observable in all democratic countries in the powers of parliaments. Professor Carl J. Friedrich (*Constitutional Democracy,* Cambridge, 1956) is only the most eminent of those who have treated this theme. In France the most eminent work is Georges Burdeau, *Droit Constitutionnel et Institutions Politiques,* Paris, 1962. If the prestige of popular assemblies was due to the belief that they were authoritatively translating a higher law (Vox Dei) into contemporarily useful terms, it is not surprising that the abandonment of that lofty realm for divisive struggles over who is to get "what, when and how," resulted in a decline of prestige in favor of administrators, whose job had always been to decide how and when services were to be performed.

[9]Joseph Schumpeter in *Capitalism, Socialism, and Democracy,* New York, 1942, shows how the growing desires of modern liberal democratic societies have made it very difficult for them to maintain highly differentiated institutions of government.

[10]Under the IVth Republic, the two houses of Parliament were: the National Assembly (or Chamber of Deputies) and the Council of the Republic, a nonpolitical "consultative" upper house composed of local notables. The government was responsible only before the former.

[11]Georges Vedel, in his report to the International Political Science Congress (1958, *op. cit.,* p. 764), divided regimes into two categories: those "in which the executive and the legislative are but two branches of the activity of a political party occupying power, the problem of their relationship being then largely reduced to problems of life within the party or of relations between the majority and the opposition (and) . . . the regimes in which either because of the absence of majority party or because of a lack of discipline

within such a party, there is no simple articulation between the chamber(s) and the Government . . . ."

Such differences as exist between the Soviet Union and Great Britain, Vedel points out, are not due to the separation of powers between executive and legislative. In both countries, the party in power has complete control of *The Power.* Sovereignty in both is one and indivisible. The differences lie in the purposes which animate Britons on the one hand and Communists on the other.

[12]The definitive analysis of the effects of proportional representation in the IVth Republic is found in Ferdinand A. Hermens, *The Representative Republic,* Notre Dame, 1958.

[13]See Pierre Avril, *Le Régime Politique de la Vᵉᵐᵉ République,* Paris, 1964, p. 34. By the 1950s, political scientists recognized the sovereignty of "governments" throughout Europe. This was evidenced by the debates which followed Georges Vedel's report to the International Political Science Congress on the relationship between the legislative and executive. The following sums up the conclusion of these debates: ". . . The task of government is not the executive (function), but prevision, general direction, and synthesis. The function of Parliament is not legislation, but critique, control and assent." (Vedel, *op. cit.*)

[14]*Ces Princes qui nous Gouvernent,* Paris, 1957 and *La Mort de L'Etat, Républicain,* Paris, 1947. In the latter see especially pp. 194-5 for an analysis of the effects of P.R.

[15]"In fact, the only question which now posed itself to the political system was that of the way in which its self-renunciation would be accomplished." de Gaulle, *L'Effort,* p. 26. In fact, in 1958—as in 1940—the only party capable of "mobilizing" supporters was the Communist Party, but on both occasions it refused to do so for its own reasons.

[16]*Les Dernières Nouvelles D'Alsace,* 14 April 1972 and 16 April 1972. Prior to the presidential trip, the major topic of speculation in the newspapers was what sort of presents the President would bring in his pocket.

[17]Jacquier Bruhere (Michel Debre and Emmanuel Monick) *Refaire la France: L'Effort d'une Génération,* Paris, 1945, p. 108 as quoted by Nicholas Wahl "Aux Origines de la Nouvelle Constitution," *Revue Francaise des Sciences Politiques,* 1958, p. 33.

[18]*Le Renouveau,* p. 8.

[19]*Ibid.,* p. 10.

[20]*Ibid.,* pp. 10-11.

[21]*Ibid.,* p. 28.

[22]*Ibid.,* p. 30.

[23]Georges Burdeau, *op. cit.,* p. 92, cf. Voegelin, *op. cit.,* Chap. II.

[24]De Gaulle, *Le Salut,* pp. 234-240, is only one of the many places he makes this, the classic monarchical argument.

[25]If no candidate receives a majority, a runoff is held between the two candi-

dates who, after possible withdrawals of better-placed candidates, had received the highest number of votes on the first ballot. This method assures the winner of an absolute majority. The tendency has been for groups to "test" their appeal on the first ballot, confident that if enough do it, no one will have a majority, then bargain to form coalitions for the second. Prior to the Constitutional Amendment of 28 October 1962, the President was elected by an electoral college comprising some 70,000 notables; mayors, delegates from municipal councils, etc.

[26]*Le Monde,* 15 Dec. 1970.

[27]The notion of two majorities within one electorate is not peculiar to France. Willmoore Kendall's essay "The Two Majorities in American Politics," in *The Conservative Affirmation,* Chicago, 1963, distinguishes between a presidential electorate voting on issues of such magnitude as to be presentable only in generalities which are at best oversimplifications and at worst an invitation to misconstruction, and a congressional electorate, voting on candidates and issues intimately known by communities of citizens who know and care about their common good. The latter produces a congressional majority impregnated with common sense, while the former invests Presidents with vague "mandates" for actions so loosely conceived that they often have unforeseen noxious effects on the Republic. On the other hand, James McGregor Burns *(op. cit.),* among others, claims the presidential majority in American politics, composed of the forward-looking, modern sections of both parties, produces the enlightened leadership of America. The congressional majority represents America in its particularity and acts as a constant brake on the presidency. Burns's view is, of course, far more akin to the distinction made in France, for example by Burdeau *(op. cit.)* than Kendall's.

[28]De Gaulle, *Le Salut,* p. 502.

[29]Macridis and Brown, *op. cit.,* p. 131.

[30]This is also congruent with contemporary political science, vide Hans J. Morgenthau's definition of prestige as "a reputation for power" and of power as ability to get one's way.

[31]*Le Monde,* 4 Sept. 1970.

[32]A "strong" prime minister, in order to overawe the President of the Republic, would independently have to head a solid parliamentary majority capable of weathering a dissolution of Parliament which would surely be pronounced by a President whose prerogatives were threatened. In such a case a situation resembling that which followed the dissolution of 16 May 1875, by Marshal McMahon would obtain. However, were such a strong prime minister to arise, the main Gaullist concern would be taken care of: the country would have a *Pouvoir.* No constitution can insure a country against weak political men, but precedents of strength which achieve success are as likely to be followed as those of weakness which end in failure.

[33]Quoted from Goguel and Grosser, *op. cit.,* p. 207.

[34]*Le Monde,* Sept. 4, 1970. Art. 52 of the Constitution gives the President the authority to "negotiate and ratify" treaties, and Art. 51 the command of the armed forces. There is nothing in it, however, about a "reserved domain."

[35]It will become clear below that in order to get its way, the government does not need a solid majority in Parliament, it only requires that there not exist such a majority *against* it.

[36]This occurred on 23 Nov. 1960, the censure motion receiving 214 votes, 277 being the bare absolute majority of the National Assembly. The Senate is not considered able to deny confidence as it did in the IIIrd Republic.

[37]Pierre Avril, *Le Regime Politique de la Veme Republique,* Paris, 1964, p. 16.

[38]This, according to Michel Debré, is the only real reason why the Vth Republic constitution included a senate, and is consequently the reason that we mention the upper house only in passing. We will look at this institution at somewhat greater length when we examine Gaullism.

[39]Avril, *op. cit.,* pp. 42-43.

[40]Referring to "Vox Populi, Vox Dei," *Le Renouveau,* p. 87.

[41]The council is composed of nine members, each appointed for a non-renewable nine-year term. Three members each are named by the President of the Republic, the president of the Assembly and the president of the Senate, who, along with the Prime Minister, are the only parties who can call upon the council for a decision on the constitutionality of laws. On its own initiative, the council can only examine "organic laws," that is, laws bearing on the organization of the organs of government as well as the rules governing the functioning of Parliament.

The saga of the bill modifying the law of July 1, 1901, was front page news for weeks. Some of the most informative articles appeared in *Le Monde* on June 30, July 16, 18, and 20, 1971. The law of July 1, 1901, was actually a far more repressive instrument when it was adopted—its purpose then was to stamp out religious societies—than it is today. Its Article 3 forbids all associations "contrary to the laws, to good morals, or which have as their purpose the infringement of the integrity of the national territory or the republican form of government." But for most organizations the permit is granted routinely. The two organizations which had been denied their permit while the new law was pending—"Red Aid," a sort of revolutionary boosters club, and the "Movement for the Application of the Treaty of 1532 between France and Brittany"—received their permit almost simultaneously with subpoenas. The whole matter did not portend immediate serious practical consequences. In 1973 two political organizations, one of the extreme Left, the "Communist League" and one of the extreme Right, "New Order" were disbanded using the old procedure in a show of determination and evenhandedness by the government.

[42]*Le Monde,* 19 Sept., 1970. Edgar Faure was president of the Council of Ministers under the IVth Republic.

[43]*Op. cit.,* p. 170-173.

[44]The elections of 1956, the last under the IVth Republic, were contested by 10 major groups. By 1967, the number was down to six. By 1973 it was down to two major coalitions, the "Majority" and the Union of the Left, two minor "reformist" groups and a few insignificant splinter organizations.

[45]In a featured article in *Le Monde,* July 1, 1971, Maurice Duverger, citing these and other figures, argued nonetheless that the Communist Party (PCF) could draw great benefit from a majority system because it provides a strong incentive for a broad "coalition of the Left," one of the party's perennial aims. However, other figures cited by Duverger, as well as ones cited by F. A. Hermens *(op. cit.)* for earlier periods, show that "majority" systems tend to favor the "moderate" elements of coalitions against more extreme ones. For example, whereas the PCF gained 33 chamber seats in the 1968 election (majority system) against 57 for the Socialist Federation of the Left, PR would have given the two 117 and 94 respectively. What finally belies Duverger's argument is the testimony of the party itself: Duverger cites Georges Marchais, general secretary of the PCF saying, "Very solemnly I challenge all parties, whether they be of the Left or Right, without exception: if you are ready to decide that the proportional system is going to be the electoral law for all elections, the French Communist Party commits itself to respecting the will of the majority." Marchais' attachment for P.R., Hermens shows (p. 262), was also shared by Togliatti, longtime Communist leader in Italy.

In a similar article on 15 March 1973, immediately following the legislative elections, Duverger seemed to follow the logic of the figures, stating that a "majority" electoral system, at least on the second ballot, tends to push political forces into two large coalitions each dominated by its moderate elements, coalitions so large as to leave no room between them. The center, he declared, no longer exists.

[46]Vide C. L. Sulzberger in the *International Herald Tribune,* Jan. 12, 1972.

[47]Philip M. Williams, *op. cit.,* p. 171, is not the only commentator to note that in de Gaulle's case, "the pursuit of grandeur abroad does not preclude the practice of pettiness at home." Williams referred to the general's managing of the state broadcasting monopoly to give himself and his party what in Anglo-Saxon countries would be called unfair advantage. The general himself, in *L'Effort,* pp. 81-82, agrees that he so managed broadcasting while in power. There is no lack of examples of Gaullist low politics.

Chapter 4
Political Parties
and Representation

The Fifth Republic's Constitution is the first in French history to mention political parties.[1] But the de Gaulle Republic, as it is called, was also constituted as a modern democratic remedy to the strength of antagonistic political parties, which were depriving the state of its strength. Paradoxically, the Fifth Republic is also seeing the growth, for the first time in French history, of government based on a party.

Charles de Gaulle came out of retirement in 1958 to rescue France from the parties which had divided her. He never claimed that they did not faithfully represent Frenchmen, rather that they reproduced within the leading organs of the state the divisions which had plagued Frenchmen for centuries. The parties represented Frenchmen insofar as they differed from each other economically and ideologically but who, besides the old general, represented France? Since the state is perforce the representative of France, its strengthening at the expense of the parties would not deprive Frenchmen of representation; it merely changed the image to one of renewed unity. This was the purpose of de Gaulle's anti-party, the *Rassemblement du Peuple Francais* (RPF, Rally of the French People), formed in 1947 to draw voters and political men away from the regime of the parties, to support the strengthening of France, the national interest over that of particulars, etc. But although the RPF achieved a stunning success in the 1951 elections (21 percent of the seats in the Assembly, the most numerous parliamentary group after the Communists), the logic of the Fourth Republic soon made of it a "party like the others." The partisans of France were, it appears, just another faction in France obliged to join in the game of parliamentary coalitions. De Gaulle disowned the venture and waited for the state to be delivered into his representative hands.

The Party System

Political parties in France as elsewhere exist to exercise influence. Their organization and to some extent their appeals are shaped to take advantage of the electoral system, the geographic and juridical divisions of the state. During most of the Third Republic, the single-member district, two-ballot electoral system, coupled with the diffusion of governmental power among a large number of members of Parliament, made it difficult for parties to form. No single group could hope to gather enough support to exercise power alone, much less could it hope to exercise it over its parliamentary supporters. The electoral system of the Fourth Republic, PR and two ballots allowed the leadership of political parties to control the members they sent to Parliament, but also made it virtually impossible for any one party to gain control of Parliament. Consequently, with the notable exception of the Communist Party, it was never clear whether any given party was a government party or an opposition party. The deputies were bound to vote as they were told, but it was never clear whether they were bound to the leadership of their group in Parliament — whether it happened to be part of the government at that time or not — their departmental party committee, which actually determined their place on the electoral list, or to the national party committee. On controversial issues such as the European Defense Community, for example, the Socialist Party National Committee might order its deputies to vote "no," while the majority of the Socialist deputies would decide on "yes." For the national committee to sanction a defiant *depute* who was in agreement with his departmental committee and with his own leadership in the chamber made little sense. Even party responsibility did not hold. As a result, at election time the public could not, by voting for any party, support or sanction any government or even necessarily take a stand on any given issue. It could only express a general attitude on ideological matters it knew little about.

The Fifth Republic has given France a government party simply by making the government both largely independent of parties and dependent on one man: deputies and senators who belong to the UDR and the other groups making up "the majority" have their electoral platform ready-made. Their very acceptance of their label signifies their identification with the President's government and their election binds them to support it. Withdrawal of the party label to a *depute* of the majority has been an unambiguous sign to his constituency that if it cares to support the government, it had better do it through another candidate. Thus it has been the willingness of Frenchmen since 1958 to have a strong government, made possible but far from inevitable by the Constitution, which has allowed the rise of a government party. It would be wrong to attribute the success of the government parties to a positive will to be governed in a particular manner, however, for in every election since 1958, the government has spared no effort to convince voters that the only choice other than itself is chaos followed by communism. The existence of the government party depends on the starkness of this choice.

Even after fourteen years of constant reduction in number, the opposition parties still number five. These were divided into three electoral groups for the 1968 elections: the Federation of the Democratic and Socialist Left, then including the Socialist, the Radical and the United Socialist Party; the democratic center; and the Communist Party. The 1973 elections were contested by two major coalitions: the "majority," made up of the Gaullist UDR, the Independent Republicans and the Center for Democracy and Progress, and the Union of the Left, comprising the Communist, Socialist, and Left-Radical parties. The other participants can only be characterized as minor. We will now take a closer look at the parties in the French political arena, while, however, reserving our analysis of the most important political tendencies they, albeit imperfectly, represent until Chapter 6.

The Line-up: The Majority

UDR (Union of Democrats for the Republic), which won 46 percent of the vote and 291 Assembly seats in 1968,[2] and managed to remain the largest party in 1973 with 24 percent of the vote and 184 seats, is only the latest name for the Gaullist Party. In 1947 it was called the Rally of the French People (RPF) and in 1958, the Union for the New Republic. (UNR). The changes in name show at a glance that this party is defined by adherence to the plans of a given leader or set of leaders rather than by a self-standing set of principles. Through the years as the leadership's policies have changed, important persons have left the party. For example, Jacques Soustelle and Georges Bidault, mainstays of the RPF and of the UNR in its early years, left when the general decided to abandon Algeria. Other politicians of national fame from the old center, e.g., former Agriculture Minister and President of the Assembly Edgar Faure; from the Right, e.g., Tixier Vignancour, and from the Radical Party, e.g., former Prime Minister Jacques Chaban-Delmas have joined the fold, together with persons taken from the state administration, e.g., former Prime Minister Couve de Murville or from private life, e.g., the President, Georges Pompidou. The party is ecumenical in its openness to ideas on matters where the leadership has not pronounced itself. De Gaulle, of course, never considered it a party but a grouping of patriotic Frenchmen of all persuasions united in the recognition of France's basic needs, first among them the general.

The party has no experience in choosing its leaders: the general was the founder and Georges Pompidou his heir who proved himself an effective party leader during eight years as Prime Minister. The four party congresses it has held since 1958 have been without struggles for leadership. For as long as the party remains in power, its leaders are likely to rise through prominence in government service, and something like a British style dominance of back-benchers by front-benchers is likely to remain. Away from the government, the UDR, like any new party shaped by the exercise of power and lacking a specific ideology, revolutionary fervor, or a coherent nationwide organization, would escape fragmentation only if it were the only alternative to the government.

The UDR "believed" in Charles de Gaulle but is now perhaps more comfortable with his heritage than it was with the man. The main points of allegiance are simple: above all, order must be maintained and the government must be *sérieux* about its business. UDR supporters in high stations or low stress their pride in the seriousness and *efficacité* (effectiveness and efficiency) of the state whether or not they agree with the government's policies. General de Gaulle would smile on them, especially on those Gaullists who had opposed the amputation of Algeria from the body politic as treason, but who are now reconciled to the party that supported it because it succeeded in carrying out the operation in fine surgical fashion. Nothing demonstrates the character of Gaullism better. The prestige of France abroad is something else the UDR agrees upon. Gaullists like, and know that Frenchmen like, to think of France as something the world cannot do without. Some, not many, like to stress military strength, others, more numerous, speak of industrial and financial self-sufficiency, and nearly everyone mentions something about a cultural or diplomatic presence around the world. In order to assure these things Gaullists are committed to the somewhat vague goal of social peace at home through participation and cooperative consultation.

The UDR is inescapably conservative: its supporters among the population are the millions of Frenchmen who like to think mildly nationalistic thoughts, "a certain idea of France," and are more than mildly unfriendly to social upheaval. Outside of Gaullists who consider themselves intellectuals, one finds little comprehension of and at best tolerance for the idea of participation. The defeat of de Gaulle's referendum in 1969, due largely to the alienation of mayors, communal and general councilors who saw their positions threatened by the proposed reforms, shows how dependent the UDR is on the support of this sort of conservatism. As the government party, however, the UDR knows it must act against the interests of some, for example, small businessmen, if it is to further its larger plans for modernization of French society. Its leaders hope to tackle antagonists one at a time, even as de Gaulle in effect completely expropriated the one million Frenchmen in Algeria while keeping the rest of the country behind him. But since the inconveniences caused by future reforms, leading Gaullists feel, should not fall upon nearly that many people at once, there is no reason why the resentment they will cause should be politically harmful, especially if general economic conditions continue to improve. What the UDR as a conservative government party fears most of all is that a series of scandals, of which the French are avid spectators, might spoil its image. Confident that it has mastered the political passions of the French, it knows it is at the mercy of the antipolitical ones.

The UDR's junior partner in the government is the National Federation of Independent Republicans (RI), a small party composed of rather bright young "principled" conservatives led by the minister of finance, Valéry Giscard d'Estaing. The RI received but 4 percent of the vote in the 1968 elections, but by virtue of second-ballot alliances with the UDR, amassed 61 seats: the second largest bloc in the Assembly. In 1973 it received 6.9 percent of the vote and 54 seats—no longer as important a force in the Assembly, but proportionately more powerful *vis-à-vis* the senior partner in the "majority," the UDR, which dropped from 291 to 184 seats, and lost its absolute majority.

Formed in 1966 by 16 deputies who had split off from the National Center of Independents and Peasants (CNIP), itself a heterogeneous group reminiscent of traditional Third Republic conservatism, the RI immediately joined the Gaullist majority. Most of the rest of the CNIP rallied later. Valéry Giscard d'Estaing had caught the fancy of Charles de Gaulle, who paid him the compliment of calling him "a young man who has a sense for the state"[3] and made him his minister of finance in 1962 at the age of thirty-six.

Although Giscard d'Estaing is not the national secretary of the RI (M. Poniatowski is), the party's fortunes are tied to his. These appear bright indeed. The news media portray him giving lessons on economics — on France's behalf — to the world. This and his virtuosity in explaining the tax system to Frenchmen has added popular admiration to widespread recognition of exceptional ability. He is a very serious prospect for the presidency.

The Independent Republicans are generally thought to be in favor of a free enterprise economy, although as finance minister, Giscard d'Estaing more than any other man actually controls the French economy, something he defends as necessary to achieve modernization with a minimum of social friction. Giscard's men are known as technocrats. Their success is also that of their style. They dress and act American while taking the United States as their point of reference in politics as well as economics. They are enthusiastic partisans of the "majority" electoral system focused on presidential responsibility for government policy. It is this system, after all, which has turned a small loosely bound group of conservatives into the leaven of the majority. They are more sanguine than the orthodox Gaullists about holding out in the face of interest groups' demands. This brought them into conflict with de Gaulle, when, during his last months in office, he raised wages to appease the various demands which had arisen in the course of the May 1968 crisis, increases which were ultimately covered by a devaluation of the franc. They are also far more willing to allow local autonomy and somewhat more "serious" than the Gaullists on both the subject of European unity and of national defense.

Rounding out the majority with the remainder of the CNIP are the conservative remnants of the MRP (Popular Republican Movement),[4] and Tixier Vignancour's Republican Alliance for Liberties and Progress, the remnants and successors of the old Right. These small groups depend for their influence within the majority on the personalities and considerable ability of their leaders and on their ability to wed to the majority the groups they used to represent. They ran in the 1973 elections under the name, Center for Democracy and Progress, as allies of the UDR and RI. After the elections they formed a parliamentary group of 23 called the Centrist Union, still a part of the majority. Like the RI, they saw no future, no possibility of being effective in the Fifth Republic, outside the fold of the majority. But they are strangers to its spirit.

The Radicals

The history of the Radical Party is an important part of French democracy. The battles which surrounded the birth of the Third Republic brought forth an upper middle class of local notables defined by their victory over the Right, sharing republican, progressive ideas and empowered to govern France. In 1901 these notables, physicians, teachers, freemasons, and the deputies who depended on them for election, formed the first political party in France: the "Republican Radical and Radical-Socialist Party." Obviously heterogeneous ideologically, and based on the belief that every deputy individually represented the whole people, it was held together by the exercise of power which, until the First World War, it monopolized and diffused among its leading members. On the eve of the conflict it had 172 deputies. Between the wars and again after World War II, it was the vital center of politics since it could ally with both the socialist left and with the right to form government coalitions. It formed the Popular Front of 1936 as easily as the center-right postwar governments. Almost half the cabinets prior to the Fifth Republic were headed by radicals, who figured prominently in all but a very few. Radicals were tied to the living structures of French society: from thousands of local notables came a constant flow of ideas, recruits and requests. Unlike other parties, the radicals had no self-contained political program; within broad guidelines its politics were elaborated by its office holders. Nearly all the great men of the Third Republic were radicals: Waldeck-Rousseau, Clemenceau, Daladier, Herriot and Reynaud are only a few examples.

Radicalism was severely shaken in the late 1950s by the efforts of Pierre Mendès-France to enforce party discipline, something totally foreign to radicalism. In addition, although its members exercised power, most, along with their electorate, were just as interested in limiting it. Radicalism was finally brought low by the appearance of the semi-presidential system of the Fifth Republic, which made it possible for the electorate to confide government power to a united conservative force. The appeal for Frenchmen to put government above representation was launched from outside radicalism. When the electorate gave de Gaulle a mandate to govern, radicalism was excluded from power. Has the very powerful tradition of centrist power-limiting coalitions been ended? It would seem that as long as the basic dividing line in French politics is drawn by the presidential election and that both Gaullism and communism remain strong, the center, of which radicalism is the archetype, can only decline.

The Radical Party fought the 1968 elections as part of the Federation of the Democratic Left and shared 21 percent of the vote and 57 Assembly seats with the Socialist Party and with M. Mitterand's political clubs. Since 1969 it has been under new management, that of Jean-Jacques Servan–Schreiber. The latter, the author of the well-known *The American Challenge* and *The Spirit of May*,[5] founder and former editor of the leading weekly news magazine *L'Express,* has tried to make the party a vehicle for his own flamboyant style of politics. He has tried to make himself by virtue of "American" publicity techniques into the leader of the democratic opposition, champion of local liberties against an oppressive state, advocate of modernization and true participation, advocate of European unity, patron of youth and freedom as well as technology, etc. These themes are very much in the air.

What first convinced Frenchmen that he suffered from a lack of *sérieux* was his quixotic campaign against the Prime Minister in the latter's own constituency. Servan–Schreiber first led his party into a search for a deeper alliance with the socialist Left, then concentrated on building a "reformers' front" with the democratic center party of Jean Lecanuet, in which the radicals fought the 1973 legislative elections, then turned again toward the Socialist Party with a fruitless request that it turn away from its perennial attempts at alliance with the Communists while making known he would consider an offer of a cabinet position under President Pompidou. The offer did not come. The Reformers Front did not do well in the 1973 elections, receiving only 12.4 percent of the vote and 31 seats. Servan–Schreiber then found himself criticized for frivolity, inconstancy and bad judgment by his principal partner in the front, M. Lecanuet, and deserted by leading members of his party, some of whom joined Robert Fabre in a new party, the Radicals of the Left. This new party fought the 1973 elections in alliance with the Socialists and Communists and held its first national congress on December 1, 1973. One of these rebels, Pierre Naudet, indicted the entire concept of a centrist party— no matter how well led—given the polarizing pressures of the present political system.[6]

His opinion fits with that of the French political scientist Maurice Duverger,[7] who believes the existence of a centrist bloc of 31 deputies hides the fact that its electoral supporters' primary motive was no different from that of supporters of the majority, that is to say, anti-communism. In Parliament the bloc's only meaningful action could be to sell its support to either the majority or the opposition. Servan–Schreiber tends toward the latter, but the electoral system, the existence of the Communist Party, and the nature of the radical electorate in southern France argue against an upturn in his fortunes.

The Democratic Center

Those members of the MRP and CNIP who for one reason or another refused to rally to Gaullism gathered under the centrist label in 1967 under the leadership of Jean Lecanuet, who had come in third in the presidential election of 1965. By 1968, with 7 percent of the first ballot vote, they managed 33 seats, almost an equal percentage of all seats in the chamber thanks to the traditional privilege of moderates in France: ease in forming second-ballot alliances.

Its hopes had been greater, though. A respectable centrist, Lecanuet had hoped to draw moderate Gaullists and moderate socialists away from the poles to which they were attached, toward a traditional French centrist coalition. The center's positions were eminently simple and moderate: support for a united Europe in the tradition of the MRP and Robert Schuman, friendship with the United States, more local autonomy, etc.—appeals different from those of Gaullism above all by the absence of the tone of authority. The CD is more of a flag of convenience for individual deputies, often prominent in their own right, than a party. As a whole, together with what remains of the Radical Party, it is a remnant of the old system of personal representation. But the logic of the regime is against the "center":   since it is in opposition, its leaders stand no real chance of being the President's choice for Prime

Minister or the latter's choice for government posts. Hence those electors wanting to bring the democratic center's generally moderate policies into the government have to cast their ballots elsewhere. Neither is the center convincing as an opposition party, for not only are its views fairly close to the majority's, but it reflects its electorate's antagonism toward the Communist Party which, as everyone knows, is the main political force in opposition. Aware of this, Jean Lecanuet, even while leading the Reformer's Front in the 1973 election campaign, began trying to adjust himself to the realities of two-bloc politics. In the course of a debate on national television on February 23, he asked in effect to be allowed to join the government, asking only that it make some political changes in its stance. The Gaullists replied that they would indeed be happy to receive the centrist reformers into the fold, but would not pay in the coin of their principles. Obviously it would no longer be a question of anything but the price to be paid for the integration of an old firm, slowly going out of business, into a new, powerful, if shallow-rooted, conglomerate.

To prove the sincerity of their offer, Lecanuet and the centrists, after the first ballot of the 1973 elections, decided to withdraw a number of candidates who stood no chance of winning their districts and whose candidacy might draw enough votes away from the "majority" candidate to elect a member of the Socialist-Communist Union of the Left. Not a few political observers credit this move with providing the winning margin for the "majority" on the second ballot. Doubtless also every potential "majority" candidate for the 1976 presidential election put such a deal with the center fairly high on his list of things to do.

But Lecanuet has not been able to bring himself simply to dissolve his movement into the "majority" and work for his ends as, for example, Giscard d'Estaing works for his within the team. Yet as time passes and the constraints of the system weaken it, the price the Democratic center can ask for its support is not likely to rise.

The Socialist Party

The Socialist Party is a true opposition party, but it too has had difficulty adjusting to the Fifth Republic.

It is, first of all, the heir to the S. F. I. O. (French Section of the Workers' International) which was founded in 1905 and ran for the last time under that name in 1962. From the SFIO the Socialist Party has inherited an impressive base in local government (almost a fourth of all towns over 9,000 inhabitants have Socialist mayors), a fairly faithful, if aged, electorate of civil servants and some manual workers, a relatively extensive, if faction-ridden, organization and the standard of democratic socialism in France.

Since 1920, when a majority of the party left to form the Communist Party, the relationship between the two, euphemistically called the "problem of leftist unity," has been undoubtedly the single greatest source of hope and trouble for the Socialists. Briefly realized in 1936 and 1944, Socialist-Communist coalitions ended with the Socialists allying with the center or the Right in order to escape the totalitarian power of their offspring's organization.

The Socialists are not Marxists, but rather heirs of a Marxist tradition. Belief in the infallibility of Marxist analysis or even acquaintance with its principal details remain in the memory of very few Socialists. A desire to transform society through state action remains, but both means and ends envisaged are influenced more by the experiences in office of party members than by any comprehensive view. This poses problems: how to differentiate modern socialism from the enterprises of both Communists and Gaullists who also want to transform society by state action; especially from the latter who first instituted national economic planning and carried out more nationalizations in 1944-45 than the Socialists had ever proposed during the Third Republic. The center and the Radicals are different, their commitment to reform is uncertain, they are undisciplined, and still skeptical of government power. But if Socialists condemn them as nothing but *petits bourgeois,* won't that push them into the arms of the majority? That would leave the Socialists alone in the opposition except for the Communists and the wild men from the extreme Left. A step in this direction has already been taken by the breakup of the old Federation of the Left and the formation of the Union of the Left, which fought the 1973 elections. As for the Communists—well, they offer strength, also indisputably the will to change society in a socialist direction, but at what price?

The leader of the Socialist Party at this writing is a man who did not come up through Socialist ranks.[8] It is thus not surprising that François Mitterand envisages an entirely different sort of solution. His experience in the 1965 presidential election convinced him that the institutions of the Fifth Republic make it possible for the first time for the Left to gain the whole of government power in France in one election, that the power would be stable, and not necessarily dependent on the support of the coalition which helped gain it. Most of all, so runs his reasoning, the Communist Party knows that although it is indispensable to such a coalition, this must be headed by a non-Communist—like Mitterand—because neither the majority of the Left nor even a majority of Communist voters would vote to be *governed* by a Communist President. Someone with his independent status, he concludes, can strike a modus vivendi with the Communists which would oblige them to support him in the presidential elections while not offending the moderate elements necessary to fill out the opposition. Thus, the institutions of the Fifth Republic can serve to place the entire center and Left under the dynamic leadership of the force which stands at its ideological center, the Socialist Party or rather François Mitterand.

Not only do the Communists interpret differently the possibilities offered by the Fifth Republic, but many Socialists, led by the powerful Guy Mollet, do not cease to chastise Mitterand for his "Gaullist" interpretation of the Constitution. They remind him that the party has long officially supported a revision of the Constitution which would lessen the powers of the presidency and make the stability of the executive depend on a constitutional provision requiring the dissolution of Parliament in case a government was forced to resign by the withdrawal of support of any part of its "majority." This amendment would be a long step back to parliamentary supremacy, also desired by the Communist Party. Bargaining over the form of its proposal seems without end.

The latest Socialist Party program, like other party programs, is not particularly exciting to Frenchmen. Upon its adoption M. Mitterand expressed the hope they would come to believe that a socialist victory "would not only be a change of *Patrons,* but also a change in a way of life."[9] Thus does the party program try to draw a distinction between socialist nationalization of enterprises, which would turn them over to the workers' democratic control, and state-ization, which merely changes the boss. The Socialists are no less in favor of "participation" than the Radicals and not much more than the Gaullists, no more in favor of European unity than the Independent Republicans and somewhat less than the Radicals, and not much more anti-American than the Gaullists.

The party program is, however, less important to the role the Socialists will play in French politics than the actual alliances that this party, still firmly anchored in French life, concludes from time to time. These depend on the constant struggle for leadership in this the most faction-ridden of French parties.

Undoubtedly the biggest political news of the 1972-73 season was the agreement between the Socialist and Communist parties and, incidentally, the Leftist Radicals, to unite upon a single "government program," i.e., campaign platform, and a single list of candidates for the 1973 parliamentary elections. The agreement of July 12, 1972, was carefully worded to allow divergent interpretations by the several parties, and capped negotiations characterized by diffidence and bitter polemic on matters such as freedom in Czechoslovakia, under what conditions the workers would relinquish power, etc. The union's biggest asset was that it alone had a realistic possibility of displacing the UDR and its allies as "the majority." It sought votes on this basis. This, however, was also its greatest weakness, for the great number of Frenchmen who expressed dissatisfaction with a Gaullist regime a bit tainted with corruption and in power for fifteen years could not bring themselves to vote for a coalition the biggest member of which is the Communist Party.

Françqis Mitterand was always well aware of this, both as a particular feature of the current situation and as a general feature of democratic politics in France, as evidenced by one of the more quotable statements of the campaign:

> On Monday they (the people) throw artichokes into the prefectures' courtyards. On Tuesday it's the potatoes' turn. On Wednesday they barricade the roads, on Thursday they block the Avenue de l'Opera and spit upon the minister of finance. On Saturday I don't know what they do, and on Sunday they vote for the government . . . .[9]

It has been pointed out that Mitterand's interest really did not lie in a victory by the Union of the Left in 1973.[10] Such a victory, even with more Socialist deputies elected than Communist deputies, would still have been a Communist victory, for Mitterand has no illusions as to where the advantage would be in a struggle between his loosely organized Socialists and the Communist Party apparatus for something as ill-defined as control within a parliamentary majority. Mitterand did not want to share parliamentary power with the Communists, but rather primarily to make a big down payment for Communists' support in the 1976 presidential election. In 1973 he would once more help the Communists out of their isolation and into some seats they could only get by second-ballot alliance, and he would habituate the party to democratic cooperation which would continue in 1976, when he would run for President with its support. If he won, the powers of the French state would insulate him from his redoubtable allies' effort to collect on whatever promises he might have made.

Thus Mitterand, according to charges by the general secretary of the Communist Party, Georges Marchais, did his best to ensure the Union of the Left, but especially the Communist Party, would not gain too much. The Socialists' conspicuous effort to present themselves during the campaign as quite different from the Communists on matters as important as civil liberties, private property, and the ominous events behind the Iron Curtain, not only took votes away from the coalition, but also took votes away from the Communists within the coalition itself. In his report to the Central Committee, Marchais said:

> The Socialist Party...has, one must say, deployed efforts similar to those of the big bourgeoisie to try to weaken our party by taking up on its own certain anti-Communist themes.

Be that as it may, the Socialists were the big winners of the 1973 elections, winning 91 seats with 19 percent of the vote, more than doubling the number of their deputies, whereas the Communists, who also doubled the number of their deputies (to 73) were clearly the number two party of the union though their share of the vote, 21 percent, was higher. Their anger is understandable.

Mitterand's Socialist Party is engaged in an ambitious enterprise. The Socialist deputies of the class of 1973 are a large infusion of new blood into an old decadent party. Almost half have no previous experience in elective office. Their roots in their districts are shallow. For about another decade, therefore, the fortunes of the Socialists will depend largely on Mitterand's high-level deals.

The Communists

The Communist Party's size and unity make it the natural core of the opposition. The PCF, however, has found it difficult to play that role because, alone among political parties, it considers itself the particular representative of a part of the population, "the working class," instead of, as the others, potentially the representative of the heterogeneous majority of a heterogeneous people.[13] This theoretical difference is also illustrated by certain practical ones: for example, while the deputies adhering to all other parties receive their salaries from the state (about 7,000 francs per month), Communist deputies turn in their state salaries to the party, from which they receive about 1,800 francs per month. Of course, they also get numerous perquisites, but the principle is established: they do not "belong" to the nation, but are the agents of an organized group which not only pays them, but tells them how to vote, hires and fires them as well. Of course, the party is not *the* representative of French workers. Public opinion polls published in *Sondages* year after year confirm what anyone can discover by talking to his neighbors: only about a third of manual workers vote Communist (one-fifth of the whole population does). However, about half of the Communist voters are manual workers, most of the rest being either "intellectuals" or employees. There are few farmers among them. In sum, the composition of the Communist electorate, although weighted toward manual workers, is not so different from that of most other parties.

With its nearly 300,000 dues-paying members, the party has more members than all other French political organizations combined.[14] Whereas during the nineteen-fifties its membership dropped and aged, it has been expanding and including ever-younger people since 1961. Today its membership is almost one-third larger than it was at the beginning of the Fifth Republic and almost half have joined the party since then. But not all is as the leaders would want it: membership used to be a million in the nineteen-forties, and the party's daily newspapers used to sell over two and one-half million copies, whereas they now sell a bit more than one-tenth that many. No doubt also the new members are not as disciplined as the old. The party's mystique has been damaged by de-Stalinization and, most seriously, the party now faces competition on its left. But all French newspapers and parties have suffered tremendous disaffection. Proportionately, the party is holding its own quite well. The majority electoral system, however, has chopped the average of Communist voters from 5,227,382 per election under the Fourth Republic to 4,436,172 under the Fifth.

A new glass and concrete party headquarters in the Paris suburbs testifies to the party's opulence. Its annual budget has been estimated at about 10 million dollars without counting the much larger expenses of its "mass organizations." These are the party's eyes, ears, hands and feet, as well as its pride and joy. Chief among them is the General Confederation of Labor (CGT), the nation's largest labor federation, headed by a member of the PCF's Politburo, Georges Seguy, and a model of Communist organization: whereas only one in ten of its one million members is Communist, advancing up its organization chart, the proportion of Communists increases geometrically until at the top they dominate.[15] Young people, women, lawyers, farmers, practically every sector of the population has a "mass organization" which "serves" it with efficient and always evident representation of its interests, political and cultural activities, vacation camps, etc. The towns in the Paris suburbs run by Communist mayors are usually models of civil administration, its leaders working tirelessly to get every possible swimming pool or concert series available from the state. Finally, of course, Communists enjoy the not always covert sympathies of many French teachers and intellectuals.

As a result of all this wealth, discipline, and practical experience, the leader of the PCF, Georges Marchais, could declare without boasting—though not without distortion—on the party's fiftieth anniversary that "thanks to their Communist Party, French workers, manual and intellectual closely associated, can tomorrow effectively administer the state."[16]

Yet nearly all Frenchmen have some idea how this serenity and power are achieved: when Charles Tillon, a high-ranking member of the party defected and told radio audiences how party congresses are "fixed" by the leadership according to directives from Moscow,[17] he really did not shock anyone. The possibility that the Communist Party might be evolving rapidly away from its totalitarian ways and its allegiance to Moscow does not appear to have spread beyond moderate leftist intellectuals. Even people quite willing to admit to voting Communist often express fear that Communist power in France would entail the sort of oppression and privation which are now the lot of Eastern Europe.

The PCF tries to calm these fears in several ways. Its spokesmen promise at every available opportunity both that socialist power is by its nature liberating and that anyhow conditions in France would allow the coming of socialism without the inconveniences observed in the East. The common statements of the Socialist and Communist parties usually contain such declarations, along with indications from the Socialist side which show it is not quite convinced.[18]

The party has been more successful in changing its image from that of a party of social disorder to that of perhaps *the* party of order. The loud accusations of social treason on the part of the various New Left groups has helped, as has the thoroughly proper legal conduct of the CGT. Unlike the Italian Communist Party, the PCF does not openly wage campaigns of violence any more, and does not approve of those who do. When, for example, a young ultraleftist demonstrator was killed in a clash at the Renault factory gate, the Communist apparatus, from the chairman of the CGT at the plant to the general secretary of the party, accused the leftists of provoking incidents in collusion with the government to bring repressive measures on the head of the Communist Party. "The Communist Party knows how to stop a strike" is a saying not limited to the extreme Left. Party members are instructed to be orderly not just on the job but also in the army. Military men who have handled draftees report that young men from Communist families or who are themselves party members make the best recruits. They are told by their Communist superiors that their duty is to learn all they can about army methods and equipment, and above all that, if at all possible, they are to become noncommissioned officers, gaining valuable experience in leading their comrades. Causing trouble or undermining discipline is out of the question for them. The party sees military service as an excellent—and rare—opportunity for modern youth to acquire the habits of self-control so essential to communism. Whatever the party's ulterior motives, the somewhat strange-sounding words "He's a Communist, he can be counted on," are being heard in the French Army.

Most embarrassing to the PCF has been the behavior of the Communist states. The party has attempted to preserve both the reassuring image it is trying to project to the French public and its fidelity to Moscow by following events such as the invasion of Czechoslovakia, the trial of Jews in Leningrad, and the Polish workers' riots by brief statements "for the record" expressing disagreement followed by long campaigns of support for the Soviet Union and denunciation of the enemies of socialism who are allegedly behind all the troubles.[19] In debate after public debate[20] the party's tactic is the same: when confronted with what socialist brother parties have done when in power, party spokesmen briefly say their party is not for such measures and then charge the other side with trying to draw attention away from the troubles of present-day France! Only the repeated commission of frightening acts by Communist governments keeps this tactic from being very successful.

The Communist Party must overcome all these fears if it is to forge a union of the dissatisfied.[21] Without it the party is condemned to a choice between sterile opposition and trying to come to power by exploiting crises such as the one of May, 1968. The latter course of action, the party believes, would pose unacceptable dangers. The French Army, it knows, was almost called on to liquidate the 1968 crisis. Had it received the order, it would have performed its job with a zeal fed by the rancor of half a century's conflict. The army remembers the Communists hindering the fight in World War I, playing their part in the defeat of France in 1940 at the time of the

Stalin-Hitler Pact, and "stabbing the army in the back" in Indochina and Algeria. The party is determined not to give the army the chance for revenge for which it fervently longs.

The PSU

Founded in 1961 by leftist socialists from the Radical Party and the SFIO, the United Socialist Party is the main representative of the New Left in France. Long considered the personal vehicle of Pierre Mendès-France (who has since left the party to join the Socialists), the PSU came into its own in May of 1968 when, more than any political group, it tried to fan the rage and discontent in schools and factories into a general conflagration. At that time it made lasting friends and enemies by organizing and sending into the streets adolescents from Paris Lycées. In the elections which followed the riots, it lost all four seats it had held.

Among its 13,500 members[22] one finds undisciplined young people who fancy themselves "real" Communists, Trotskyites, "advanced" Catholics dominated by social concerns, as well as a few technocrats. Members of the PSU are usually quite well off economically. Under the leadership of Michel Rocard (a graduate of the ENA and an alumnus of the Council of State and deputy from a Paris suburb, a post he first won in a by-election in 1969), the party shows little of the lack of discipline it recommends. The PSU is the only party that habitually stands up in Parliament for the civil liberties of revolutionary organizations and individuals.[23]

The PSU is less worried than other political parties about appearing frightening. Its appeal is simply that people should stop living their lives according to decisions made by others and follow no directive they did not individually help to shape. Still, it is careful to point out that it would retain, if in a less rigid form, planning and "social responsibility" for the welfare of all.[24]

Clubs and Unions

The decline in the influence of parties under the Fifth

Republic has been accompanied by a certain renaissance of clubs where politically active gentlemen elaborate political alternatives. The Federation of the "Perspectives and Realities" Clubs was founded by Valéry Giscard d'Estaing in 1965 during the brief period when he was not occupying the post of minister of finance. It is an auxiliary, political as well as intellectual, of the Independent Republican Party. The "Republican Institutions Convention," a network of clubs founded by François Mitterand in 1964 was once almost a full-fledged political party, but since its leader has taken over the Socialist Party, has become its adjunct. The best known network of clubs, the Jean Moulin, gained prominence in the early 1960s with a series of publications discussing policies and institutions from a literate modern socialist perspective. Generally, the clubs have survived insofar as they have been connected to parties. In France as in other democracies, politics appears a thing more amenable to action than to discussion.

The two largest labor confederations are at least as important in the political as in the economic life of France. The CGT, of course, is the secular arm of the Party. The CFDT, though more independent, follows the line of the PSU. In so doing, however, the CFDT is above all trying to keep up with a trend in labor relations evident in Europe since the mid-60s. The strikes of 1968 were not the first started by non-professional organizers in which exorbitant demands were pushed by the fanatical zeal of employees. Gone are the days when professional organizers had to work long and hard to foment a strike, and even harder to have it last more than a week. The new militancy is not inspired by political purpose, nor is it usually violent. The demands are for changes in working conditions and for much higher wages. They are politically significant because although not directed against political authority, they are carried out with complete disregard for rules governing strikes, with no apparent concern for ulterior effects of the settlement on the enterprise or on the nation, and with savage tenacity.[25] The labor unions soon step in and conduct negotiations, sign agreements and get them ratified but they, especially the CFDT, would like to take the lead. They know that money is not the main motive of strikers, but rather the resentment of authority coupled with the desire for security, hence the stress on promises of "worker power," "plants run by workers," etc.

Political Representation
Access to Power

In modern parliamentary governments political parties can be said to have two basic functions: the exercise of government power (or preparing for it while in opposition) and the representation of an electoral clientele. The latter can be divided into representation of particular interests and representation of concerns about the state in general. During the Fourth Republic nearly all parties were government parties and all shared the monopoly on both kinds of representation, but in the Fifth Republic only the Gaullist and the Communist parties fulfill the first function. As for representation, although members of Parliament of all parties remain important persons, parties themselves can no longer be the intermediaries, the brokers, between the people and government power. That is now the job of the hundreds of consultative committees which connect the state with the nation. A mayor who wants to see new industry or a new swimming pool in his town no longer goes to the departmental party committee, but through the appropriate consultative committee to the appropriate officials. As for concerns about the state in general, these seem in short supply everywhere.

Similarities and Differences

The student who approaches modern French democracy expecting to find it an arena where political parties, each representing a distinct socio-economic class and spiritual family, give each other battle in behalf of mutually incompatible views of society will be disappointed. First, although one can still detect "class" differences in the electoral constituencies of political parties—Communists have a higher percentage of manual workers than the Independent Republicans and the PSU, who have a higher one of managers—the socio-economic differences are not great. Second, it is no longer a question of each party representing a separate way of life. Most people are employees: the percentage of self-employed people in France is now below 25. Thus the socio-economic basis of the turn of the century battles between the classes whose farms, crafts, or businesses made them independent, and the "working class" which wanted to be cared for, has disappeared.[26] Even managers are employees, and even the self-employed, as we have seen, unceasingly petition the government to be taken under the umbrella of social legislation guaranteeing them vacations and pensions. Disagree as they might on everything else under the sun, today Frenchmen and the parties which seek their votes nearly unanimously share the concerns of dependence.

People who vote Gaullist, no less than those who vote Radical, expect the state to provide them with the opportunity to get more for themselves and their children: this means stability, the availability of goods at low prices, and of jobs at higher rates of pay. The source of conflict here is that it is difficult to find an employee, whether he works for the state or for another *patron,* who not only wants more, but who wants the gap between himself and those below him to do anything but widen, while that which separates him from his superiors closes. The latter is shouted from the housetops by political leaders, the former, perhaps because it is too obvious, is mentioned much less readily.

The omnicompetence of the state is not questioned by political parties with the exception of some Radical leaders. Everyone, though, from the Gaullists to the Communists, wants to "democratize," to introduce "participation" in his own way.

The several parties are also fairly close in their structure.

Only the PCF, which is exceptionally well organized, can claim that as many as one out of fifteen of its electoral supporters actually participate in its affairs by attending meetings, voting the resolutions which are due to be consecrated as party policy at the national congresses, etc. How much of a voice democratic centralism gives Communist Party members is another question, but at least they believe they have enough of a stake to participate a little. In the Gaullist or the Radical parties, for example, the active membership is a smaller proportion of the voters.[27] With the exception of the Communists, French parties also resemble each other in not asking much of the voters; not money or time for the party nor sacrifice on behalf of the nation.

Parties also resemble each other in that they all appeal to the voters strictly on the basis of their self-interest. Even a quick perusal of French newspapers before the war or immediately after it yields images of Blum, Thorez, Reynaud, Maurras, Herriot, Schumann appealing to nationalism, to history, even to God in their presentations to the voters. Now, unless they are attacking each other as *technicians* (i.e., "They couldn't or wouldn't do what they promised"), parties vie with each other in describing how prosperous and participatory their reign will be.[28]

What about elections then? Are they just an uncertain way to decide on the partition of the pie? One can say with confidence that they would be precisely such dull and meaningless affairs, but for the presence of the Communist Party. When, as at the time of the 1967 and 1973 elections, party policy and Soviet policy let the character of the Communist alternative fade into the background a bit, electoral politics consists of personalities trying to outbid each other as at an auction. One of the main features of the Fifth Republic, however, has been that the government has presented itself at each election as the representative of perennial France, the only alternative to which is, after a period of chaos, domination by the Communists. Frenchmen have thus been presented with a choice between parties which is eminently political. During the 1973 campaign, for example, President Georges Pompidou, officially above the battle, gave a very short speech at a time (Feb. 8th) when the polls were predicting a serious defeat for the "majority." Clothed in the majesty of his office, he told the nation the choice before them was "between the Communists and all the others," between a society imperfect but free and Communist collectivism, statism and oppression. He didn't have to tell anyone how to vote to hurt the Left badly. From that day the polls recorded a reflux toward the lesser evil. The Communist leader Georges Marchais simply reported the truth to the Central Committee when he said:

> The principal means by which electors who might have supported us were driven back was above all the violent anti-Communist campaign.

The principal question of French politics is simply how long the image of a very great evil which is not yet will loom larger in the popular mind than a number of small evils at hand.

To conclude, we should point out how little the parties and programs and campaigns sometimes have to do with politics in France. The Socialist Raoul Bayou, five-term deputy from the fine wine-growing *département* of Herault in southern France, explained to a reporter the secret of Socialist success in his area: "First of all, the great fear of 1968 disappeared. Secondly and above all, the UDR deputies have never understood anything about wine." The reporter commented:

> In order to be elected one must of necessity do two things: commit one's self to defend and uphold the price of *Le Produit* (the product, wine) and do everything to bring all pressures to bear to stop the scandalous campaign waged by the public authorities against wine.[29]

Less amusing examples from other areas dealing with other interests could be mentioned, but none more typical. Over the course of a year, one can "feel" public moods and feelings about the government change according to what happens to be in the news, whether it be political or not, and, yes, according to the weather. Opinion analysts have long known this. For example, *Le Figaro,* July 13, 1971, published a poll conducted by the National Opinion Research Organization, SOFRES, showing a dramatic rise in the popularity of the government, related apparently only to the return of good weather after months of rain!

Notes to Chapter 4

[1]Article 64 says in part, "Parties and political groups vie for the expression of the suffrage. They form and exercise their activities freely. They must respect the principles of democracy and of national sovereignty."

[2]The figures for the strength of all parties in the 1968 elections should be understood in the light of the unusual circumstances at that time. France had just been face to face with social disarticulation during the riots of May, and it appeared to Frenchmen that only the Gaullists and their allies stood squarely on the side of order. Their victory was the largest of any party in French history. The opposition parties, notably the Communists, have not failed to point out that these circumstances were made to order for the typical Gaullist appeal, and that the figures from these elections should not be interpreted as a rejection of leftist ideas. In fact the figures from 1973, a more normal year, are far less unfavorable for the Left.

[3]*Le Figaro,* 14 September 1970. The only other man to reach the post of minister of finance at that early age was Joseph Caillaux at the turn of the century.

[4]The emergence of the MRP immediately after World War II (it gained 24 percent of the vote in the elections for the Constituent Assembly in 1945) was a break with French tradition. It was a party of Catholics, conservative on social matters and deeply anti-Communist, but quite close to the Socialists on economic affairs. It was part of the Christian Democratic movement which at that time brought to the fore Adenauer in Germany and de Gasperi in Italy. The MRP will be remembered in France for the contributions its leaders, especially Robert Schuman, made toward a Franco-German rapprochement and European unity. In fact, the MRP in the persons of Schuman and Bidault was in charge of French foreign policy for the first postwar decade. Gradually, however, it divided into left and right wings, a process which accelerated under the Fifth Republic. Thus Pierre Pflimlin, a member of the MRP and last Premier of the Fourth, first joined Gaullism and then retired to the job of *maire* of Strasbourg; Georges Bidault, an early de Gaulle supporter finally moved off to the Gaullist's right—now largely empty—while Maurice Schuman and Pierre Henri Teitgen remained within the majority.

[5]Paris, 1965 and 1968. One can safely say that these books, like their author, have been far more influential abroad than in France.

[6]*Le Monde,* 11 August 1973.

[7]See p. 180 (ff), *supra.*

[8]Francois Mitterand came to the Socialist Party by way of the Democratic

and Socialist Union of the resistance, where he worked with (and against!) such non-Socialists are René Pleven, and by way of the Convention of Republican Institutions, a group of "independent" leftist political clubs allied with the Socialists and Radicals in the Federation of the Left in the 1967 elections. His principal claim to leadership of the federation is the race he ran for the presidency against Charles de Gaulle in 1965. On the first ballot as the candidate of the Left—including the Communist Party—he received 34.7 percent of the vote to de Gaulle's 44.6 percent, forcing a second ballot in which as candidate of the whole centrist and leftist opposition (a veritable popular front!) he received a respectable 44.8 percent. On the basis of this he overshadowed and eventually replaced M. Alain Savary as Socialist leader in 1971. However, given the organization of the party based on several powerful departmental committees headed by men who *are* the party in their area, e.g., Guy Mollet in Calais and Gaston Defferre in Marseille, his hold on the leadership is far from firm.

[9]*Le Monde,* 14 March 1972.

[10]*Le Monde,* 13 March 1973.

[11]Claude Harmel in *Est et Ouest,* 1 February 1973.

[12]*L'Humanité,* 30 March 1973.

[13]The "Account of the Conversations among Socialists," the published result of the negotiations between the Socialist and Communist parties in 1970 (*Le Monde,* 24 December 1970) reads in part as follows: "The French Communist Party defines Socialist power as the power of the working class and of other sectors of the working population. The Socialist Party defines it as the power of the majority expressing itself through universal suffrage, freed from the de facto restrictions which the domination of the capitalist class impose on it."

[14]For only slightly divergent but complete breakdowns of figures for Communist Party strength, see the special section published by *Le Monde* on 25 December 1970, and by *Est et Ouest* (Paris), December, 1970, on the occasion of the 50th anniversary of the foundation of the French Communist Party.

[15]See Jean Ranger et al, "Les Liens entre le PCF et la CGT", *Revue Française des Sciences Politiques,* February, 1969.

[16]*Le Monde,* 25 December 1970

[17]*Ibid.,* 24 July 1970.

[18]*Ibid.,* 24 December 1970. In the "Conversations among Socialists" there is evidenced agreement that socialist power would respect the "will of the people," but while the Socialist Party underlines that it would give up power if refused confidence by the electorate, the Communist side affirms that since their "socialist" government would rule to satisfy the working masses, it would enjoy their ever-growing active confidence.

[19]Readers of *L'Humanité* know that not one of Alexander Dubcek's Communist followers, many of whom took refuge in Paris, have ever appeared in its pages. This tactic has been diagnosed in *Le Monde* by S. Karol (23 October 1970), and in *Est et Ouest* on many occasions.

[20]For example, the televised series *A Armes Egales* on which Communist leaders such as Jacques Duclos and Roland Leroy have appeared.

[21]It should be pointed out that the party since the 1930s has tried to keep open the option of two distinct, if not always separate, types of coalition: the *Popular Front,* an alliance with all who feel they would benefit from social change, and the *National Front.* The latter is an alliance with certain forces of the Right on the basis of nationalism directed at enemies internal or external which the party considers especially dangerous. The wartime resistance had certain aspects of a National Front, as did the Communist alliance with certain Gaullists to defeat the European Defense Community Treaty in 1954 and to oppose the unification of Europe since then.

[22]*Le Monde,* 11 February 1972.

[23]From time to time PSU deputies publicize cases such as these: the government of France forbidding for "diplomatic reasons" the publication in France of a book by a Congolese revolutionary, the seizing of the *Little Red Book of the Lyceé student,* etc. *Le Monde,* 14 March 1972; 6 July 1973.

[24]Michel Rocard, column in *France-Soir,* 12 January, 1972.

[25]This phenomenon has been well commented on: e.g., Maurice Duverger in *Le Monde,* 23 September 1969, and, in the context of the United States, A. H. Raskin in a column in *The New York Times,* 14 December 1970. The latter writes, "They don't give a damn about anyone else. They see everybody getting away with murder, and they don't want to be left out. No union leader can afford to be a statesman under these circumstances." The former stresses the example provided young workers by the success of "confrontation" movements in the universities and churches. The strikes are carried on not so much in opposition to the social structure, but as if it did not exist.

[26]See Seymour M. Lipset, "Class Structure and Politics" in S. Graubard, et al, *op. cit.,* especially pp. 340-355.

[27]Cf. Robert Michels, *Political Parties,* New York, 1962, p. 86: "In the life of modern democratic parties . . . it is only a minority which participates in party decisions, and sometimes that minority is ludicrously small. The most important resolutions taken by the most democratic of all parties, the Socialist Party, always emanate from a handful of members."

[28]Cf. Michels, *op. cit.,* p. 85: "Stirner makes fun of all those who in accordance with the views of Kant preach it to humanity as a 'sacred duty' to take an interest in public affairs. Let those persons who have a personal interest in political changes concern themselves with these. Neither now nor at any future time will 'sacred duty' lead people to trouble themselves about the state, just as little as it is by sacred duty that they become men of science, artists, etc. Egoism alone can spur people to an interest in public affairs and will spur them—when matters grow a good deal worse."

[29]*Le Figaro,* 3 April 1973, as quoted in *Est et Ouest,* 16 April 1973

Chapter 5
The Agenda

Having examined some of the organs of the state as well as the government and parties, all means by which the polity articulates itself for action, we now turn our attention to the substantive matters which are its day to day concern. Although an objective observer might conclude that the state of national defense preparations is more important than the corruptibility of the people who run the state television network, it is significant that in normal conversation one finds the latter question preoccupies Frenchmen more than the former. By the same token, quite as significant for the character of a democracy as the purposes the actions of government are intended to serve, is the manner in which they are received, for according to a saying popular in political France today, the people are the consumers of public services, and the customer is always right.

Our discussion of what is before the people will be limited here to ordinary matters. Also before France are several comprehensive questions: European unity, and other rather ill-defined reforms springing from Gaullism and modern social-ism. These will be examined separately.

National Business
Economics

The desire of each for economic progress both absolute and relative was recognized by de Gaulle as "the principal object of public preoccupations"[1] in modern societies. He enthroned its pursuit as the task toward which the single greatest portion of the state's energies would henceforth be bent. Though they profoundly bored him, he admitted to spending one-half of his time on economic affairs. But what are the economic issues in French politics? What is at issue?

Economic growth is a general desire, not an issue. When Sicco Mannsholt, the chairman of the Common Market Com-mission, wrote in March, 1972, that growth should be re-placed as the paramount economic objective by the search for harmonious co-existence with the environment, the public out-cry was severely limited by widespread disbelief. We found no one, even in the upper middle classes, blasé on this matter: the environment, yes, for after all we need places for vaca-tions, but above all, growth. Only one thing is valued above growth: price stability. In the fall of 1967 a poll found 72 per-cent preferring the stability of prices and currency over a high rate of economic expansion.[2] To repeat, this is not an issue. Neither are rising prices: everyone from Giscard d'Estaing, to Georges Pompidou, to Georges Marchais, to manufacturers, to consumers deplores them. Only farmers partially approve. But how to hold them down? Madame Crespelle knows and cares nothing about what goes to make up the cost of her washing machine. She just knows it costs too much. Her opposition is visceral, but non-political and non-economic. Besides, it is not for people like her to decide on such matters. These are settled in the plan. Newspapers carry stories of arguments within the various organisms of the plan over whether the growth rate should be 5 percent or 5¹/₂ percent, whether the former entails too much stability, the latter too much inflation, but by no stretch of the imagination can this be called a public issue. Furthermore, among those who know something about how indirect taxes make up the better part of many prices, no one suggests eliminating the services financed by those taxes. So although prices are a point of economic discontent, and an occasion for accusing "those responsible," they are not really a point of *contention.* The government is nonetheless held completely responsible for the non-satisfaction of economic expectations and for the price rises.[3]

There are, of course, economic matters before the government or before the various planning boards which do raise public controversy, but these have a particular character, constituting an issue among the groups directly affected but of little interest to those who are not. Typical examples of these conflicts are: pressure exercised by coal miners and farmers for the maintenance at public expense of their ways of life; the demands of small businessmen that their painful adjustment to modern conditions be financed both by the general public and by supermarket chains; the demands by certain artisans (plumbers, etc.); and finally the demands of striking employees in any given industry.

The case of farm price support is well known. Industrialists deplore the ever-growing sum, now more than six billion francs per year, which goes largely into the pockets of efficient farmers, helps maintain the small inefficient ones at subsistence levels, encourages farmers to produce for the "supports" and not for customers, and forces consumers to pay doubly: in higher prices as well as in taxes. Yet price supports are not a public issue except for most farmers to whom they are sacrosanct. No political party wants to alienate farmers. Other pressure groups, e.g., industrialists, have chosen, it seems, to spend their energies to get their own advantages from the state rather than to cut down on those of others.

The retirement of aged small shopkeepers whose business

has been declining is one of those issues which sets one pressure group squarely against another. The government's proposed law to tax business establishments, and especially supermarkets, to help pay for the scheme was so vigorously opposed by the supermarket lobby, along with garage owners' associations,[4] that the whole matter was reconsidered. One of the unwritten rules of cooperative consultation is that although groups will not always get the positive measures they want, no group should normally be made to swallow anything it absolutely detests. The supermarket interests argued that the care of unfortunate shopkeepers is incumbent on the state, not on them—for it is not they who have forced the public to abandon their old suppliers. The question was not whether the small shopkeepers would get their "departure premium," but what portion of the cost would be spread over the whole population. The supermarkets' resistance resulted in the state and the taxpayer assuming a larger share of the burden. The matter is simple. An organized, vociferous and sometimes violent group wants benefits which another influential group is adamant about not paying for. The path of least resistance leads toward at least partial state satisfaction of the demands. When two interests clash head–on, neither loses—the state pays. As for the taxes required to cover the added expenses, the Ministry of Finance reports that only 9 percent of state expenses are covered by direct income taxes, the rest by indirect taxes, primarily the T.V.A.[5] The people, they say shaking their heads, would not want it any other way.

"Black market work" above all worries artisans and persons engaged in service trades. As we have seen, most of the prices charged by service establishments are set by the prefecture. At the heart of the problem is the fact that tradesmen registered with the authorities, such as plumbers, barbers or landscapers, are obliged to pay a percentage of their gross income to their trade's state-supervised retirement fund, and to Social Security. Each tradesman must also pay part of his employees' "social dues." This makes for relatively high prices. Therefore in innumerable cases, persons who want electrical wiring fixed, a tree cut up for firewood, a car started, or even a haircut, turn to people they know who can do the work regardless of their official job. The pay might be in money, in eggs, chickens or wine, or in other services rendered, and is usually below the official rate; but whatever it might be, it belongs entirely to the worker. "Official" artisans have long pressed the government for prohibition of this sort of thing. On 29 March 1972, the Council of Ministers agreed on a proposed law that would punish "black workers" with fines and jail terms, and would do so unless *they* could prove they had received no remuneration for the work performed. That this law will stop the exchange of nonofficial services any more than the law long ago passed at the behest of large vintners stopped the unlicensed sale of wine is to be doubted, but it will make services scarcer. When an interest group's demand goes directly against the public's interest, the latter is not likely to fight the demand but rather will use its ingenuity to defy the authorities' attempt at enforcement. Of course the public will exercise its right to feel bitter.

One cannot open a regional newspaper or talk with anyone engaged in any sort of business beyond shopkeeping without coming face to face with one of the thousands of economic "issues" the state or, for the largest, the government must deal with. Applegrowers *(La Societé Pomologique)* require help in the search for foreign markets and authorization to distill unsold products, the winegrowers ask that no French wine be allowed out of the "air of production" unless first bottled there. Although, for example, in support of the latter demand the Vintner's Congress staged a street demonstration, such economic issues draw little sympathy from persons not concerned.

On the contrary, strikes for higher wages often do draw expressions of sympathy from the nation and sometimes even material help from neighbors, especially in small towns. For example, strikes in small factories in Saint Brieuc, Brittany and Besançon were front page news throughout France for weeks, the strikers being portrayed as paradigms of little people holding out for a decent living against the rich and powerful. In such conflicts public opinion demands the state be on the right side regardless of cost to the taxpayer.

Harmonizing particular prices, wages, advantages, incentives, etc., with a view to fostering the economic growth of the whole is a technical problem. Whether or not it can be authoritatively resolved, surely translating the alternative choices available into political terms, as the Poujadist Movement did in the 1950s, can be dangerous, especially when the contending groups are powerful. Yet precisely such groups are likely to find politicians to champion their cause.

The resentment of hundreds of thousands of shopkeepers, artisans and their families at the passing of their independent way of life is always ready to manifest itself in support of some anti-government political movement. Since these voters are basically conservative, the "majority" has gone far to appease a group it really cannot do without in a national election. If shopkeepers in a mood of spite were to mobilize about four million votes behind their own presidential candidate, they could well hand the election to the Left.

But what is the government to do when the shopkeepers' demands overflow the limits of its ability to pay and put it in a position where it must alienate another group to keep them? Precisely such a situation faced the government in 1973. The shopkeepers found support from Jean Royer, mayor of Tours and Gaullist deputy, who introduced a bill permitting local government units, often controlled by shopkeepers, to exclude shopping centers from their jurisdiction. The shopping centers in turn mobilized a sector of public opinion behind them. Their prices average about ten percent below those of small shops, and the public is not indifferent to *that*. The "majority," behaving as if in a classic two-party system, did its best to keep the growing Royer movement within itself, making Royer a minister, but the success of such a two-party maneuver depends on the Royer forces' willingness to see things in the same way, to prefer what real advantages can be gained as a part of a heterogeneous coalition—though it might well involve watching the defeat of a bill they have called "a law to restore the balance of civilization"—or resignation and departure into the political no man's land from which, empty-handed, to watch their erstwhile comrades get their comeuppance. Governmental resolution of the crisis brought on by the Royer bill, by giving neither side a victory at the direct expense of the other, would not discourage other groups from attempting similar bargains.

Economics is a politically dangerous area for government to operate in. Given the necessarily divisive nature of the matter (not everyone can have everything at the same time) and the fundamental role of material things in the modern vision of the good life, it chances drawing unto itself the most powerful frustrations, not the thanks of the people. Its actions, favoring now one group, now the other, necessarily set one against the other. But if several groups disagree on what is due each, each one individually agrees that it should receive more, while all can point together to the source of their individual griefs: the government.

Economics is obviously a promising area for political opposition.[6] Fortunately, most economic interests represent such powerful portions of the population that no political party, especially in a majority system, can afford to ignore or exploit any one of them. Less fortunately, all the parties can try to advance their interests by exploiting general vague feelings of dissatisfaction that exist in all the interest groups.

There appear in fact to be more sources of dissatisfaction than ways of satisfying. Take for example the widely acknowledged fact that French workers by nearly two to one prefer increases in their vacation time to increases in salary.[7] This is but one indication that Frenchmen consider work as something not quite noble, something that one ought to do as little of as possible, consistent with economic well-being. Not only does France, never having been a Protestant country, not have a tradition which glorifies work, but the modern emphasis on economics seems curiously weighted on the *consumption* rather than on the production side. Nonetheless, the two must of necessity be balanced. Furthermore, while the efficacy of the cooperative consultation process is undoubtedly great for every person associated with any decision by the good feeling which comes from sharing power, thousands must be left out. These still refer to the whole decision-making apparatus as "them."

Finally, how to defend one's self and family against economic decisions made by "them," though it does not appear in the newspapers, is the biggest of preoccupations. The French, like most peoples who have known economic controls, "thesaurize" rather than save. Estimates of the private gold hoard range from 15 to 25 billion dollars. Very privately held gold is safe from tax collection, inflation or devaluation. Traditionally, Frenchmen also like to put their money into land, houses or durable goods, and consume the rest. "Why put good money into the bank to take out bad money?" The consequences of this attitude for business investment are plain. The trend toward smaller bank accounts is, however, also due to a new concept of family responsibility. Formerly, within the memory of most adults, the primary economic objective of each was *accumulation* of wealth, whether in land, gold or goods for transmission to one's children, who, it was presumed, would do the same for theirs. Good families would ultimately be well off. Few families with bourgeois aspirations did not do this. In fact, not many years ago inheritances were one of the chief subjects of private conversation. Now the concept of family responsibility has changed: to be a good responsible parent one need not pass on one's wealth to one's children; one is free to consume what one produces. Parental duties appear more and more limited to seeing to it children get a good education.

Education and Technolatry

Education, as we have seen, is the business of the state. Educational issues are, perforce, issues of national political significance as well. Education was one of the most burning political subjects of the early Third Republic. It was the focus of the controversy over what kind of people the French should be, what kind of polity they should have, the role of the sacred in human life—in short, it was at the center of politics in the truest sense of the term. Several key elements in the Third Republic's solution to the educational question, however, have recently been reformed without even a hint of the fierce antagonism which marked their original adoption: thus in 1959 religious schools entered into a contractual relationship with the Ministry of Education, which now supports them, and in 1972 the half-century old institution of the free Thursday passed away. Thursday had originally been left out of the school week of elementary pupils as a means of assuaging the objections of the majority who objected to compulsory secular education on the grounds it infringed upon their religious liberty. Churches have traditionally held catechism classes on Thursday. Significantly, during the discussions which surrounded the switching of the midweek rest period from Thursday to Wednesday and the possibility of switching Saturday morning classes to Wednesday, not a major newspaper article, not a speaker on television brought up the subject of religious instruction. One should not, however, draw the conclusion that education is no longer a question which arouses passions in France: it suffices to recall the May, 1968 disorders and the riots of March, 1973 which closed down the nations *lycées.* But although in both cases the troubles were *in* education, they were not fundamentally *about* education.

On most matters related to education there is general agreement: every course of study should lead to a socially useful and remunerative career. French schools should not follow the example of their European neighbors, but should continue to exalt French heroes, glorify the tricolor flag, etc. What are the issues? What is "up" in education? The actual search for ways to mesh the educational system with the economy takes up the largest amount of public attention. Plans for work-study programs are popular. After all, the state is responsible for the economy on one hand, and for education on the other. Why should it work at cross purposes? But there is nothing here for the public to decide on. As consumers of decisions, more or less affected by them, people just approve or think what is being done insufficient.

Of more burning interest is the question, or rather, the affair, of the new math, which in 1970 the Ministry of Education ordered taught in all schools. The suicide of a mathematics teacher who believed the new math to be against his students' interest is the most tragic example of the unsmiling seriousness with which the entire matter of modernization is regarded. Jokes about computers are very rare in France, and futurologists' predictions about what life will be like in the year 2000 are taken far more seriously than in America. The new math, computers, and all that sort of thing, are indispensable if France is to survive in the modern world, anyone who cares enough to talk about it will say. But if one probes a bit, one will find people usually do not know what they are saying. Surely most do not think these things important because they are useful in weapons technology. They would rather not talk about weapons or about making military efforts. It seems the interest is due to a general awe before things pregnant with promise and to a felt need to keep up with the latest world trends in intellectual matters.

There are, of course, many particular issues in French education: the university library system claims it is falling apart due to lack of money. Several branches of the University of Paris claim to be without money to pay their water bills, and so on. Sometimes these issues lead to demonstrations, as in the case of Paris medical students in 1970, who demanded the expansion of facilities, and sometimes to violence.

The problem of violence caused by *Gauchistes* who don't like a professor or just want to cause trouble is not really an issue for most Frenchmen. They want order, while at the same time enjoying the sight of someone letting the state have it.

Once again, issues are made more for—and by—pressure groups. They propose, demand, cajole, while the state, having taken them under advisement and perhaps obtained their consent, makes decisions. The list of such groups is long: three national parents' associations, the various teachers' unions, the national union of Lycées and Colleges, the National Confederation of Autonomous Groups in Public Education, and so on.

One of the reforms which followed the 1968 disorders involved the establishment for each school in France of a school council composed of parents, teachers and administrators. In 1972 the minister of education gave these councils their first real powers: each council could decide whether or not to *recommend* to the rector of the academy (geographic administrative unit for the ministry) that the classes normally held Saturday morning be switched to either half of the new midweek rest day, Wednesday. Heretofore, the council's main function had been to consult on personnel matters, extracurricular activities and to ask the rector for more money on behalf of the school.

Culture, the Intellectuals and the Church

A people's object of worship, the thoughts of those it considers its leading thinkers, its mores . . . what could be more important to a people, especially to a democratic people, than that which forms the basis of its character? Both Montesquieu and de Tocqueville, without knowledge of whom no Frenchman passes his *Bac,* taught that above all in democracies the quality of politics depends primarily on the *moeurs* of the people. Indeed, French politics from the Revolution through the first half of this century was marked by an evident concern for *moeurs,* and by controversy among intellectuals of the caliber of Jaurés and Barrés as to what they ought to be.

Intellectuals are still politically important in France: Pompidou is a *Normalien,* some deputies in the National Assembly (M. Foyer, Gaullist) also teach in the university, while others (Jean Charbonnel, Gaullist) write with authority on theological and political matters. Charles de Gaulle was, not counting his last two volumes, a first-rate author. French politicians probably write more serious books than the rest of the world's politicians combined. Public men read the book section of *Le Monde,* probably the only newspaper of its kind to carry literate articles, for example, on Plotinus, and of course, Jean-Paul Sartre is more active than ever in the revolution. But no one can doubt that here, too, things have changed. When the now aging son of the fiery nationalist royalist intellectual Maurice Barrés told how, before the turn of the century, his father had helped a young Socialist by the name of Léon Blum get into print, he was in effect recounting the history of a time now past when *engagé* intellectuals, bound by a common intellectual tradition, loved talking to each other, and when their arguments constituted real political issues. No politically relevant living intellectual controversy has, however, quickened the French intellectual scene since the Sartre-Camus battles of the immediate postwar period. It appears that even in France, culture is becoming something packaged, something one must have a certain amount of. Not only does politics not appear to be *about* matters about which intellectuals might have something important to say, but intellectuals do not appear to have much that is engaging to say about politics. Levi-Strauss? Most of those "who count" have read him, but what does he really have to say about how we are to keep up economic growth and institute participation? Even Jean-Jacques Servan-Schreiber is more relevant than he. Jean-Paul Sartre? Above all those who are older remember being moved by his portrayal of modern man's alienation, but as the years pass, he becomes just another *notable* of the revolution. The time of correspondence between intellectual and political leadership appears over.

Of all free nations, though, France is the one which most cares about its culture. While the United States Congress was debating in the 1970s whether to come to the aid of the arts, the French state had been for almost a century the owner of nearly all theater, orchestra and opera companies, ranging from the famous *Comédie Française* and the Paris Opera to the not-so-very-humble national theaters located in provincial cities. A ministry is charged with cultural affairs. The state radio-television monopoly is criticized in the press for giving in to base desires when it presents popular American series such as Elliot Ness and the Untouchables *(Les Incorruptibles)* and Columbo. Even the Communist *L'Humanité,* the paper of the people, agrees television exists for the cultural elevation of the people. Culture is, it appears, still a political preoccupation of French democratic politics, though it is no longer as close to the center of political controversy as it once was.

Typical of the role of culture in current French politics was a debate in January, 1972, on nationwide television on the subject: "Culture and Ideology in French Society." The participants, high ranking members of the Gaullist and Communist parties, both showed respectable intellectual credentials. The former's presentation, punctuated by Mozart's music, attempted to distill the essence of Western civilization and tie it to the Gaullist party. Culture is knowing how to understand and how to choose so as to realize one's personality fully. True culture leads to the realization of each in his own way and to the participation of all in the organs of public decision-making. The Communist's line was twofold: culture is the way one lives. For those who work, it is an endless succession of *boulot, métro, do-do* (shop, subway and sleep). Culture should mean leisure to change the world. The Gaullist, though, spent the greatest amount of his time pointing out how much universities have been expanded and how many cultural shows are on television and how education is being geared to the job market, while the Communist spent most of his denigrating the quality of television shows and claiming schools are producing unemployables—and that people do not have enough vacation time. Although there could be no doubt that the two sides rested on different intellectual traditions, even as it was clear that the practical consequences of Communist power would be far more serious than a change in television shows, the debate was only indirectly about culture.

Frenchmen, like other democratic peoples, always have before them the possibility of changing their way of life, their priorities, their culture. The Communist Party, of course, does not specifically advocate a new way of life—nowhere in the immense corpus of Marxist-Leninist literature is the promised future Communist society described other than by stating it will be characterized by the absence of this or that feature of present-day society. But the Communist appeal to leave one's troubles behind is powerful, all the more so because it is made by a physically vast organization. Only the Catholic Church has as many "persuaders" out on the job as the party. The non-Communist political parties not only do not have comparable organizations, but they also are not quite sure what sort of culture they are advocating. De Gaulle himself, though quite conversant with the intellectual heritage of Western civilization, did not, it appears, see it mirrored in modern French society. His description in *L'Effort* (pp. 115-117) of the lives Frenchmen live today might well be condensed into *boulot, métro, do-do.*

The Catholic Church, officially non-political since 1905, continues day in day out in nearly one hundred thousand parishes to explain, to advocate, the way of life personified by Jesus. Communist intellectuals speak with awe of an organization which has at its service even in the most out of the way corners of the country, men, usually quite intelligent, who have spent years at rigorous study and have sacrificed their private lives in order to propound to all who will listen a way of life and a perspective on death. Even if only 37 percent of adults describe themselves as "believers,"[8] they make up by far the largest group of Frenchmen who firmly believe in any one thing. Despite a half century of official laicism and ten years of internal turmoil, the church retains both size and coherence.[9]

It is, in fact, only when opposed to the official teaching of the Church that the other civilizational alternatives before France stand out in all their difference. The televised encounter of Cardinal Daniélou and the Communist theoretician and Senator Jacques Duclos in 1971, and the *tête-à-tête* between the former and the Gaullist Edgar Faure, formerly a prominent Radical, published in *Le Figaro,* July 28, 1970, provide unusually clear examples. Duclos, an orthodox Marxist, spoke of a future realm of freedom for men in which "culture," real knowledge of the world, would be so widespread that external constraint would not be needed to enforce social harmony. People would no longer be ruled. Faure, for his part, after outlining many possibilities, chose to believe that "It is not unthinkable that it might be possible to diffuse culture the way health has been spread to all. . . ." On the basis of this he looked for the elaboration of a "charter of full partnership" for each man, "a life comprising the elements of knowledge, formation, elaboration, decision. It would be a true democracy. . . ."

To Marx's contention that humanity poses for itself only the problems it can resolve, he opposed Maulnier: "Progress must supply the means to resolve the problems it poses." The cardinal, on the other hand, stressed that the basis of society must be recognition of what the human person is, the creature of God, born free and bound to the will of no other human being: ". . . if I can submit to a law which is the expression of an order which is above me and to which all are subject, I have on the other hand no reason to submit to the arbitrary will of another." Law, it seems, is either "writ in the hearts of free men," as the Marxists claim (but since all men are not yet free, it is in the hands of the vanguard of freedom) or it is, as the Gaullists hope, the result of widespread cooperation and consultation among interested parties (but, insofar as interested parties do not agree, there must be a supreme arbiter among them), or it is, effectively, the consensus of men—in a democracy, of the majority—on how the will of God applies to any given subject.

The Church in France does not speak with one voice, especially in political matters, and the dialogues described above are unusual in their clarity. In fact, the Church, associated with the monarchist Right before World War II,[10] changed after the war to support the moderately reformist MRP. The postwar period also saw the worker-priest movement: about a hundred priests took factory jobs and involved themselves in Socialist and Communist activities on behalf of the "working class." When in 1954 the Pope condemned the movement, about half their number left the church. The movement, however, affected a far greater number of priests, as did the popularity of the pop-theologian Teilhard de Chardin. By 1965, in concert with the Vatican's worldwide policy of *Aggiornamento,* the worker-priest movement was back, though under Church control. If one were to go by official Church publications, for example *Living Parish,* a monthly magazine, and most articles which appear about the Church in the press, one would have to conclude the Church has wholly dedicated itself to the earthly pursuit of socio-economic equality. But since to most the Church is their parish priest, the matter is more complex.[11] In any case "modernism" in the Church is old hat by now and stories about religion usually appear on the same page as art and entertainment. An exception which proves the rule was the participation by various bishops in the campaign conducted by the Left, led by the Communist Party, against France's testing of nuclear weapons in the Pacific in the summer of 1973. In the course of the campaign enough of the Church publicly disassociated itself from the entire French defense effort to prompt the press to comment that the "sacred union" between the Church and the armed forces of France had been broken, and lead Admiral de Joybert, chief of the Navy, to deliver a lesson on the principle of separation of Church and state to the Roman Catholic hierarchy. The admiral, to the subdued cheers of the "majority," in effect asked the Church if it could not bring itself to sanction the efforts France has to make to survive, at least not to add to the country's difficulties by trumpeting its scruples.

Only briefly was the Church a public issue. At least on defense matters, it is less likely to be one in the future.

Politics as a Spectator Sport

What did Mitterand really say about J. J. S. S.? What is the meaning of the Socialist-Communist alliance? Will the PSU finally break with the Maoists? What is the Radical Party's latest statement on European Unity? This type of question, amply treated in the press, is considered somewhat in bad taste in polite conversation. Anyone who brings it up is sure to be considered an incurable bore. As a general rule, politics, that is, the interplay between political men, is of interest to the extent it bears on strengthening or weakening the government. News of trouble within the majority, speculation as to the enmity between Giscard D'Estaing and Chaban-Delmas, why Pompidou replaced Chaban, are seen as somewhat more worthy of attention, but still one does not normally talk of it with friends, unless the matter looks like it might lead to a change in the government. The same is true of partial elections. Some, like the one which opposed Chaban-Delmas and Servan-Schreiber in Bordeaux in 1970, are followed because they have a bearing on the question of who will hold power, while others arouse no interest. A prime example of the latter is the referendum of 23 April 1972, on the enlargement of the Common Market. Despite the majority's best efforts, since nothing tangible, no one's head, was on the line, Frenchmen shrugged, smiled, and failed to vote in droves. This, however, was considered a failure on the President's part, and during the May 1st holiday, Frenchmen asked each other without embarrassment how much Pompidou had been hurt. By May 2nd the IFOP measured a drop of 6 percentage points—since the previous month—in the President's popularity.[12]

Since politics is understood primarily as a question of who does what to whom, the character of the personages involved, their personalities, their backgrounds, their concerns are deemed quite as important as the policies with which they might be identified from time to time. Thus, when one mentions the name Giscard d'Estaing, one is met first of all by accounts of the early age at which he performed his exploits. He stands for a type of bright young man. His fortunes are seen as those of a class. A question concerning any political man is likely to elicit details about his personal life rather than about policies with which he is associated. The human drama of the rise and fall from power appears to exercise a powerful attraction on democratic peoples.

Of a higher order of interest are the so-called *revendications,* social demands, some of which are also *contestations,* that is, those acts by individuals or groups which challenge the power or legitimacy of government. Here is fare sure to liven any evening before the *Télé.* Those who engage in that sort of thing, called *contestaires,* or, when they engage in violence, *"casseurs"* (breakers), are the object of mixed but usually strong feelings on the part of their countrymen. When "plain folks," e.g., striking workers, protesting farmers, etc., are involved, public sympathy is overwhelming, but even when the government is "contested" by students, the most widespread answer to the question "Why do they do it?" is that life in modern society is so trying.[13] There does not appear to be, at least in French public life, any such thing as an illegitimate grievance. In fact, government leaders when asked about this or that *contestation* invariably reply that although much progress has been made in alleviating admittedly undesirable conditions, the effort must continue. They ask only that legitimate grievances should not be pursued in illegal ways. Nonetheless, it is difficult to find working people who think the police should be less severe in handling demonstrators. This is a curious situation which Gaullists describe in all too simple terms: everyone wants progress, but no one will stand up for disorder. More to the point is that even the "conservatives" like to describe themselves as enemies of present-day society, which really had no defenders. Only "progress" has partisans. But the meaning of progress is, as always, problematic.

The most interesting normal business, however, concerns scandals in government. During the Third and Fourth Republics scandals, i.e., more or less well-founded allegations that persons connected with the government were using their power to enrich themselves, vied with clashes between personalities and policies for first rank in the causes for the fall of governments. In the Fifth Republic, the place of personalities and policies within the government is very largely influenced, not to say determined, by the President who, up to this time, has also been the only man who can authorize changes in government between elections. The role of scandals in the Fifth Republic has therefore changed: more powerful than ever because they are now the only issues placed on the agenda directly by force of popular opinion, they cannot immediately break a government, but they can quite effectively use up its, the majority's, and the President's "credit." No one ever accused de Gaulle of veniality and the same has been true of his successor, but the charge that the official family is contaminated necessarily redounds on its head, the President.

Scandals do not have to be very big to be politically significant. During the Pompidou presidency one Gaullist deputy and one low ranking member of the government have been convicted in civil court: the former, M. Rives-Henrys, of allowing his title of deputy to be used by a company engaged in fraudulent real estate dealings, and the latter, M. Dechartre, of misusing his political influence in his private business dealings. In addition, during this time five mid-level employees of the state radio and television monoply were fired for having surreptitiously introduced disguised commercial advertising into television programs.[14] No one suggested the government approved of the infractions, which are themselves hardly self-evident proof of widespread corruption, yet the prime topic of political conversation in France is scandals. On the Right, M. Poniatowski, a member of the majority, demanded the guilty be cut off, while on the Left, the Communist Jacques Duclos echoed the thoughts of Frenchmen of all political persuasions when he said that a few resignations are but a touch of the feather duster where vigorous sweeps of the broom are needed.[15] Are you surprised that people in high places should behave like this?, we asked a young engineer. Not at all, came the reply; we are mature in this country, we know that people help themselves to what they can when they can.

But the most typical scandal of all goes under the name of the *Affaire de L'Avoir Fiscal,* the affair of the tax credit. Here is how it developed. In order to breathe some life into the Paris stockmarket, long one of the most sluggish in Europe, to encourage investment in stocks and the modernization of industry, the government in 1965 decided to lighten the tax burden on common stock dividends by taxing them only once, at the moment of distribution. Every taxpayer is notified that the amount of tax taken out of this dividend counts against his total personal tax obligation. Naturally, the more one's income is made up of dividends, the more of one's taxes are paid this way. Furthermore, since French income taxes are low compared to other taxes—including the ones on dividends—it is quite possible for someone to fulfill his fiscal obligation by his dividend income alone. In this case, he may be liable to no direct income taxes at all or might even get a refund. The scandal consisted in the revelation that some people, including the Prime Minister, because of this fiscal credit paid little direct income tax. Now, no one at all ever directly suggested the Prime Minister had done anything illegal, but for several months the main topic of political conversation was *L'Avoir Fiscal.* These reactions are typical: a rather well-to-do lady, shaking her head and saying, "Ah, the system, those who know how to profit always make out;" and a pro-Gaullist army officer, "This is just a hint of how many injustices we have."

Foreign Affairs and Defense

We have left these subjects for last because that is where they belong among the concerns of Frenchmen. That is not to say that France has closed her eyes to the rest of the world: quite the contrary. No country in the world spends proportionately more on foreign aid: about 2 percent of GNP compared to a little over half that amount for the United States. France even boasts of a highly successful Peace Corps: each year 7,000 highly qualified young men, teachers of French, engineers and technicians, are sent to former French colonies or French-speaking areas of other nations, e.g., Quebec, Canada and Southern Louisiana, U. S. A., to spread French culture, which France believes no civilized people should really be without. One does not hear many objections to this. Further, the French news media do a remarkable job covering foreign news, which their audience consumes quite avidly, and one finds a surprising number of Frenchmen aware of names, places, and events in Asia, Africa and America, as well as Europe. But the French, save some "professionals" in the army and the diplomatic corps, are quite glad to be only critical spectators of world affairs.

It is a peculiar sort of isolationism. Certainly more than ever people believe—it has been said for so long, it would be believed even if false—that in a shrinking world no nation escapes the effects of major events anywhere. Yet as Servan-Schreiber remarks every time he has a chance, what does France, what does Europe as a whole, do with regard to the wars which are deciding the control of vast areas of the world? A few more ask what France is doing in the face of the Soviet Union's great naval power in the Mediterranean and of the ever-growing insecurity of its vital oil supply? However, when President Pompidou says "We are not the strongest, but we count," most are delighted to take his words at face value. It is, in fact, with considerable pride that the French people watch on television the arrival of foreign heads of state in Paris and hear that their country's advice and support on global affairs is sought by leaders around the world. Paris, as everyone knows, is the political capital of Europe. Can any other city even contend for the title? The feeling is all the more pleasant because largely without cost, except for the money spent on former colonies, France is involved in no one else's quarrels and does not cease to congratulate itself for being in a position to observe, offer advice, without compromising itself. Finally, the logic of its strategic interests binds America to come to France's aid *in extremis* whatever France's foreign policy might be. Thus, in apparent defiance of the maxims of *Realpolitik* according to which prestige is a reputation for exercising power successfully, the French rejoice in their country's prestige among nations.

There have been in the course of the Fifth Republic several basic foreign policy choices before France (excluding colonial matters), some of which have aroused public interest:

(1) Should France work closely with the U. S. within NATO? For or against *Atlantisme* is the way the question is normally put. Most are quite satisfied with the explanation that too close a relationship with America is not necessary to obtain either friendly cooperation on trade or defense *in extremis.* These are in the American national interest and will come no matter what France does. Furthermore, close cooperation in the 1950s did not prevent America from working against France's retention of Indochina and Algeria. Besides, why be anyone else's subordinate? Why be concerned with anyone else's quarrels? The Communists charge the government with being too *Atlantiste,* while Servan-Schreiber de-

clares there should be greater Atlantic cooperation. President Pompidou declares that Europe's independence must be defined vis-à-vis the United States, but this matter barely stirs polite conversation.

(2) Europe is something just about everyone is for, but no one is really concerned about. This President Pompidou learned when his referendum (April 23, 1972) on the entry of England into the Common Market provoked the highest rate of non-voting (43 percent of the electorate) in French history. The rapprochement with Germany has been accomplished, the horrible memories of the past officially forgotten, and the French are just as glad that the government is putting a strong public accent on cooperation with Britain, a European partner with fewer potential quarrels on its hands. But barely more than half of the electorate could be induced to make the effort to say their "yes" at the polls.

(3) The government, while gearing the national defense effort against the Soviet Union, treats the latter with nothing but friendliness. Frenchmen, when they think about Russia, which they really try hard not to do, hope she will reciprocate.

(4) The only real foreign policy issue of the Fifth Republic was the pro-Arab stand taken by General de Gaulle at the time of the war between Israel and the Arab states in 1967. There were marches and heated speeches against the President, and people became excited about foreign affairs in a manner to which modern France is no longer accustomed. But neither did the issue last long nor were feelings so strong on the matter that the next electoral campaign was run on the subject. By 1968 foreign affairs were not even a minor issue. By the 1973 Arab-Israeli war, France was congratulating itself that the Arabs had made a partial exception for her in their oil boycott of the West.

It was not always thus. International affairs once played a very great role in the political life of France. The Communist demonstrations against NATO in 1948 and in favor of the Stalin-Hitler Pact of 1939 were, in comparison with the great storms of anti-British and anti-German passion in the mid and late nineteenth century respectively, the mild agitation of a limited sector of the population. In fact, from its revolutionary beginnings, the French state tended to define itself in relation to its enemies. No less a student of democracy than John Stuart Mill considered the existence of strong feelings on foreign affairs essential to the state's survival in France:

> [I agree with what you say] that the feeling of Orgueil National, which is the only feeling of a public spirited and elevating kind which remains, and that it ought not therefore to be permitted to go down. How true this is, every day makes painfully evident—one now sees that the love of liberty, of progress, even of material prosperity are in France mere passing, unsubstantial, superficial movements on the outside of the national mind and that the only appeal that goes to the heart of France is one of defiance to L'Etranger—and that whoever would offer to her satisfaction to that one would find the whole of her wealth, the blood of her citizens, and every guarantee of liberty and social security flung down at his feet like worthless things. Most heartily do I agree with you that this one feeling of public and therefore, so far, of a disinterested character must not be suffered to decay.[16]

Today it is easy to see that this collective selfishness has broken down—into its component parts. The grandchildren of the young men who marched joyously off to the First World War, the sons of those who went off to the second full of doubts, speak very clearly: if love of country means the possibility of war, and insofar as dealings with foreign nations involve the danger of war, they will have nothing to do with them. National stereotypes of foreigners remain very widespread, but very strong feelings are not. These have been shown by all too many wars to cost too much; and besides, why fight anyone for anything? What will violence ever get you? But to elicit this sort of explicit renunciation, one has to persist in his questioning, for even the possibility of going to war on behalf of one's country is very far from the minds of most.

France, the President told the army, must develop a new patriotism—a patriotism without enemies since in modern times nations have only competitors, not enemies. True or not, this is believed. This is not to say Frenchmen in high places entertain many illusions about the Soviet Union; Pompidou is just as sanguine as de Gaulle ever was on the need to keep France armed and has, moreover, modified the absurd "all points of the compass" defense strategy, turning the armed forces' attention exclusively eastward. Also, from time to time, one finds editorials in *Le Figaro* expressing worry about the ability of France and her allies to defend their interests in the Mediterranean. But attempts to start conversations on defense matters, whether with military men or civilians, educated people or villagers, are usually met with the rhetorical question why should anyone—meaning the Soviet Union—want to attack *us?* One articulate person summed up most of the elements we found in the many arguments on this point. He held that in the modern world, especially where developed countries are involved, conquest, even easy conquest, does not pay. Modern wealth consists not of things which can be taken easily from a country, such as corn and iron, but rather of very highly technical and highly organized productive activity which depends for efficient operation on the contentment of personnel. Our suggestion that conquests are often undertaken for non-economic motives was agreed with only after many examples, including that of Hitler's enterprise, were mentioned.

Among those who agreed that the country might be menaced, a surprising number said, well, France has been invaded before and we're still here, and so is (Paris, Strasbourg. . . etc.); why risk getting people killed and their way of making a living destroyed by fighting? Yes, let's have an army and even a *force de frappe* to discourage an aggressor, but it would be foolish to ever use them. Those who suffered under the German occupation, former prisoners of the Soviets, do not feel this way, but for most, the liberation of 1944—in retrospect—is something which, although very welcome when it came, was bound to come sometime.

Does this mean people really wouldn't mind being invaded by Russians, we asked an army officer? Of course they would. After all everyone knows all Russians are savage animals. But, he added with characteristic directness, *"Cela n'empêcherait personne de se mettre à table,"* that wouldn't keep anyone from sitting down to dinner.[17] One of the most sanguine persons in public affairs on matters of foreign policy, M. Servan-Schreiber, a man with fine anti-Communist credentials, wrote in *L'Express* (15 May 1972) that after all it may be counterproductive to fight to keep peoples from coming under Communist domination. War not only destroys those it is intended to save, but hardens the oppressive characteristics of communism. The best hope for liberty lies in a relaxation of tensions which, in the end, will permit all that is irrepressibly human in both oppressors and oppressed to come out and life to normalize. This somewhat vulgarized version of General de Gaulle's view on the matter is very popular. Nonetheless, France spends about 3.5 percent of its GNP on defense.[18]

The defense of France is not something normally discussed, yet the French people seem quite willing to let the government do as best it thinks in this area. "The people care nothing about defense," complains one reserve general, "But is it up to them to care?" answers another. The uncertainty which surrounds the French defense establishment cannot be attributed to popular resentment of the military. These generally are well-esteemed: streets are named after generals, officers have a social rank their American counterparts would envy, and the recruits who come to fulfill their military obligation (universal) are as disciplined as any in the Western world. An undeniable malaise affects the entire structure, though. One can see it in the dead silence aboard trains loaded with young conscripts, where up to the nineteen fifties a sort of carefree bedlam reigned (a popular expression for raising the roof translates as "acting like a conscript"). One can see it in the attitudes of soldiers and in high level debates over strategy.

The attitude of soldiers has been explained by the fact that military service, although theoretically universal, now for practical purposes excludes those well-educated young men who "do their time" as cultural ambassadors. Thus, there is inequality. Both officers and young men agree, though, that a more significant cause of disaffection among the young is due to what actually happens to them in the army.[19] Morale is far higher in combat units (only one in three men serves in them), than among so-called support troops, higher among those who handle rifles than among those who handle brooms. "They love to play war," says an officer. "When we do that, I have all I can do to hold them back, but when we stop, it's another story." And a young man: "No, I don't like the army. I mean I'm as patriotic as anyone, but how does a fellow help to defend his country by serving at the officers' mess?"

A still more serious problem is that, although the vast majority of Frenchmen, left or right, support—even if passively— the existence of a national defense establishment, very few have any idea of what it is supposed to do and few think France is actually capable of defending itself alone. The defense establishment itself is unsure as to its role and still suffering from the trauma of Algeria, once part of the French Republic, which the army abandoned with very great bitterness after achieving a military victory. The shock of defeat in Indochina and the debacle in 1940 are not forgotten. Nor have the armed forces recovered from the decade of dominance by Charles de Gaulle, who purged them of some of their most combative senior officers—some of whom had been involved in plots against him—re-organized the forces, dispersing or reducing elite units such as the *paras* and the foreign legion, building the entire military structure around nuclear weapons, and withdrawing France from the integrated NATO command structure.[20] In fact, he attempted to form a new army from the standpoint of motivation as well as of armament. But the difficulties have been many. Technicians prefer the freedom of the civilian world, officers of the old school see little reason for dedicating their lives to technical pursuits without a sense of mission. Military leaders without a combat record have had a difficult time winning the respect of their subordinates. The regime has tried to make officers' careers more attractive, but some have called it an "inflation" of rank. It has proven difficult to graft a system based on personal incentives on an army which lived for centuries on its sense of honor and of duty. Certainly, also, there was something unrealistic about the notion of an "all points defense" and there is much discouraging for an army about a "world without enemies."

The transformation of the army has been accompanied by a debate on its uses. This, however, seems to interest only politicians, military men and journalists. De Gaulle, wanting to rely exclusively on French forces, and deeply mistrusting the willingness of Americans to make sacrifices when interests vital to France but marginal to America are threatened, built the nuclear force around the notion of "minimum deterrence." That is, France does not pretend to be able to defend itself from attack by the Soviet Union, but lets it be known to the latter that in case of attack, France would, before succumbing, be able to "tear an arm" from its aggressor with nuclear weapons launched from bomber aircraft, (27) solid fueled missiles from "hardened" silos in southern France, and from a fleet of nuclear *Redoutable* class submarines (five planned). Even before the Soviet Union built ballistic missile defenses, this sort of planning was severely criticized by, among others, General André Beaufre (Retired).[21] He argues that deterrence occurs only when a potential attacker is faced with a force actually capable of frustrating its designs or of inflicting upon it damage which is at least comparable to what it can, for its part, cause to the nation attacked. Deterrence succeeds only when it can plan to cope successfully with its own failure. In other words, he maintains that any potential aggressor knows quite as well as Frenchmen that no French President, as the numerically inferior French forces were being defeated and France invaded, would launch his small nuclear force just for spite and assure the destruction of his own country in return. The *Force de Frappe,* argues Beaufre, makes sense only as the "trigger" for the far larger American force. He views the semi-departure of France from NATO as against common sense, while men like General Laffargue call it treason against the natural strategic interests of France.[22] Ground forces, even when completely armed with tactical nuclear weapons, can only make sure the conflict, if engaged, would be a nuclear one and thereby can force the Soviet Union, if it has designs on France, to make a major effort. This is hardly an inspiring mission for the French Army. As General Beaufre says, the well-equipped French Army could certainly defend itself against anyone in close concert with other European armies, but European military integration is on no country's agenda.

Finally, a project dear to the heart of General Beaufre should be mentioned, though, since it has been under review for the better part of a decade, it is hardly pressing business. It involves the actual defense of French territory in support of— and even after the failure of—the regular troops, by a sort of militia modeled after the highly admired Swiss reserve system. This would involve keeping virtually all able-bodied men in the ready reserve until at least age 45, equipping them with good equipment, kept in working order but not used up as is the equipment of the active forces. This system allows little Switzerland to muster fully 36 divisions in case of war and would allow France to raise well over 100. The system is also inexpensive to operate. The army, it is true, has some doubts about the effectiveness of reserves just as all active-duty forces everywhere do, but the greatest objection to the plan is political. In the name of what are Frenchmen to be asked to submit to military service longer than any in their history? The mere introduction of such an item on the public agenda would so profoundly clash with the spirit of every other item on it that it might not be taken seriously.

What Else Is Before the Public
Human Interest

Lest we give the impression that the matters mentioned above constitute the bulk of the public domain, we are obliged to mention that they do not. People seem to be interested above all in the personal affairs of people. Thus, more people read *France-Soir,* a tabloid which is short on politics and long on sensation and human interest, than the prestigious *Le Monde.* It has been said that to know what France is really thinking about, one must read Page 3 of *France-Soir.* But even readers of *Le Monde* are more likely to remember, for example, that in January, 1972, a 17-year-old Lycée girl secretly gave birth to a child and put him in a garbage can where he was found safe and sound, than any political event of that month. By the same token, there are surely more people of all classes in Strasbourg who know the name of Simon Schneider, a local boy turned bandit, escape artist extraordinaire, and lover of fast BMW getaway cars, than know the name of the mayor.

The event which held the attention of most Frenchmen in 1971-72 combined criminal, sexual and political interest. In the small town of Bruay near Calais, a 15-year-old girl was found naked, murdered. On the basis of purely circumstantial evidence a local judge indicted one of the town's leading citizens and kept him in jail despite the prosecution's plea he be released for lack of evidence until, months later, he was released by the order of a superior court. During this time news of the case overshadowed just about everything else, and actually brought out here and there snide remarks about the rich and powerful who think they can get away with anything. In the town itself, television reporters showed almost daily meetings of sullen citizens demanding justice against the accused. The stock of revolutionary leftists in the area soared.

Local Interest

It is an old adage that people who live in big cities hear more about what is going on on the other side of the world than they know about what is happening next door. France, however, although dominated by the metropolis of Paris, is rare among democracies in the modern world in its attachment to small town ways. One hears in fact that there is only one city in France. However that may be, the items on the national agenda, and even the great crimes do not vie for attention on equal footing with matters of purely local interest, such as we described earlier. A road, a spectacular traffic accident, the doings of the town's oldest person, the opening or closing of a store, the career of a local boy, marriages, first communions, the mayor and his enemies, these are much more likely topics of conversation than national politics. By the same token, people will gladly lend their time to the local *Centre Culturel* or *Maison Des Jeunes* (the names for young people's canteens), whereas they would not spend time worrying, much less doing something, about politics. These things are, as we have said, close to home.

Private Interest

It is at home, in the family, that the concerns of Frenchmen lie. Visitors never fail to be impressed with how closed the family circle is to outsiders. There is traditionally less visiting of one another's home in France than in America, hence the greater importance of cafés and other public meeting places. The warmth, privacy and intensity of home-centered life, so difficult to perceive from the outside, is of tremendous importance for public life because it is what the lives of individuals are almost all about. One fortunate enough to observe it can easily see why Frenchmen love it so to be *chez eux*. There are, in France as in other advanced democracies today, some signs, notably the increase in the number of nursing homes for the elderly, and shifting of parental responsibilities for vocational guidance of the young onto the state, that the family is breaking down or at least consolidating into the nucleus of parents and young children. Nonetheless, more than in years gone by, the family seems to be the sole source of individual fulfillment. Life at work, in the innumerable clubs and associations is, in a sense, lived abroad for the purpose of bringing home a livelihood and many little pleasures. The number of friends from these realms who enter the home is small. Certain activities, for example the work of politically or socially active persons trying to solicit support for a candidate or a cause, rarely if ever cross the threshold of the home. Perhaps in the past there were allegiances of class or party which contended with those of the family. There are none now. Certainly the family is not independent in fact, for as we have seen, the state regulates and assures the way of life of all, but on the other hand it is very much self-sufficient in spirit. All our previous discussions should be understood in this light.

Summary: Depoliticization

The proper role of the individual is first and foremost to live his daily life; his personal family cares absorb him: the number of citizens who follow public affairs with the desire to take part in them is limited. It is good that it be thus. The polity, the nation where each day a great number of citizens discuss politics are close to ruin! Democracy is not the permanent attachment of passions or popular feelings to the discussion of problems of state. A simple citizen who is a true democrat silently makes his judgment upon the government of his country, and, when he is consulted, at regular intervals, for example the election of a deputy, expresses his agreement or disagreement. After which, as is normal and healthy, he returns to his personal preoccupations, which have their own grandeur if only because they are necessary not only for each individual, but for society as well.[23]

These prescriptions of Michel Debré do bear a resemblance

to the political culture of modern French democracy, but although there does seem to be less desire to participate in public affairs than in earlier periods, and interest in personal preoccupations is certainly not lacking, there are fewer signs of the docile willingness to support massively, to take as one's own, the actions of governments democratically approved.

Political scientists have disputed whether the apparent loss of interest in public affairs, not only in France but in other democracies as well, constitutes a sort of depoliticization.[24] If this is intended to mean a lessened participation in the consummation of democracy, i.e., voting, there is no depoliticization.[25] Other meanings attributed to the term point to more significant possibilities, e.g., loss of interest in political parties, in ideology, in class identity, national identity, etc.

As we have seen, the level of interest aroused by public things varies: in some matters active, in others passive, depending on the nature of the thing. Nearly everyone wants to benefit from social security, nearly all are interested in the personalities of top leaders, but the political process by which national power is won is not so interesting. "Politics is ideas," Thibaudet used to say. But insofar as it is, France today is not interested. Parties used to represent more than a choice on the ballot: Socialism, Radicalism, Communism, the Right, each was a way of life. "My party gave me my life. . ." is a saying all too familiar, all too vivid in the memory of most adults. But disenchantment with that sort of politics is deep: "What good did it do?" That was the politics of the bad old days of social strife, etc. As for patriotism, that is almost in the same boat: "How many good men died in Algeria and Indochina, and in the war? How stupid! Some people actually went off of their own accord to get themselves killed in Spain in '36. Hard to believe, eh?" The conclusion is plain. No contest, no party or idea, not even perhaps a nation should mean that much to people. If it exists, depoliticization means not indifference to the state, but rejection of a certain kind of politics without the affirmation of any other kind—more like divorce than like celibacy. Therefore, when private men act in the public domain at all, it is not to shape general policy, nor even as in the Third Republic is it to limit the exercise of public powers. The typical public act now aims at enlisting *Le Pouvoir* on the side of one's particular interest. After all, that is the job of the state, to increase the well-being of one and all.

Politics is seen by the French as a means of pursuing one's interest—that goes for the membership of labor unions, for the industrial associations, farmers, etc., and naturally for those who do the governing as well. They are seen at best as no different. People are just no longer ready to believe that someone else, unless constrained to, might govern in their interest. They know very well what interest is, they know that the state is there to give to one and take away from the other, and for a long time they have heard that when it is a matter of interest, it is each man for himself. What has happened perhaps should be called a re-privatization. But if the type of thing expected from the state has changed, and people are less willing to participate politically, they nonetheless expect more from the state. It is quite a good bourgeois attitude, really, to want to get more for less.

Political professionals know very well that success lies in appealing to the electorate outside recognizably political categories of issues, and going to what concerns people in their *private* lives. The Communist Party, for example, has long based its power over the masses in "mass organizations" that wed people to the party's political aims by serving the particular, even private needs of, for example, youth with recreation, or laborers with on-the-job services, vacation camps, etc. The Gaullist movement for its part has had de-politicization emblazoned on its banner. Its weakness today comes from having become the establishment and, therefore, itself the focus of antipolitical feelings. Its strength lies in the fact that, since in power, Gaullism has been the only political alternative to communism.

Although privatism is pervasive and indignation about the things which do not concern one is out of style—even in the movies in this age of anti-heroes,[26] there are more enraged grouplets of Trotskyites, Maoists, assorted extreme leftists and anarchists than ever before. This, together with the growth of the PSU into a considerable political force and the "radicalization" of the CFDT, points to a certain need for the politics of great changes. By the same token, the massive adherence of the French people to Charles de Gaulle was not in itself an antipolitical phenomenon despite the general's attitude toward internal politics. It is well known that the general's following was heterogeneous, and that many saw his return as a way of galvanizing the nation for concerted action abroad.

No doubt the presidency of de Gaulle heightened the already great interest of Frenchmen in foreign affairs. In 1969, for example, a public opinion poll found three foreign political leaders, Ho Chi Minh, Fidel Castro and U Thant among the ten most admired living persons.[27] But these names sandwiched those of a sports personality and of a singer. No Frenchman in his right mind, of course, would want to be governed by any of these men. Clearly, interest in international affairs is not of the sort to engender popular participation. The world is a stage and the people like to sit in the audience. De Gaulle himself found that although he had a relatively free hand in foreign affairs when his policies were of a purely verbal kind, e.g., his "long live free Quebec," or when they involved cutting off Algeria from the body politic—the number of opponents to his policy was not much greater than that of those who had a stake in Algeria—he found that he could not call forth from his countrymen the strong enthusiasm needed to carry out his European projects. The population was not hostile to a Franco-German rapprochement—it takes, after all, little effort to resolve not to hate—but was not at all warm to plans for coordinated Franco-German defense. Not to quarrel with the Germans is one thing, but to take up their quarrels is quite another.

It is not surprising then that perhaps the most common theme in French politics today is the search for a solution to the problems of participation, nor should it be a surprise that it has been placed on the agenda not by private groups or by the intellectuals, but by national political leaders concerned that French politics is, as some political scientists would say, excessively output-oriented. Political leaders have felt, especially since the war, how separated they are from the rest of the country. They know they form a class apart: the political class, and that they cannot bridge the gap between themselves and their neighbors merely by being competent drivers of the machinery of state. Well versed in history, French political leaders know that every form of government, every regime, has a peculiar manner of marshaling the human resources of its country behind itself. The absolute monarchy of the Bourbons claimed divine origin for its powers and let the nation take vicarious part in the glory of the king's crown. The early republics, imperfect democracies as they were, lived by the interested attachment of the propertied classes and by the vicarious participation of all in the great adventure of nationalism. Feelings of racial and cultural pride were mixed with noble causes. In the name of *La Patrie* "we" would defy barbarians, make the world safe for and from . . . a whole list of things. But nationalism no longer finding any defenders among the political class itself, on what basis is it to ask for the support it needs to govern? People can be appealed to on many bases: they can be called upon in the name of good things or for the avoidance of bad ones, as, for example, the Christian Democrats of the postwar period based their appeal on the worth of a threatened civilization and on the evils of communism. Or they can be called to associate themselves with something appealing by its greatness, for example, a colonial enterprise. Peoples can also be assembled about the pursuit of wealth or comfort, or they can be appealed to insofar as they differ from their neighbors in matters of race or religion. Appeals to the self, individual or collective, of course, are ambiguous given that people are quite capable of having several conceptions of themselves. In any case, different appeals will have different results.

The problem of democratic participation is all the more pressing because, according to democratic theory, it should not exist. After all, *the* characteristic of democracy is precisely that there is no distinction between the rulers and the ruled. But the fact is that where there is little local government to speak of, and few offices in national government are filled by election, no matter how large the bureaucracy the overwhelming majority of people must be the ruled and a relative handful the rulers. The problem of the relationship between ruler and ruled, at least in a democracy, must be solved by some sort of participation, but of whom, in what, and for what purpose?

In our next chapter we will examine the meaning of this most thaumaturgic political term, participation, in modern France.

Notes to Chapter 5

[1] *Le Renouveau,* p. 140.

[2] *SONDAGES,* 1968, No. 1, p. 19. All social categories joined in this massive judgment except graduates of higher education. These also preferred price stability, but only by a narrow margin. On the other hand, it is significant that knowledge of what brings price stability about is not widespread. Hence many workers believe that escalator clauses in wage contracts guarantee increases in purchasing power!

[3] Some price rises, of course, are imposed by the government for basic services such as electricity, gas, railroad, transportation, etc. One is much more likely to find resentment at rises in these parts of the "public domain" than at rises in, say, the price of sugar. See *SONDAGES,* 1968, No. 1, p. 19.

[4] The proposed tax would have been assessed on the basis of the number of square meters occupied by the shop. A garage would thus pay disproportionally more than a jewelry store. The "departure premium" to be paid to each shopkeeper over 60 years of age who qualifies is between about $2,500 and $4,600.

[5] See below. A well-educated man told us, "You know, this is the only way a modern tax system can work." In fact, we have found very little awareness on the part of even educated people of what a large proportion of their taxes they pay every day through higher prices. The finance minister seems to be quite alone when he expresses the desire to switch to a totally direct,

above-the-board fiscal structure based on the personal income tax. "What does it matter if it's heavier? The present system is almost painless," we have been told.

⁶Politicians and journalists, government and opposition can all quite as easily deplore France's place far ahead of the rest of the world in per capita consumption of alcohol (23 litres a year; Italy is second with 15.2, according to *France-Soir,* March 3, 1972). Even alcoholics, one imagines, are not proud of being what they are. But only the government is blamed by those inconvenienced by the high taxes on liquor.

⁷*SONDAGES,* 1970, No. 1.

⁸The French Public Opinion Institute, IFOP, did a study on religion in France, published in *France-Soir* from 28 March through April 1972. According to this poll, 73 percent of the population describe themselves as believing in God, but only about half of these are "believers in the sense that they wholly accept the teachings of the Catholic Church." Only about a fourth of the population attends Church every week, and this group is disproportionately feminine. This poll also revealed some very interesting facts: one-half of the population believes Jesus is the Son of God, but whereas only 8 percent and 7 percent respectively either believe Jesus a mythical personage or refuse to answer the question, fully 36 percent believe either that he was a prophet or a great moral teacher. Now, the last are absolutely incompatible with official Church doctrine. Since Jesus is either who the Church says he is, or never was but a figment of the imagination, one can hardly explain such a high proportion of the people *misconstruing* (as opposed to accepting or rejecting) Jesus except by a certain lack of clarity in the Church's everyday teaching.

⁹This is not to say that France is, as it was in the early Middle Ages, "The firstborn daughter of the Roman Church." Christianity, even as communism, is a regional phenomenon in France; very prominent in Alsace, hardly noticeable in the Paris suburbs. Even where it is strong, the influence of laicism is unmistakable: occasionally men occupy a half of the church apart from women and even the regular church-goers crowd toward the rear and go to Communion only on feast days, because it just would not do to be seen too pious. Even in Catholic eastern France, there is general applause when courts pronounce acquittals in euthanasia cases. Even the general French revulsion to the idea of abortion is due less to immediately religious than to social causes: "It is a shameful thing" and "one should bear responsibility for one's acts," one hears. Certain other common attitudes irrespective of region show how much the Christian way of life is in retreat: according to the poll mentioned above (footnote 8, *France-Soir,* 30 March 1972) a majority of the population and a strong minority of "believers" hold that people are not responsible for their actions, but rather what they do is the product of a certain manner of education, etc. Common experience, of course, shows this to be primarily a verbal attitude—people just don't live that way—nonetheless, its expression is significant.

[10]See Ernest Nolte, *Three Faces of Fascism,* New York, 1969.

[11]We had occasion to witness an embarrassing incident. A village priest, thoroughly dedicated, orthodox and obedient to the suggestions as well as to the orders of his bishop, had called a meeting of the young people of the parish. The way to capture young souls for the church, he had been told, is to join with the young in their demands for redress of grievances at home, school and work. Only the more devout youth bothered to attend the priest's meeting and these, though they respectfully listened to the call for a public manifestation of their grievances, remained silent. Finally the priest had to ask each whether there was anything, anything at all, in his life with which he was not satisfied. Each answered briefly and respectfully. But one, his face blushing, asked, but *Monsieur L'Abbé* what does all of this have to do with the church?

[12]*France-Soir,* 12 May, 1972.

[13]Poll published in *France-Soir,* 12 May 1972.

[14]The first affair involved the *Garantie Foncière,* a company whose directors would, at the expense of the stockholders and with partial financing from the government, buy property at relatively high prices from a "front" company which had previously bought them at lower prices. The affair dates from January, 1970. The second scandal is known under the name of Dechartre and took place in 1971, while the third, called the affair of the *Publicité Clandestine,* took place in 1970-1972.

[15]*France-Soir,* 17 May 1972. In this case, the Prime Minister felt compelled to ask for a general vote of confidence from the Assembly on his government's behalf. His purpose was primarily to pressure members of the majority who had been criticizing the government, such as M. Poniatowski, to come out in public support of it. This is the traditional use of "the question" by a Prime Minister.

[16]Letter to A. de Tocqueville, 9 August 1842, in Alexis de Tocqueville, *Oeuvres Complètes,* Tome VI, Paris, 1954, p. 337. In fact, at least half of the force which staged the Paris Commune of 1871 was animated by this feeling, and General Boulanger, because presented as *Le Général Revanche,* the man who would lead France to victory over Germany erasing the bitter memories of 1870-71, almost had the lives and liberties of Frenchmen cast at his feet. The sources of the feeling of nationalism have been analyzed at length by, among others, Hans Kohn in *Nationalism, Its Meaning and History,* Princeton, 1965 and by Ernest Renan in *Qu'est-ce Qu'une Nation,* Paris, 1882.

[17]William Shirer in his account of the fall of France remarks that people were concerned about not being caught in a battle zone, not about avoiding capture. Opposition to the occupation grew proportionately to the inconvenience it caused. Also cf. Joseph Schumpeter, *op. cit.,* pp. 128, 160-1.

[18]More than a third of the amount is devoted to the nuclear striking forces. In 1971, the proportion of the budget devoted to defense dropped for the first time below that of the Ministry of Education, something for which the

government publicly congratulates itself. The United States spends about 6 percent of GNP on defense, and the Soviet Union, between 11 percent, the official figure, and 40 percent. These, however, are raw figures, more indicative of national priorities than of military strength. For example, the proportion of these expenses devoted to salaries is far higher in the U. S. than in France, and higher in France than in the Soviet Union.

[19]A good feature on this subject appeared in *Le Monde,* March 30, 1972 and July 31, 1970, and an interesting poll on the subject appeared in *SON-DAGES,* 1968, No. 4, p. 19. According to it 63 percent of young men 15-20 years old—and 81 percent of the women of that age!—agreed that military service adds something useful to the formation of men. However, by a margin of over two to one, young men preferred "national service" such as that performed by cultural ambassadors, over the normal military service.

[20]French conventional forces now number 350,000 men as against 1,100,000 in 1955. On the whole, they have superb equipment. The AMX 30 tank and the *Pluton* nuclear system for the army, the *Exocet* surface to surface anti-shipping missile for the navy and the *Mirage* III, IV, V and F, and *Jaguar* for the air force are only some examples. The pace of technical development, especially for aircraft, is quite high. De Gaulle acted against the elite units because in his opinion, they had been molded by a decade of war into psychologically self-sufficient groups, whose allegiance was to victory rather than to the political leadership of France. The army had brought him back and he was afraid of its power. (For this reason, the brightest spot for the army in the Gaullist decade came when, at the height of the 1968 riots, General de Gaulle flew to Baden-Baden to ask the former military commander of Algiers, the personification of the *Para*, General Jacques Massu if the army would, on command, descend on Paris. See *Le Renouveau,* especially p. 79.) His withdrawal from the NATO command structure posed the problem of the strategic role of the French armed forces. The arrival of nuclear weapons in quantity has no doubt strengthened their firepower, but has not begun to answer basic questions about the conditions under which they would be used and about coordination between nuclear and conventional forces.

[21]General Beaufre, the author of many books on military strategy, including *La Stratégie, La Défense et La Dissuasion,* is one of the world's foremost writers on military strategy. His career in the French Army was ended by Charles de Gaulle. Among those foreigners who have argued along General Beaufre's lines is Herman Kahn, author of *On Thermonuclear Warfare,* New York, 1960, and other works.

[22]*Le Figaro,* 28 October 1970.

[23]Michel Debré, *Ces Princes qui nous gouvernent,* Paris, 1959, pp. 59-60.

[24]Georges Vedel, *La Depolitisation, Mythe ou Réalité?,* Cahiers de la Fondation Nationale Des Sciences Politiques, Paris, 1962. An interesting compari-

son is made between Debré's often quoted desire to depoliticize those matters essential to the national interest and nearly identical statements on the matter by Napoleon III in 1860 and Philippe Pétain in 1940. See the contribution of Marcel Merle, pp. 49-60.

[25]It has been argued, though, that only when crises loomed, e.g., 1958, 1962, 1968, was voting heavy, while under "normal conditions," e.g., 1967 and 1972, it was quite low. Be that as it may, variations of 10 percent in the percentage of registered voters voting are probably not significant.

[26]It is interesting to note that the French have no popular culture hero like John Wayne. In fact today no country other than the U. S., with the exception of Japan, does. Brigitte Bardot is quite another symbol. However, the extreme antipolitical Left does have contemporary heroes and presents them in the movies, e.g., *The Working Class,* a prize-winning movie at the 1972 Cannes Film Festival.

[27]*SONDAGES,* 1969, Vol. 1.

Chapter 6
The Principal Proposals
for Revitalizing
French Politics

Gaullism

For over a third of a century the ideas as well as the person of Charles de Gaulle have inspired a movement dedicated to reforming democracy in France so that citizens might thereby be brought closer to the state and to one another. Fundamental to the Gaullist idea of participation is the belief that a state which shoulders vast responsibilities but lacks strength and unity in its several corps, as well as the active support of its citizens, cannot endure. Long before it succumbs completely to its maladies, it will have been put out of its miserable independence by a foreign *pouvoir.*

Weakness within the state inevitably entails the disaffection of citizens from their institutions.[1] Weakness repels and strength attracts. The basic tenet of Gaullism is especially important in democratic politics: the strong man, the strong institution do not have to constrain or even threaten in order to get their way. Power is something human beings instinctively bend themselves around. The desire to possess it is also "the profound animating force of the acts of the best and the strong."[2] Furthermore, political existence itself requires the outstanding success, that is, the demonstration of power by one man or one united elite. The more outstanding, the more social cohesion benefits. "What legitimate prince," de Gaulle asks, "was ever obeyed like any dictator [whose authority has] come from nothing other than his daring?"[3] The source of authority in the modern world, be it in military, political, or whatever sort of affairs, lies less in the leader's official position than in his ability to impose himself by identifying his leadership with common enterprises attractive to many, and to justify himself by success in these endeavors. Not the least of the causes which provide the occasion for leaders to exercise authority is the very existence of the group (the state, corporation, etc.) itself.[4] He leads the group toward its common ends but does so less by virtue of those ends than by that of his success.

His own ascent to sovereignty, he attests, was not made legitimate by any of the usual principles: kings claimed divine right, emperors relied on plebiscites, and republican officials on election,

> But I, it is without hereditary right, without plebiscite, without election, at the sole call, imperative but mute, of France, that I was earlier led to take charge of its defense, its unity and its destiny.[5]

He did so in the name of no doctrine, no principle, but in the name of his country. Throughout his career he offered his collaborators a share in the love he bore for his country, a love which absorbed him.[6] He hoped that they, like he, would be filled by participation in her grandeur and seek their own in hers. But far from being empty of content, such allegiance to a nation is all too full: a nation of 50 million souls with a long history necessarily means different things to different people. The effect is almost the same as if the object of allegiance were void of content. The question of "politics (or sacrifice) in the name of what?" cannot really be satisfactorily answered with the name of a country other than in exceptional times.

Even today a "modern" Gaullist describes Gaullism as "less
a doctrine than an exigency." In fact, necessity in the form
of imminent dissolution of the French polity was the midwife
of Gaullism. For his part, the general handled every problem,
made every speech with his attention fixed first of all on the
fundamental question of political existence—more important
than the fate of Algeria, farmers, or any particular problem.[7]
Even democracy itself was subordinated to basic needs: there
must be a French state before there can be elements of democracy in it. Consequently only as many such elements can be
allowed as are consistent with the state's existence. This sort
of politics can be described as the politics of the bare minimum.[8] In fact, it is the bare survival of France which he symbolized both in 1940 and in 1958, and it is efficacy, stability,
continuity as opposed to chaos that he promised in the successful electoral campaigns of 1958-1962 rather than specific
goals. Of course, he was not without proposals of a specific
kind, but the only time he ran a campaign on the basis of
them, in April, 1969, he was defeated and left the political
scene for good. As we examine Gaullism, we must keep in
mind the question of what makes the politics of the bare minimum necessary, and ultimately if the bare minimum is really
enough.

Modern society, according to de Gaulle, characterized as it
is by the elaborate organization essential to production for
mass consumption, has habituated men to a discipline at work
and play, "the rigor of which would have revolted our fathers."[9] Not only must general discipline be maintained, but
each person must make an individual effort in what is allotted
him if the whole system of production and administration is
to flow smoothly. Modern society either functions very
smoothly or does not function at all. Now, this means modern
nations are faced with a future that can either be very brilliant

or quite terrible, for the disciplined effort of many necessarily produces great things, whereas the disorganization of a mass which draws what it considers most important in life from organized activity is disaster itself.

Charles de Gaulle spent the largest part of his life as a soldier of France. Although in his youth he neglected neither philosophy nor the political battles in Paris, his main concerns up to the beginning of World War II were of a military kind: how to forge for France the most effective armed force. Since foreign and defense politics are closely related, he became interested in the former as well: after all, a nation's glory exists most evidently in the behavior of other nations toward it. He was never particularly interested in social or economic matters.[10] After the war, when called upon to decide what the essential affairs of state are, he did not hesitate to express the formula: "The diplomacy which expresses it, the army which supports it, . . .the police which covers it."[11] Economic and social matters, even a nation's mores, evidently fall under the category of things which must be looked after in order to cover the state's strength. To this day Michel Debré thinks of economic development primarily as something affecting national security.[12] The same goes for constitutional and social arrangements. Thus, the Gaullist plan for giving new life to the French polity would appear divided into two unequal but tightly interdependent halves: solidity within and grandeur without.

Solidity Within

Having earlier discussed in some detail the constitutional framework of the Fifth Republic, we turn to the principal projects of Gaullist social engineering.

Local Government and Regionalization

Why should a regime essentially concerned with foreign affairs want to transform local government? De Gaulle, once convinced that like it or not France had to "marry her time," decided that local collectivities are

> . . . too small for modern life where economics dominates everything with its requirements for planned large scale public works and improvements. Now, three-fourths of our towns do not have the resources needed to provide these insofar as they are concerned. . . . It is only by making a great number of municipalities disappear by means of fusion of boroughs that the basic element of local administration will be raised to the required scale.[13]

A twin concern underlies this: people will not be happy unless they have all the sewage treatment plants, swimming pools, etc., they think necessary, while industry in order to grow will need more roads, etc. If citizens are not happy, they might not be so loyal, and if industry does not grow, the nation will not have the economic infrastructure necessary for national defense or for "keeping up" with the rest of the world. Thus, laws were passed authorizing prefects to group small municipalities (16 July 1971) and to establish "urban communities" around large cities, that is to say, to place the suburbs under the control of the central city administration for purposes of urban planning, transportation, and industrial development (31 December 1966).

The same thinking originally went into the plans for the creation of regions. De Gaulle decided the framework of the *département* was too restrictive "to practical life and to development," and since the identity of the old royal provinces still survives despite their official abolition long ago, "it is but necessary to resuscitate them for economic purposes under the form and the name of regions; each having the size required for becoming the framework for specified activities."[14] Thus, in 1960, a decree commanded the bureaucracy to think in terms of the 21 regions when making plans for public works, and in 1963, it was decided that in each region one of the component *département's* prefects be designated "regional prefect," given a special staff and powers over his other colleagues. To advise the super-prefect and act as liaison with the "living forces" of the region, a Regional Economic Development Commission (CODER) was set up in each region. Its members are delegates from general and communal councils, mayors, and representatives of major interest groups. Their powers are purely advisory, though they are called on to discuss and approve the Regional Development Plan submitted every five years. They are, of course, informally consulted much more often, and semiformally together constitute regional pressure groups, excellent cooperative interlocutors for the state.

But even as the underlying purpose of cooperative consultation is a sort of political articulation, the general began to think of his regional plans in political terms. His referendum proposals of 27 April 1969, were intended to make of the regions centers of popular attention, participation, veritable breeding grounds of wholesome civic feeling, as well as more efficient intermediaries for the central administration. Whether the actual provisions would have done this[15] is open to question, but this was the intention. The defeat of the referendum, by the way, was certainly not a rejection of the idea of regionalization. This is very popular.[16] If anything, the measures were thought insufficiently far reaching. The issue in 1969 was, as usual, the general himself.

The purpose of the new regional statute (Law of 5 July 1972) is quite similar, if the means are somewhat different. In presenting the law, the Prime Minister—as well as virtually every Gaullist from the President on down—stressed political necessity over and above economic and administrative reasons. He stressed, though, on every available occasion, that under no circumstances would the regions be given *the* power—that is, the ultimate say-so and *a fortiori* the only political one—even over economic affairs which concern them, or for that matter, over any affairs at all. The state's power is inherently indivisible and requires an absolute monopoly on representation. No other organism may pretend to take binding action on behalf of any group of Frenchmen. But, in the words of the Prime Minister, since ". . . the problems of economic organization and social progress are at the heart of the debates of our democracy, the region imposes itself more and more as the appropriate level to discuss these problems concretely. It is also the occasion and the means of a deepening of our democratic life."[17] Concretely, this means that the regions, as provided by the 1972 law, are not territorial units but *public corporations* which it is hoped will become foci of "convergence, confluence and concentration."[18] Insofar as people are concerned with the larger aspects of economic development, such as infrastructures, and insofar as they do decide to act on their concerns through the new regional institutions, democracy will in effect have been brought "closer at hand" as the Prime Minister wished. Whether, as he and all Gaullists earnestly assert, "regional vitality is a force for national community" is another question.

But the powers of the new regions are small. They now have two-chamber "legislatures": the first chamber includes representatives of Communal and General Councils together with the regions' delegations to the Chamber of Deputies,[19] while the second brings together representatives of interest groups— labor unions, industrial, agricultural, educational and professional associations. The financial attributions of the council are symbolic: only the tax on drivers' licenses has been turned over to the regions, providing them with about 24 cents per person per year. In addition, they can levy "additional centimes" (see above) on local taxes so as to raise a maximum of about 5 dollars per person per year. On the other hand, the councils are free to make all the socio-economic recommendations they wish and to spend their money for any socioeconomic purpose approved by the prefect. The latter is the most obvious gainer from the new law. His powers are clearly heightened, since as a measure of administrative decentralization local representatives of the ministries are put more unambiguously than ever under his control. His office is also the natural target of the councils' recommendations, that is to say, of their requests.

The two purposes of local reform, rationalization and participation, are only in conflict if one does not regard politics from the Gaullist perspective: i.e., from the equation of domestic political life with economic life. Gaullists believe the various groups contending for economic advantage must do so in a way which does not conflict with national unity. Therefore, a free market, whatever other effects it might have, tends to reinforce the feelings of isolation already so strong among democratic peoples. A system which channels disparate economic pursuits through institutions where representatives of all interests must come together to agree to recommend how the pie is to be sliced, is believed to engender notions of the common interest. In any case, at the top of the process sits the guardian of the common interest, the state, with its guarantor, the President.

There are, admittedly, troubles in this scheme. For example, the decentralization law of December, 1970, allowing a bit more financial latitude to towns, and the law of July, 1971, allowing the fusion of towns by decree, although intended to make local government more efficient and spread its cost more evenly, work at cross-purposes. Gaullists proudly cite the poll according to which 66 percent of the people are for the fusion of small towns and only 22 percent against, but this is a verbal attitude. We have met very few people who have lived in their town for more than a couple of years who want to see *it* fused. Others' are quite another matter; *they* can be as rational with *them* as they like. Prefects have experienced very great difficulties in "grouping" towns, even under the "association" scheme. Most of the time the *maire* simply states he and the council will resign. Prefects have, in most cases, not forced the issue. It would not be seemly to establish democracy that way. High officials are very bitter at this sort of resistance. M. Andre Bord, once the member of the government charged with implementing the policy, told a dinner in

Strasbourg that this could lead to grave consequences and pleaded that in local as in regional matters everyone in a position of responsibility seek only the general interest, while Camille Laurens, general secretary of the CNIP (now part of the majority) asked that local democracy be respected because it is the only means to wed the people to the planned reforms.[20]

As for the regions, Gaullists think it will be easier to establish a model participatory regime where no regime existed before than it is to reshape the established institutions at the national and local levels. Regional feeling no doubt exists. What can be built upon it is another question. Some regions, for example, Brittany, Alsace, Languedoc, to name but three, have languages fundamentally different from French. The people of Languedoc, for example, are quite conscious of belonging to a large international community, part of which lives in Spain. One does not have to go far to hear talk of French imperialism there.[21] But this sort of regional feeling is not at all what Gaullists have in mind. Still, all the talk of "making the regions," the emphasis on regional identity, folkways, noticeable on television—a half-hour regional news program every evening and numerous regional programs every week—are feeding the fires of regional nationalism. No doubt the movement toward European unity is influencing people in the same direction: people from Provence can now turn their attention toward very profitable exchanges with prosperous nearby northern Italy rather than toward their depressed countrymen to the west; Alsatians need no longer feel uneasy about their strong ties with the people of Baden-Würtemberg across the Rhine; people from Tourcoing and Lille feel the attraction of lower prices just a few kilometers away in Belgium. The Gaullist nightmare is that of France ceding national prerogatives to European authorities from above while growing regional feeling attacks its sovereignty from below. Not without justice do they bitterly reproach Servan-Schreiber for advocating this sort of thing. But how can the 1972 regional law really engender the sort of regional feeling desired? Participation, Gaullists agree, is a personal matter. The industrialists, mayors, persons representing interest groups who will actually participate in the regional organizations have now long participated in countless committees. The unorganized, all-too-private citizens are the real target of participatory schemes. But if they are allowed to elect representatives by universal suffrage, might they not through them, region by region, express disapproval of schools, officials, prefects, policies? In a modern democratic country, that would mean the death of the state.

Cooperative Consultation

Someone watching the process work in 1972 in the case of French butchers, some of whom, in the Paris area, decided to raise prices beyond the levels set at a meeting between the national butchers' federation and M. Giscard d'Estaing, and found a confiscatory tax applied to their new profits, might conclude that participation is merely a matter of agreeing to the inevitable. That would be oversimplification, as are the summary negative judgements one hears from workers regarding the effects of the 1967 law requiring companies to share profits and stock ownership (25 percent of assets) with their employees. This is a significant participation (for Renault, that means three million shares), even if only employees with seniority benefit. The workers' even quicker dismissal of "enterprise committees" intended to associate employees at all levels with the running of the company also does not seem justified. Every day one hears of new agreements reached between representatives of employee groups, interest groups, and the state. Bargains seldom seem to be one-sided. M. Jean-François Revel, not known for authoritarian views, even complained in *L'Express* that the Gaullist government's policy since May, 1968, has been merely to allow pressures from any and every group to build to a certain level, then move in to satisfy them. Officially sanctioned anarchy, he calls it.

But nowhere does one find the psychological reasons for the shortcomings of this sort of participation as clearly stated as in the writings of Charles de Gaulle himself. With characteristic directness he once described the Senate as useless because only endowed with consultative powers: "Consultative, naturally little consulted"[22] are his words. Commentators such as M. Raymond Aron long ago noted the anomaly of a system based on talk, compromise and agreement, proposed and headed by a man who abhorred that sort of thing.[23] If the general's successors are personally more disposed to conversation and compromise, the system is not thereby altered. One cannot easily at the same time glorify power, espouse the doctrine of democracy which demands that every citizen have his full share of that of which the regime consists, and then ask that all be content with having representatives of their economic interests consulted. Clearly there is a difference between being able to say something about one's own destiny and being its master. One cannot even begin to confuse the two unless one thinks of one's self in purely economic terms, and even if one does, given the particular nature of economics, one is more likely to give one's allegiance to the group one fights with than to the arena one fights on—or to the referee.

Many Interests, One France

De Gaulle was under few illusions as to how much his representative scheme could accomplish by itself.[24] After all, one does not cure a people of a soulless preoccupation with private material advantage by turning them exclusively to the cooperative search for economic growth. This sort of preoccupation with interest, coupled with political institutions based on the power of a relatively inaccessible presidency, may very well smother interest in party politics and generally attenuate noxious political feelings, but at the price of also attenuating feelings of nationhood. For this reason de Gaulle placed his confidence on his ability and that of Presidents who would follow him to engage popular interest in ventures which would remake the grandeur of France. The President and his foreign policy would act as a catalyst, transforming a placidly docile, unpolitical people into political France.

Grandeur

The efforts of Charles de Gaulle's provisional government, first in London in 1940, then in Algiers in 1943 and in Paris in 1944, to save the empire for France against any possible encroachment from Britain and America were as successful as they were energetic. His war memoirs, written before 1954, show clearly that he thought France without a world role, in politics as well as culture, would be not only drastically reduced in power, but also without the stimulus for life, the evident reason for being one people, which great enterprises abroad alone can give.[25] He did not hesitate in the darkest days of the war to threaten the British and American governments with the fire of French troops if French rights in (respectively) Lebanon and little St. Pierre et Miquelon (islands off Nova Scotia) were not scrupulously respected. If ever a Frenchman in the twentieth century could have been expected to defend to the last the least of French possessions, that man was de Gaulle. The efficient cause of his decision to give up *Le Pouvoir* in 1946 was the mere possibility that the Assembly might cut his proposed defense budget, even as the efficient cause of his return in 1958 was the evident failure of the Fourth Republic to defend the twelve *départements* of France located in Algeria to the satisfaction of the army, the civilian population of Algiers, and most of France. The character of the Fifth Republic and of its Gaullist *Logos* cannot therefore be understood apart from the first and most important matter they dealt with, and which shaped them even as they fashioned its solution.

Algerian Policy

The elements of the Algerian situation in early 1958 were

as follows: about 1.5 million Europeans, mostly French, held most important positions in the twelve Algerian *départements* while almost nine million Moslems, though permitted by law to exercise any profession (some even sat in the French Parliament in Paris), occupied generally subordinate ones. The rebellion which had broken out on November 1, 1954 did not at first have much support among the Moslems—who made up the overwhelming majority of the victims of the FLN—nor had it been taken seriously. By the end of 1956 the European community had been affected, had taken rather indiscriminate measures of reprisal—as per the FLN plan—and had begun to receive the massive assistance of the French Army. The latter was carried on in a thoroughly effective manner by men who had learned much from Communist tactics in Vietnam; and, by the end of 1957, the battle of Algiers had been very decisively won.[26] All leading revolutionaries were either dead, in jail, or abroad. However, although the governments of the Fourth Republic had given General Raoul Salan full civil and military powers, they had not ceased to criticize the conduct of operations, notably the use of torture in interrogations during the battle of Algiers. More significantly, the constant talk of a search for a negotiated solution angered many in France and nearly all Europeans in Algeria. Most important, the recurring government crises lent an atmosphere of indecision quite inconsistent with the firm policy being pursued on the scene. The fall of the Gaillard cabinet in April, 1958, followed by a month's interregnum before the investiture of Pierre Pflimlin, gave the several groups of plotters (some field-grade army officers, some Gaullists, other European Algerians) working separately the chance they needed: on May 13 a fairly well-handled crowd of Europeans, Moslems and military men took over the governor general's building on the forum of Algiers, and a Committee of Public Safety (the term dates from 1789) composed of leading officers and civilians from both communities was formed in open defiance of Paris. By May 24 elements of the 10th and 25th airborne divisions, the *paras,* had landed in Corsica and a landing in Paris was imminent.

Only the person of Charles de Gaulle at the helm would reassure these ardent partisans of French Algeria that their cause would find the needed firm support in Paris, and only their threats could have convinced the Fourth Republic to pronounce its own abdication in favor of de Gaulle. As for the latter, he had no particular plan. He knew he would be obeyed by all, at least at the beginning. As for the rest, he said "I'll go and I'll see." In his first six months in office (he was officially Premier until after the new constitution was adopted and presidential elections held), he made five trips to Algeria. During the first, after having declared, "Now I am Algeria, and General Salan is my representative," he answered the cheers of the crowd at the forum with the words, "I have understood you!" and, "In all of Algeria there are none but full-fledged Frenchmen." and the next day, "Long live Oran . . . great French city" and finally, "Long live French Algeria." His most ardent supporters and closest collaborators, M. Debré, Georges Bidault, and Jacques Soustelle were all firmly on the side of French Algeria and were to remain there while the general's policy of withdrawal took shape. It is essential to note that the Gaullist Algerian policy developed not as a result of pressure by public opinion, but according to the logical interplay between the general's priorities and the realities of the rebellion. He shouldered the full responsibility for the conception, and the execution of the Algerian operation.[27] He changed executors at will, one set for each phase of the operation, and often left his ministers to find out his intentions, e.g., that he would give up the Sahara, from the radio.[28] He was quite conscious that the stakes in Algeria were high: far above the interests of over a million *Pieds Noirs* (black feet, as Frenchmen born in Algeria are called), were the fabulous oil and natural gas fields of the Sahara, Hassi-Messaoud and Edjele, discovered and developed by Frenchmen in a *départment* of France. Their products are piped to the sea at Bougie. Algerian oil is strategically far more important to France in the late twentieth century than the coal and steel of Lorraine, for which hundreds of thousands of French soldiers died, had ever been fifty or seventy-five years before. Even more important than oil was the state of mind of Frenchmen. How would they take to being closed in between the Mediterranean and the North Sea?

Public opinion, as usual on an external matter, was not ada-mant.[29] Frenchmen overwhelmingly shared their leaders' con-cern over Saharan oil and most believed the army's policy of firmness was paying off. More than in previous years they felt that Algeria not only should but would remain part of France. Observers at the time note that patriotism was very much in the air.[30] There was no significant popular pressure to get out of Algeria. Even the powerful Communist Party was silent on the issue, and the Jeanson group which aided the FLN was isolated, convicted, and jailed. The army and the *Pieds Noirs* were, of course, very much for French Algeria. It is of the greatest importance that the general feared their attachment to a mere policy of France was stronger than their attachment to its *Pouvoir,* that is, to himself. Hence the establishment of the *Pouvoir's* supremacy over the army and anyone else will-ing or capable of contesting it took precedence over every-thing else, including the war. For that matter, by late 1958, there was not much of a war left.

From June, 1958 to September, 1959 he temporized, offering the grand Constantine plan—one of every ten young men coming into the administration, the army, the teaching corps, the judicial corps, would be a Moslem Algerian—but most im-portant removing from positions of power in Algeria, one by one, strong leaders with personal followings who could op-pose him. Thus General Salan was warmly and publicly con-gratulated for the job he had done, addressed as a personal friend by de Gaulle and ordered to Paris to become inspector general of the armies (the highest uniformed post) in De-cember, 1958. One month later the job was eliminated.[31] Soon after, the very popular General Jacques Massu was transferred from Algiers. In the course of his press conferences and speeches, however, de Gaulle continued to describe the future of Algeria with phrases such as "in close association with France," "Its transformations must be made along with France," and continued to reassure the public that everything would work out for the best.

In fact, there were three possibilities for resolution of the conflict: complete integration of Algeria with France; complete independence, with the *Pieds Noirs* either leaving North Africa or grouping themselves along the coast (the "Israeli solution"); or a sort of cooperative "special relationship" between a sovereign Algeria and France which would safeguard the *Pieds Noirs,* and France's economic and strategic interests. In his speech of 16 September 1959, de Gaulle stated for the first time that Algerians would at some future date be allowed to choose the solution, and indicated he preferred the latter. The possibility of Algerian independence suddenly became thinkable by the vast majority of Frenchmen. If vital interests could be safeguarded anyway, and if General de Gaulle does not worry about it, why make a big thing of those twelve *départements* being part of *La Patrie?* As for honor, keeping France's word and all that, the general did declare in unmistakable terms that if France would give all Algerians a choice, it would not allow that groups of cutthroats from the FLN, the type of people who plant bombs in bus stations and restaurants, "the privilege of imposing themselves by the knife and submachine gun."[32] As for the *Pieds Noirs,* they too would be taken care of.

But if the September 1959 speech had a calming effect in France, it served to usher in a new and more violent phase of the war in Algeria. The revolutionaries took heart, while the Europeans, feeling betrayed, began their own rather indiscriminate campaign of violence both in Algeria and in France. This progressively alienated them from metropolitan Frenchmen who had no immediate stake in Algeria. The President of the Republic appealed to the latter's sense of interest: "Algeria costs us—that is the least one can say—more than it is worth us."[33] At the time of the Europeans' revolt in 1960 and again during the generals' attempted putsch in 1961, he assured all that everyone's interests would be safeguarded, but that France as a whole would not continue to pay a price for the privileges of that part of its citizens residing in Algeria. Thus, for Frenchmen at home, the enemy in Algeria slowly changed from the FLN who wanted to chase France out, to the *Pieds Noirs* who wanted to keep it in at heavy expense and for their own gain. The whole matter was reduced to familiar terms: should *this* particular group get its way? This was also the theme of the FLN's propaganda in Paris. The campaign of terror waged by the *Pieds Noirs'* secret army organization in Paris (OAS) made the operation of abandonment palatable to public opinion. By the time de Gaulle first uttered the phrase "an Algerian Republic" on 16 November 1960, the public was ready. By December 1960, the general was greeted in Algiers by a Moslem crowd waving FLN banners, shouting *vive de Gaulle* and by some very unfriendly Europeans. He never returned to Algeria.

Having a plan and breaking internal resistance to it do not guarantee its results. The FLN, though militarily far weaker in 1961 than before 1958, had become politically stronger because of de Gaulle's policy. He had promised the French a way out of the war, so it was sure France would go. Given then that all properly Moslem centers of power hostile to the FLN had been eliminated, the Moslem population of Algeria saw who would be their masters and began to obey them. Under the circumstances it was clear the proposed referendum of approval by the Algerian people to which de Gaulle attached so much importance ("normally a state cannot be born except of the suffrage of its inhabitants"[34]) could not help but ratify whatever solution the FLN could extract from Paris. The FLN, with which de Gaulle negotiated and to which he made concessions, was *Le Pouvoir* of Algeria a-borning, and it had imposed itself by the knife and the machine gun. As for the general, having promised Algeria independence and thereby incurred the hatred of one part of the people, he had to deliver, or risk the enmity of another part and the disdain of all. No one understood this better than the FLN. Thus, the FLN held out for one concession after another. Most important, the Sahara and all its wealth were included in the territory of the new Algerian state. Thus also, Algerian chief negotiators succeeded one other, each "harder" than his predecessor: Ferhat Abbas, then Ben Khedda followed by Ben Bella.

The agreements signed at Evian on 18 March 1962, were described by de Gaulle as follows: after referenda in which the French people would grant and the Algerian people receive independence, there would be

> . . . the close association of France and Algeria in monetary and economic matters; a deepened cultural and technical cooperation; complete and precise guarantees to the members of the French community who would want to remain in the country; privileged rights for our exploration and our exploitation of oil in the Sahara; the continuation of our atomic and space experiments in the desert; the use of the (naval) base of Mers-El-Kebir and of several airfields assured to our forces for at least fifteen years; the maintenance of our army for three years wherever we might think appropriate.[35]

But the content of the accords clashed immediately with the realities of the situation produced over the previous three years: the OAS, after first trying to stop the European exodus from Algeria, proclaimed a new order of the day: "Let's leave it like we found it." In effect, even as they were being bombed, shot at, knifed, even as they crowded their way aboard every possible means of conveyance capable of reaching France, carrying only what they could in a suitcase, some Europeans burned their homes and businesses, uprooted their vineyards, etc. Those who did not, saw their worldly possessions sacked. Officially, 1,420,214 persons left Algeria for "repatriation" in a France few had ever seen. About 30,000 living remained behind as well as an uncounted number of dead and about 3,000 who ten years later were still classed as "missing." As for

Mers-El-Kebir, perhaps the world's most elaborate naval base, it was evacuated three years later, under threats about abrogation of the oil agreements, which were in due turn abrogated after France had fully equipped the oil fields.

The Gaullist government received the repatriated population with a ministry specially charged with their affairs. Prefects were ordered to help them find housing and jobs, and soon France had economically integrated a group amounting to 3 percent of its population. But political integration is another matter. The *Pieds Noirs* spread to those who came in contact with them a profound cynicism about national solidarity. They are quick to remind one that their part of France, their homes, were given away, and that of the 500 million francs allotted by the government for their compensation, only a tenth had been disbursed ten years after the losses occurred. On the strictly political plane a sort of reconciliation between Gaullism and the former partisans of French Algeria occurred at the time of the 1968 crisis when General de Gaulle, having need of the support of rightist leaders, initiated a law granting amnesty to all those convicted in connection with the Algerian events. This freed Generals Salan and Jouhaud from prison, but could not begin to re-unite a community so deeply divided or to erase from the memories of Frenchmen that one part of the nation had found peace at the expense of another.

Why de Gaulle acted as he did is less important than the manner in which his actions shaped the Gaullist movement. France was not defeated in Algeria; de Gaulle chose to retreat. Doubtless, although he often gives the impression movements such as decolonization are ineluctable in our time, he saw the real possibilities of resistance. If he chose to ignore them, it is because he looked beyond them. Also, no doubt he believed a bit too much in the power of his own formula of cooperative association, the attraction which the prospect of receiving large-scale help from France would exercise on the new Algerian leaders. But he also envisaged clearly and calmly the debacle which eventually took place. It seems he looked upon the retreat from Algeria as a *tactical* move. Without what he called the "Algerian mortgage," he could rebuild the *Pouvoir* of the government, discipline, reshape, and rearm the armed forces, put France at the head of a new concert of Europe and give it a new world role. If France left the vitally important southern shore of the Mediterranean alone, she would soon once again exercise new responsibilities there and elsewhere in the world at the head of the nations of Europe: on the whole, a strategic concept not without logic, but a logic in direct conflict with that of the actions by which it was pursued. Even as his idea of association between France and Algeria, his determination not to let the FLN impose itself by knife and machine gun was undermined by other concerns, so would those same concerns as well as the results of the Algerian affair affect his plans for a new France.

Europe and Defense

"There is no France worth it, notably in the eyes of Frenchmen, without world responsibility,"[36] said de Gaulle, as well as, "The state never had and cannot have any justification, a fortiori cannot last, if it does not directly assume the responsibility of national defense, . . .the military command has no authority, dignity, prestige, if it does not answer itself for the destiny of the country on the field of battle."[37] Thus all his policies from the building of the *Force de Frappe,* to his withdrawal from the NATO command, to his attitude on European matters, to his search for the accolades of foreign crowds, were intended primarily to give Frenchmen—and first of all those involved in the running of the state—the feeling, the impression, that France is worth their efforts. This means that in armaments as well as foreign policy, it was necessarily appearance perhaps even more than reality which had to be pursued for the sake of the one paramount political reality, the internal coherence of France, which in practical terms means the coherence of *L'Etat,* the stiffness of the bureaucracy's backbone.

His idea of a united Europe independent of the United

States, led by an independent France, was predicated on the certain knowledge that dependence even on a friend is habit-forming. He wanted Frenchmen once again to feel that since France is her own mistress, each of them has his part in her worthy enterprises. The feeling of independence was easy enough to produce: a word spoken and American nuclear weapons left the soil of France; another word, and American soldiers left; a veto and Britain was kept out of the Common Market. Criticism of allies is highly demonstrative, inexpensive, and likely to draw the praise of those in the enemy camp as well. Furthermore, it deflates a bit the Communist opposition at home with which those enemies are allied. Sometimes independence could be profitable: a threat to break up the Common Market, and the French saw the other five countries of the community virtually impose upon themselves the costly French system of farm price supports.

According to Gaullism, cooperation among natural allies, nay European unity itself insofar as it is to exist, must consist of consultation and agreement on particular common interests. No one ally can be expected to aid another to its own detriment. Thus he built his rapprochement with Germany on the knowledge that further warfare with Germany could benefit no one, the belief that certain specific agreements might be mutually advantageous, but with the openly stated conviction that Germany's security problems are primarily its own. In his words, "Germany . . . now has its great wound. In the name of what should it automatically become the others' as well?"[38] To some extent the verbal stridency of Gaullism gives the wrong impression. After all, it was no one else but Charles de Gaulle who, on France's behalf, stood alone on the side of Germany in 1960-1961 when first Eisenhower, then John Kennedy and Harold MacMillan wanted to give in to Soviet demands that Western troops be withdrawn from Berlin.[39] The interests of France and Germany, he decided, coincided precisely on that point. If European affairs—political as well as economic—are looked at dispassionately and *with sufficient fore-*

sight, the points where national interests converge are legion. Furthermore, if one considers that given the state of mind of Europeans, it is difficult enough for each of the countries' governments, sanctioned as it is by time and usage, to hold itself together and find followers among the citizenry, nothing makes more sense than the desire to build a new United Europe by reinforcing the sole institutions in Europe capable of exercising real political leadership—the states. In time, by dint of enterprises jointly brought to fruition for the common benefit, a United Europe would grow. Not without justice do Gaullists today, as the general yesterday, brand as futile and counterproductive all talk of European institutions. It takes attention away from concrete particular questions, e.g., a common European corporation law, monetary harmonization, detailed political coordination. If agreement is not possible on the substance of the agenda, why turn to procedural matters? What if any of the proposed European institutions were to be actually established? In the name of what would anyone sacrifice to obey them?

The one concrete problem given the least public attention by Gaullists is that of defense. Surely its importance would dictate it be among the items most often put before the French public and France's European partners. But it is not. It is different. On whatever level, national or European, defense involves, even means, sacrifices. Gaullists, above other French political groups, know that military activity is the glory or destruction as well as the foundation of political life. But immediately it means the questions which all Frenchmen are least willing to consider: whether Germany is their first line of defense and whether they are willing to put their sons' time, and to see their tax money go, into an activity productive of nothing but sacrifice . . . and perhaps nationhood.

The Gaullist defense posture falls under the category normally designated "minimum deterrence." Its purpose is to produce a modicum of military power for the barest minimum of cost. It is meant to be sufficient to give the impression,

within and without, not that the nation can really defend itself, but that it is not totally without the means of imposing
a price on a conqueror. Only in combination with its natural
allies can France's armed forces assure the nation's defense
in a *sérieux* manner. But Gaullists do not want to hear of such
arrangements. They would put into question *Le Pouvoir.* For
the same reason, neither can forces be too large or their chiefs
too popular. De Gaulle, brought to the decision to resign in
1945 by the prospect of seeing his defense budget cut, worked
far greater reductions under the Fifth Republic. But the greatest cuts of all were of a psychological order. The army was
purged of its more popular leaders, reduced in size, and assigned a new mission based on the *Force de Frappe.* The
Force de Frappe, that never-to-be-used instrument which en-
gages only a little of Frenchmen's money, and economizes
manpower to the utmost, is a new Maginot Line, constructed
by that system's greatest critic in France, and liable to the
same description:

> Such a conception of war was congruent with the spirit of the
> regime [of the Third Republic]. This, condemned to stagnation
> by the weakness of the *Pouvoir* and political discord, could not
> but espouse so static a system. But also this reassuring panacea
> answered too well the state of the country's morale, for everyone
> who wanted to be elected, applauded or published not to declare
> it good. . . . Opinion giving in to the illusion that by making
> war on war one would prevent the bellicose from engaging in
> it. . . . From the strategic point of view it gave the enemy the
> initiative in every sense of the word. (From the political point
> of view it left the aggressor free to act against the weak and iso-
> lated.) . . . Finally from the moral point of view, it seemed to
> me deplorable to lead the country to believe that eventually war
> should and would consist, for it, in fighting as little as possible.[40]

Gaullism shows a certain consistency in its approach to
both foreign and domestic matters. As long as no comprehensive ideas, no generally compelling purposes animate a group,
be it of men or nations, its coherence is to be arrived at piece-
meal, by the workmanlike resolution of the particular prob-

lems of all. In European as in national politics, Gaullists follow the general in believing that, as in an army's lower ranks,
common effort grows far less from the purposes for which it
is exerted than from the habit of its exertion.[41] But the manner
of this exercise is of the greatest importance: there is an essential difference between common and concerted action. Nothing
so hampers the foresight needed to make harmonization work,
nothing so trains men to look near to their wallets as constant
bargaining about their content.

Gaullism Today

The most striking difference between the Gaullism of the
war memoirs, of the postwar provisional government, and the
Gaullism of the Fifth Republic is the reversal of the emphasis
placed on socio-economic affairs on the one hand, and on defense and foreign affairs on the other. Of course, concern with
the coherence of the *Pouvoir* is, as always, dominant, but
whereas socio-economic participation, that is, the process of
cooperative consultation, was once in fact as well as in theory
a subordinate means of assuring it, years of practice have
made of it effectively the regime's and, *a fortiori,* the movement's major preoccupation. Not that *Le Pouvoir* does not
have the upper hand in the process. It does. But such visions
of great political ends as Gaullists might have had have not
survived the constant day to day bargaining process.

The first commandment of Gaullism[42] has to do with the
power of the state over France and of the government over
the state. We earlier described how improvements such as the
subjection of Parliament to the government, and the provision
that top leaders of the state be recruited via the ENA (National
School of Administration), are designed to assure this. But
power in democratic France confronts its holders with certain
problems. For example: in the course of the debate preceding
the 1972 (annual customary) vote of confidence, M. François
Mitterand, speaking for the Socialist opposition, read off a list
of the Gaullist movement's positions of power (majority in the

Assembly, uncontested control of the state, gatekeeper for the ENA) and said, pointing to the Gaullists, "The state is you." Then he proceeded to read a list of complaints common to Frenchmen: telephones don't work; people feel put upon. You have the uncontested *Pouvoir,* said he. If there is something wrong, if people are not finding happiness, it is your fault. Yes, the state does belong to Gaullism, but to do what? And in the name of what? Gaullism neither incorporates a vision of the good life nor can it, outside of times of crisis itself, invoke the image of an enemy which it is necessary to combat. For Gaullism today the world has neither friends nor enemies, neither good nor bad, just a lot of interests. Practical experience provides a practical orientation: satisfy, do everything possible to avoid another May, 1968, because the next one might sweep away *Le Pouvoir.*

Two levels of leadership exist in the Gaullist view: that of the presidency, exercised through the government, and that of the state exercised through efficient, serious technicians such as the graduates of the ENA. But how and to what extent can the former lead the latter? Certainly such leadership must be exercised primarily by means of ideas, visions. We need only note here that Gaullism today, as distinguished from the Gaullism of yesteryear, the Gaullism of opposition to the Fourth Republic, has failed to inspire those most necessary to the functioning of the kind of France it wants: the top administrators. Although they, like the rest of their countrymen, overwhelmingly approve of the order which the Fifth Republic has brought to France, only a small proportion are committed to Gaullist ideas. A poll recently conducted among graduates of the ENA (sometimes called Enarchs) showed that three-fourths of them favored supranational institutions in Europe, two-thirds the establishment of real regional powers in France, while nearly a half are for extensive nationalizations coupled with actual management of enterprises by employees. Nearly all, however, believe that increased decentralization of initiative must be accompanied by more forceful central administration if conflicts are to be successfully arbitrated. Moreover, three-fourths of the Enarchs thought of the growth of the new extreme Left as a good thing. Finally, the poll confirms that the political orientation of young ENA graduates conforms to their ideas: most belong to the non-Communist Left, and only little over a fourth are sympathetic to the "majority."[43] Most significantly, the leading members of the 1972 graduating class of the ENA, the "Charles de Gaulle Class," refused to enter the *Grands Corps* of the state as a gesture of protest against the government.

The Radical Alternatives
The Non-Communist Left

We may legitimately speak of the alternative approach to political life offered by the non-Communist Left, because, despite its fragmentation—under this label are classed the wildest *Gauchistes* as well as the very moderate Radical Party, *sérieux* socialist civil servants as well as modish young technocrats belonging to the PSU—despite the conflicts in programs, tactics, alliances, their views of what ails the modern democratic polity and of what sort of medicine the remedy is to consist are closely related. Only the doses and the timing differ. The non-Communist Left is also the principal heir of the democratic tradition. Neither Gaullists nor Communists so revere democracy, are so concerned with squaring their analyses, their actions, with its precepts as is the democratic Left. It is thus significant that the events of 1968, the rise of the New Left, although frightening to some, appear to have revitalized the democratic Left and inspired its contemporary democratic critique. If one reads the commentaries by members of the non-Communist Left on the events of May 1968, and listens to its spokesmen, to students, to civil servants who place themselves in this category, one cannot help but be struck by how much their words resemble those of M. Daniel Cohn-Bendit, the man who sparked the 1968 riots.

Modern society is composed primarily of proletarians, not

in the Marxian sense of men prey to poverty and the market-price of labor, but in the very real sense of total, if normally mild, subordination of nearly everyone to hierarchies beyond his control. This complex set of bureaucratic pyramids is suffered to exist only because its building blocks, the numerous subordinates, have been trained not to look at the inhumanity of the situation as a whole, but rather to concentrate on obtaining ever more material, that is to say, nonhuman, not to say subhuman, comforts for their particular selves. Paradoxically, total subordination of the individual can survive only so long as the individual is totally absorbed in himself alone. But precisely insofar as material comforts have increased, so has the realization that men need other things more. Must life consist of the ever greater production and consumption of meaningless garbage? The argument is simple: the actual purposes served by the existing bureaucratic pyramids, by the existing system of human relations, do not justify the subordination of any man to any other.

Moreover, continues the critique, unpolitical subordination brings on a measure of anarchy. The regime, in the words of Cohn-Bendit, "far from being able, as it claims, to control individual groups for the good of all, is forced to grant special favours to special groups as the hour dictates." It seems constrained continuously to rob Peter to pay Paul and vice versa. "The result might be called a return to feudalism: a new kind of guild system seems to be developing hand in hand with greater economic concentration. In fact, this growth of pressure groups did not spring up by accident, but is the natural response to industrial rationalization. These groups form what is essentially a defensive counterweight to the power of the bureaucrats."[44] People feel threatened, powerless, subordinate. That's the real reason they support particularistic interest groups, hoping by dint of concessions obtained to gain a sense of power, of independence. Interest groups, however, are not the answer; they, too, are bureaucracies, they too constrain the individual, and they also pit him against his fellow man. But the search for unity and individuality has become the order of the day, for people are showing in strike after strike that they have had enough of meaningless, powerless life. Even the best ENA graduates refuse to play the game.

But where lies meaning? The answer of the democratic Left is at least in principle that of classical liberalism: every individual must be put in a position to decide for himself what is important, and to direct his life accordingly. Here is a firm tenet: this is the best way for men to live. But since it has been generally assumed in liberal circles for two centuries that people's principal concerns are earthly ones—nothing being of real concern unless it is likely to affect health, wealth, or status, that is, unless it is political in nature—the problem of authoritative harmonization of inevitably conflicting meanings arises. Thus, even the PSU, even the far leftist Cohn-Bendit who quite sincerely profess confidence in spontaneity, who declare that each group, even each man, "must speak his own language," and that in absolute freedom natural harmony will reign, even they make it very clear that the purpose of the socialist political system they advocate is a rational ordering of the forces of society. Consequently, for democrats the problem of meaning in politics cannot be dissociated from that of power.

The more mature democratic leftists, the Radicals and the Socialists, faithfully reflect the complexity of the position. Having no doubt as to the necessity of organized power in society, they try to reconcile it with their view of liberty. Jean-Jacques Servan-Schreiber considers "the art of organizing talent the model on which our modern civilization is being molded."[45] Modernity itself means the massive reshaping of the planet to meet human needs, and this requires authoritative, powerful organizations. This is a political reality as well, for only an infinitesimal few do not favor the material well-being that only organization can bring. Moreover, Servan-Schreiber considers people not basically unfriendly to power, but rather alienated from it. This means they either resent not having it themselves or not being able vicariously to partake of its being exercised in an agreeable manner. Thus, two things must be done: power must be broken up and widely distributed, and it must be put at the service of ideals with which people want to identify.[46]

Thus does the Radical Party, followed by the Socialists, favor a greater degree of local autonomy. Thus the whole democratic Left is less interested in nationalization of industry than in the institution of *Autogestion* or self-management of enterprises by the employees. The issue, they all say, is not economic. It is not a matter of money or the standard of living, but of power—the quality of life—or rather of the *feeling* of power; above all, feeling because in an enterprise employing half a million workers, or even in a branch thereof employing a small fraction of that number, hierarchy is indispensable. As for motivating ideals, Radicals and Socialists offer the vision of France shedding the nationalism which went along with the miseries of war in the past, now blending into a United Europe and devoting itself to American-style technology while living peaceably in a participatory environment. The Socialists, while almost as strongly in favor of Europe, local autonomy and participation as the grand new motivating ideals of democratic life, also heavily emphasize (the more, the better their conversations with the Communists happen to be going at the moment) the building of socialism.

But how can extensive social reforms, whether in the pursuit of socialism or of technological status be accomplished by a whole people if any part is left free to disagree? Such was the dilemma of the first modern democrats, the French *philosophes.* No less than Jean-Jacques Rousseau devoted a book, *The Social Contract,* to the reconciliation, in a democratic context, of absolute sovereignty with absolute liberty. In it he noted that while necessarily each private citizen has only a minuscule fraction of the sovereign authority, he is under it with his whole person.[47] The problem of the democratic social engineer has always been how to make each man forget that he is but one of millions of bricks in the immense edifice being shaped and to get him to feel he is the whole thing, but not to feel it so strongly that he starts to act as though he were. A thorny problem. Though it might be easier, less unjustifiable and less harmful to confuse brick with building if many small homes were built instead of a single monument, democrats, especially in Europe, have always felt that only grand projects can elicit the sort of self-forgetfulness needed to bridge the gap between partial mastery and entire subjection.

Nowhere in the modern world has the history of democracy recorded anything but the decline of local liberties. This is, of course, no reason to doubt the intentions of the democratic Left in France when it speaks of breaking up power. In fact, Gaullists claim the democratic Left's appeals on local and industrial democracy, if followed, would amount to the breakup of the state. The democratic Left, they say, does not stand for anything which would cause the people to look to the state. At best, people may very well become more attached to their town or their job, but would it not be at the expense of France? Is not the democratic Left now advocating a type of fragmentation of the body politic not so different from the old partisan divisions which almost caused the nation to disappear as a unit capable of action in history?

When the democratic Left sets out to move the people by force of appeals, it knows it has a difficult task. The principal figure in its grand design is that of a united democratic Europe. But this, like the other figures, be it *Autogestion* or socialism, must today be presented in a particularly low-key way. Certainly, these things are not in themselves without capacity to raise a following. In the memory of all, fatherland, democracy and socialism, all inspired people to kill and give their lives. The democratic Left is the least inclined of all political groups to appeal on bases which might recall this. Therefore, though Europe as a whole may have more needs of a strategic kind than any of its component states, though socialism means upsetting patterns of life, talk of Europe must not sound nationalistic, talk of socialism or *Autogestion,* while promising relief from the strictures of hierachy, must not sound . . . dangerous. This poses a problem, for before there can be participation, even vicarious, in any venture, there must be an exciting venture in which to participate. Now, if it is impossible to obliterate the difference in the heart of democratic man between his being the infinitesimal part of master and wholly subordinate, the adventures of nations on the world scale, or campaigns against domestic enemies have historically been the catalyst setting off the swelling of the little bit of master in each by way of participation in feats of mastery. But if such adventures are disapproved of either because in the past they proved costly or because one does not believe that any people should consider infringing on any other's rights, democrats have to turn elsewhere. In the past they could hope to mobilize support by calling for the strengthening of institutions. But governments have been in possession of nearly absolute power for many years and although particular groups may loudly demand that the state assure this or that, state power itself is both secure and not popular.

The democratic Left has also rejected the option of engendering participation by the creation of one or more clienteles. It has always been easier to get people to identify their fortunes with those of outstanding concrete personages than with necessarily abstract goals, even as it has always been easier to assemble people about their particular rather than the general interest. But politics based on personality or on partisan interest and fidelity to party organizations appear to have lost their attraction for the non-Communist Left. Their concept of democratic participation has consequently drawn the criticism not only of Gaullists but also of Communists.

The Nature of Communist Democracy

Pinières, having had enough, asked Boisfeuras: "What's this about 'the internal contradictions of capitalism?'" [He answered] "Not daring to wage the kind of war needed to defend one's self. Not transforming one's self, not renewing one's self to carry the war to the adversary, . . . hiring mercenaries—us for example—instead of throwing into the mêlée all who have an interest in the survival of this capitalist system, replacing faith with money and technology, forgetting that the people are the reservoir of all energies; corrupting it with comfort, instead of marshalling it, lean and full of nervous energy, around a few valid causes."[48]

A more succinct definition of Leninist operational doctrine would be hard to formulate. In vain do democrats of the Right and Left accuse the Communists of being undemocratic, of not allowing people to participate sufficiently in the affairs of the party. Communists answer, armed with doctrinal texts and with figures showing the party has the highest ratio of participants to voters of any other in the nation, that they know better than anyone how to get people to participate, to discuss and agree on reforms of society. They claim to be at once radical, effective and participatory.

Their claims should not be too quickly dismissed. French and other soldiers who have fought against Communist forces, have remarked, as Larteguy's character, their solidity, while some journalists on visits to Communist countries have remarked how purposeful people's lives appear there. A correspondent for *L'Express,* writing from West Berlin at the time of the ratification of the April 1972 accords on the status of the population of that city, said that beyond the wall, guarded by soldiers under orders to shoot to kill, a new, purposeful nation was being born, while in Western Germany, people morosely wallow in luxury and pornography. Another, of the *New York Times,* wrote from Havana after having witnessed one of Fidel Castro's speeches, remarking how the crowd roaringly approved when asked whether one of its food rations should again be reduced to improve the Cuban balance of payments. Even if the speaker had decided on the ration long before stepping on the platform, said the journalist, how much more a part of this important decision every man in the crowd must have felt, how much more a part of the forces shaping his destiny than men who, in what go by the name of democracies, are called upon to merely cast a ballot every two years or so.

Young people who have heard nothing of communism other than that it is authoritarian marvel upon coming in contact with the fundamental rule of Communist life, democratic centralism. They are struck by the balance between the party's revolutionary purpose and its structure. The first requirement for the success of any party policy is that its rationale be assimilated by the membership, even as the party itself exists only insofar as its members have been impregnated with its reason for being. Popular support is so essential that it is not left to chance: it must be engineered. Of course, the discussions initiated by the party leadership are meant to result in assent to the party's actions. After all, as Lenin said, the party is a political organization, not a discussion club. But this does not take away from the fact that the party lives by the will of its supporters. Especially in a country like France where the party does not engage in widespread physical coercion, what can explain the adherence of so many to an organization (or to one of the front organizations thereof) which asks so much more of its members than other political groups, if not a superior grasp of how men in modern society may be got to take part in public affairs?

How precisely does democratic centralism, of which the French Communist Party is a firm champion, work?[49] Communists parties, structured according to Lenin's prescriptions set forth in *What Is To Be Done?* in 1902, and conceiving of themselves as the vanguard of a working class much larger, but also much less conscious than itself of the way out of present day society must first of all transmit knowledge of the way throughout their own ranks and then to the people. This knowledge belongs by definition to the party leadership. But, the often-made comparison between Communist parties and conventional armies is amiss. Whereas the latter's general staffs above all transmit orders which are not to be questioned but obeyed, the former's leadership, whenever possible, after it has made up its mind and before issuing directives, undertakes by means of debates and votes carefully orchestrated from the lowest level of the party on upward, to give every member the feeling that the decision taken was his own and that if the marching orders are going to come down the chain of command, it is because his assent had previously gone up it. This process, many times repeated, contributes to the indispensable party spirit far more than the adherence inspired by the party's purposes. Communists distrust the latter because the party may at any given time have to act in ways not commensurate with every member's personal view of communism. Their political soldiers stand and work together because they have been politically trained to. Gaullism, too, aims at a kind of training, but the means by which it is pursued differ.

Communist leaders proudly claim to be ever so much more aware than pollsters of what the people—especially those groups served by their mass organizations—think. The purpose of mass organizations is manifold: true they are transmission belts: permitting the party to transmit its directives to groups only marginally, if at all, in sympathy with it, but they function in two directions, allowing their members to express opinions to the party, which the latter spares no effort to publicly appreciate. The people are the only source of power.

However, since the party's reason for being is not merely the exchange of opinion between various groups but the coordination of as many people's efforts as possible in a single direction, it takes certain measures to ensure this, such as the appointment of subordinate units' chiefs from above, the predetermination of subordinate units' agenda, continuous tests of the members' degree of attachment, elimination of those who can't be counted on, etc. If organizational work is well done, it is seldom necessary to recur to falsification of internal election results or to violence. The manner in which Roger

Garaudy and his sympathizers were expelled from the French Communist Party is an excellent example of a well prepared operation: after months of organizational work, debates in dozens of party local committees, after careful selection of delegates to the congress, Garaudy could be allowed to speak his own defense before the 1970 Party Congress. The open vote against him served to cut him off democratically. Of course, in situations which have seemed to call for them, Communist parties have used far more definitive methods of sanction.

But if Communists are sometimes reproached for the illiberal means they often use, they are less often chided for the the ends they seek. In fact, nowhere in the immense corpus of Communist literature is there a positive definition of what the future Communist society will be like. The general secretary of the PCF, the Communist union leader, the organizer in Choisy-Le-Roy, are quite faithful to Marx when they answer questions about a future life under communism with a list of the objectionable features of present-day society which will be absent. Communists do not have any vision of the good life, but they can present on their behalf the living spectacle of what they and others consider bad in present-day society. When one listens to Communists explain themselves on the bulk of the French political agenda, one cannot help but be struck by how well their fundamental disposition, the total critique of society, fits into the discussion. Nearly every political party agrees on the need for reform, for helping the disadvantaged, for putting a greater share of society's products into the hands of workers; in sum, everyone wants equality. No one but the extreme Left and the Right doubt that of all political groups the Communists are the most committed to these goals; the general complaint is rather that they are perhaps too committed to them and not enough to liberty. But liberty is not on the political agenda. Up for democratic decision making, up for popular approval or disapproval, are the uses of state powers, not their extent.

Europe

We now leave the ideas of specific parties on democratic reform and turn to the brief examination of one reform which figures most prominently in the plans of all reformers (Communists excepted) and to which it is most difficult to find opposition. The phrase "building European unity" comes close to meaning all things to all men. Yet enough has been done and enough unambiguous things said by Frenchmen in the pursuit of European unity since the Second World War for us to able to say with confidence what European unity—such as it already is and such as leading Frenchmen want it to be in the future—stands for.

To begin with, we must note that "European unity" is a panacea cited by men of virtually all political tendencies. After a recital of what he believes is wrong in France, one's interlocutor is as likely as not to say "But when Europe will be made, then perhaps. . . ," and go on to describe what he would like to see, be it a vast nation taking on important tasks like sending men to the moon or even providing for its own defense, or more likely a higher standard of living, or better business conditions. Yet Europe is perhaps the political "thing" least likely to cause voices or tempers to rise. The French public's record-setting abstention (39.6 percent) and deposition of blank ballots (7 percent) in the June 23, 1972 referendum on the enlargement of the European Community, despite the government's month-long campaign to get out the vote, is an indication of how things stand. A poll taken about six weeks before the referendum also showed massive support for measures of European unity far beyond anything which any French government is likely to propose in this decade: 62 percent were for direct election of a European Parliament, and 60 percent for giving a European government power over "the most important questions." Yet, when specific important matters were mentioned, the public approved less wholeheartedly (53 percent for, 33 percent against a common monetary currency) or disapproved (39 percent for, 44 percent against a common army) of their being handled by a European government. Universal as it is, approval of European unity is problematic. There are good reasons for this.

Early Approaches to European Unity

The thoughts about European unity which are now reflected in the several European institutions[50] and in political dialogue are peculiar to the post-World War II period. Frenchmen and all Europeans have been conscious for at least a thousand years[51] that Europe constitutes one entity distinguishable from the rest of the world culturally as well as geographically. At the time of the Crusades, Europeans fought together against the Moslem enemy, but they did so under the universal banner of the Church. Similarly, in the 18th century, Europeans, especially educated Frenchmen, felt themselves in possession of precisely the right manners and liberal thoughts required for a truly human life, but these ideas, too, were seen as universal, and in a way were suprapolitical. Attempts to unify Europe politically are more recent, the most forceful ones being identified with the names of Napoleon, Hitler and Stalin. The contemporary European movement, on the other hand, has its roots in the reaction to the First World War of such men as Aristide Briand and Count Richard N. Coudenhove-Kalergi and to the Second of such as Robert Schuman, Charles de Gaulle, Alcide de Gasperi and Konrad Adenauer. What moved these men most of all was the desire to avoid the recurrence of war among Europeans. The other motivations, though significant, were of secondary importance. Since the European movement has been the work of many diverse men, we find in it, to be sure, several themes: the unity of Western Christendom against a menace worse than Islam,[52] the unity of the world's most civilized peoples,[53] and the unity of what is potentially a world military power second to none.[54] European unity today is also the work of men in the tradition of Saint-Simon for whom technical progress is the principal end of human endeavor,[55] and of men for whom the federation of Europe has itself become so important an end, that they do not look beyond it,[56] paying little attention to the *content* of European politics. As for the men in charge of the French state, they have always approached European unity with their attention firmly fixed on what the democratic French polity requires. The Europe of the Six (now enlarged to nine) which has resulted owes its character in no small part to the way French statesmen have selected among the possible meanings of Europe.

The Economic Europe of the Six and of the Nine
Dirigisme, interests and autarchy

Because of the European treaties, men and goods now flow more easily between the nine nations which adhere to them than at any time since 1914. But it would be wrong to call the regime of the Treaty of Rome "free trade." If political frontiers are today less of a barrier to economic activity, it is nonetheless true that as a consequence of the Treaty of Rome economic activity throughout Europe is more "politicized" than ever before. This means that countries like Germany and Belgium with less of a taste for politicization of trade, interventionism in economics, and inflation, have by and by adopted French and Italian habits in these matters.[57]

That the Common Market does not mean free trade[58] is obvious to every Frenchman who would like to buy a German car but knows that although there are no more customs duties between France and Germany, there are now "border taxes" amounting to the difference between the rates of indirect taxation applied to any given product in the two countries. Since the TVA on cars in France varies from 23 percent to 33 percent and in Germany it is 11 percent, that means a border tax of up to 22 percent; enough to make the inferior Citroen 2CV or Renault 4 a better buy than the superior Volkswagen Beetle, the Peugeot 505 than the BMW 2002 and so on. Despite the far higher transportation cost (about 10 times higher) and the fact that the United States does not belong to the Common Market, it was far more advantageous ($700 in 1972) for an American in San Francisco to buy a German BMW 2002 than for a Frenchman looking over the Rhine in Strasbourg to do so.

Border taxes are but one part of the problem: whenever a member country requests it (in practice quite often), the Common Market Commission must look into the problems caused any branch of that country's industry by competition from products imported from another Common Market country. This means, say, that Dutch and Italian and French clothing manufacturers have to consult cooperatively with each other and with the commission to arrive at agreements on export-import quotas and prices. When the product at issue represents an important enough part of any country's economy, the bargaining in Brussels is carried on by representatives of the several states, each charged with upholding the interests of certain groups at home. This is notably the case with agriculture, where prices and "estimated" levels of imports and exports are set at what has become a familiar European institution, the all-night bargaining session in Brussels.

Trade among the Common Market countries, no longer primarily the tool of each government's foreign policy, no longer serving the design of each to gain strategic advantages over the others, now serves in detail the desires of the interest groups of which each state is composed, be these private groups or particular government agencies. When the treaty provisions run afoul of powerful interest groups, they are simply not observed. Whereas Article 37 of the Treaty of Rome, for example, provided for modification of state monopolies to allow for free international competition, the French and Italian governments notably retain their monopolies on things like matches, salt and the importation of petroleum. Interest groups are not usually eager for competition; thus market-sharing arrangements and mergers abound: the steel giants Thyssen and Mannesman merged, as did the tire giants Dunlop and Pirelli. Thus French farmers required not free access to the markets of Europe, but *subsidized* access, and France and Italy together on behalf of their rice growers required the commission to set a common tariff virtually excluding rice from countries where it can be grown economically. The examples are legion, but in sum what has happened is that prices for any given product throughout the Common Market have tended to move toward the level of the highest price charged for that product anywhere in the community.[59] The rationale behind this has been that if every group is allowed its pound of flesh, all, and therefore just about everyone, will be better off. In fact, living standards in France and thoughout Europe are higher than ever. Just how the Common Market has affected them however is not clear. The purpose of the Common Market is above all political. It is meant to wed Europeans to one another through the process of cooperation in economic matters, much like cooperative consultation of interest groups with one another on the national level. To succeed however, this scheme must overcome the tendency of those who feel they did not get a good enough deal to blame their trading partners and the process, too.

Along with the practice of cooperation, one might say the other face of the European coin is the hope that the nations of the Treaty of Rome will learn to consider themselves a unit *vis à vis* the outside world. To this end the Common Market has been fenced in by relatively high tariff walls, and the principle of community preference established according to which the governments of the community should not as a matter of principle and within their powers authorize the purchase of goods or services outside the community which are available within. The community should live on its own resources as much as possible. Thus one does not cease to find governments, major newspapers, and banks publishing figures for production and consumption of everything from milk to automobiles for the community taken as a whole, comparing them with the figures for the other "greats" of the planet, the U. S.

and the Soviet Union.[60] The figures for the "nine" are impressive: a GNP substantially more than double that of the Soviet Union with a somewhat larger population, which very nearly supplies its own high consumption of food and most raw materials, and dwarfing their closest competitor, the United States, in the exportation of finished goods. The Europe of the Nine even more than the Europe of the Six has without doubt the material wherewithal to vie for first place among the superpowers. But if the community's external economic policy resembles that of its members before World War II when each strove to develop its capacity for autarchy, its motivation today has no relation to the traditional justifications for autarchy, that is, the economic fulfillment of the theory of the absolute independence and sovereignty of the state, and assurance of an independent capacity to pull up one's drawbridges and fight.

If modern Europe's tendencies to autarchy were moved by classic motives, the principal concerns of planners would not be the amount of frozen poultry American businessmen are trying to sell Europeans, but rather the two sets of hands on Europe's petroleum tap: those of Arab and Soviet leaders. It has been obvious since before the last war that modern Europe could not function without a large and ever-growing supply of oil. Since the nineteen-fifties, it has been clear that the Europeans who discovered and developed North African and Middle Eastern oil would be dependent on the goodwill of indigenous governments for their oil, even as these would be dependent on European markets. Since the late nineteen-sixties, it has been unmistakable that more and more Arab states, supported diplomatically by the Soviet Union and strong with the latter's promise of economic and, if need be, military aid see themselves in the position of holding Europe hostage. The Soviets for their part have made no secret of their desire to become the exclusive brokers between Europe and the oil producers. No one doubts that the price added by this middle man will be high, politically as well as economically. Not only is the European community not even talking about common action in this vital area, but each country, especially France, seems intent on making its own private arrangements.[61]

The autarkic tendencies in foreign trade result rather from many particular pressures on the part of individual groups and governments, each desiring protection for a particular product or policy best "sold" to a captive public.

Political Europe

While campaigning for a massive "yes" vote on the 1972 referendum, Georges Pompidou said on television, "let no one stay home because he believes that Europe has already been made. In fact, it has not." In part he was wrong. The main desire of the fathers of the European movement is now a reality: war between the nations of free Europe is now inconceivable, and everyone knows it. Most people have the essential of what they want from Europe: peace. This no doubt explains in part why the subject arouses less interest among peoples than it does among governments. These have been trying to agree for decades on a positive political arrangement that will take Europeans beyond a much decreased willingness to fight each other—this willingness having been for a hundred years the mainspring of political life in most European countries—to an increased willingness to consider Europe as their fatherland. Having witnessed the disenchantment of citizens with their nations, they have been searching—within the constraints of modernity—for a way to create a new European enchantment.

The formulae, the "plans" proposed have been legion: confederation, federation, supranationality, cooperation, harmonization. The position of French leaders, save a few, has been quite consistent: while other nations, either because of temporary circumstances (Germany) or temperament (Italy) may be willing to dissolve into a homogeneous Europe, France is not. The European political debate has therefore long since turned to the concrete question of how the interests which everyone agrees Europe has in common will be safeguarded.

Europe first of all has democracy in common, and that means that some way must be found to give people who normally do no more than vote in their own countries a feeling of participation in Europe; otherwise the enterprise would be false to the spirit of the times. But how? A strengthened European Parliament would have two great disadvantages: first, it would separate the symbol of authority, which it would come to be, from the realities of power, that is, from the only institutions in Europe capable of making themselves obeyed; but second and most important, why should a strong European Parliament not inherit all the awkwardness, all the difficulties which have caused most modern countries, France among them, to reduce drastically the role of Parliament at home? Parliaments are unmodern. President Pompidou thought a referendum in each country would serve to line up people solidly behind Europe. But even if France's European referendum of 1972 had been massively approved, it would not have meant that the referendum, necessarily an episodic affair, can be an efficient means of participation, except perhaps when the question asked is of unmistakably great historical significance. People like to be let in on history, but great historical events are seldom painless. Is there really any painless alternative to the sort of European participation that now exists: the frequent encounter of interest groups from every corner of Europe with their homologues, the bargaining and compromises among interested parties and bureaucrats? Why should Europe as a whole be any different from its parts?

But this sort of cooperation does not by itself foster feelings of political identification. For identification with a political Europe to be even possible there must first be such a Europe, and that can be nothing other than a single voice on world affairs, a single voice resulting from the agreement of the states of Europe.[62] The agenda on which European statesmen, led by the French, are resolved to try to speak with one voice, then, is of the greatest importance, for people are not easily moved to act: "One does not create a great power simply to better assure everyday life. . . *Le Pouvoir* wants grandeur."[63] Thus the most daring European statesmen, M. Debré and Franz-Josef Strauss, agree that cooperation on details, a standardization of patent laws, and so on, can at best only create a "commonwealth of momentary exigencies." More is needed. So they speak now and then of "making more sacrifices" or "allotting greater sums" to European defense. The year 1972 even saw the question "Who will defend Europe"[64] publicly raised by a chief of state for the first time since the early 1960s. Yet there can be no comparison between these isolated, mild statements and the massive attention initiators of the European movement gave the problem of defense in the late 1940s and early 1950s.

Far heavier emphasis is given today to a United European position in commercial and monetary negotiations with the United States and to helping underdeveloped nations develop. The former arouses no enthusiasm, the latter, except in special circumstances, nothing but opposition.

From Six to Nine

Leaders of the six nations which formed the Coal and Steel Community in 1951 affirmed at the time that their union was more than a response to economic necessity, more than a political policy, but rather an acknowledgment that geography, culture and history had made of them a unit likely in the future to suffer from the same enemies, enjoy the same friends, etc. In the six nations, few voices other than the Communists' were raised in opposition. Necessity more than positive will was counted on to achieve European unity. Much like the Swiss centuries before, the Six had realized they would have to live together for better or for worse. The nascent Europe of the Nine, though dependent on the same treaties, is a different thing, stretching as it does from the Shetland Islands, reaching toward the Arctic Circle to the southern tip of Sicily and including nations whose lots are not obviously and necessarily cast together. As such it depends far more than its predecessor on leaders who will show its peoples tasks of such appeal, dangers so appalling, as to articulate Shetlanders and Sicilians into a body politic.

Europe, What for?

Since the European debate stopped being about formulae (confederation versus federation) and turned to concrete matters, this question has been heard more and more in France. There has been no lack of answers affirming the absolute need for grand motivating purposes, yet, at least in public dialogue, discussion of purposes is completely lacking. This, too, has been widely noted.[65] *Time* magazine even devoted one of its essays (30 November 1970) to how devoid of passion and great projects Europe had become: "The peace of exhaustion after a millennium of bloodletting" it called it, referring both to foreign and domestic affairs in Europe. Having been shown by the suffering of war of what little worth all her previous cares had been, she has turned her back on the ideologies and nationalisms which had replaced the Christian faith her leaders had lost, and has turned her energies to cultivating her own garden, like a retired Don Quixote. When one asks thoughtful Frenchmen to describe what a united Europe will be like, sooner or later one is likely to be told that it would be like Switzerland, that is to say, federated, peaceful, democratic and wealthy.

But Europe cannot transform itself politically into Switzerland any more than it can erect around itself a synthetic Alpine barrier. It can neither transform itself at will from the world's richest into a relatively small prize of war, nor mobilize its whole male population for the defense of its territory on several hours' notice. European politics have also shown no signs of evolving in the direction of Swiss politics, either insofar as discipline or participation is concerned. Can one imagine a Frenchman or a German or an Italian being deprived

of citizenship or exiled for refusing to serve in the ready reserves of his country's armed forces until age 48? The Swiss
are proud of this discipline. The differences between modern
Europe and Switzerland are apparent in other fields as well.
The economic integration of the Swiss cantons, often mentioned as a model by partisans of the Common Market, is an
entirely different beast, based as it is on free trade. Furthermore Swiss democracy is based on the greatest possible autonomy of the smallest possible territorial units. Not surprisingly
the meaning of the term participation in Switzerland and in
modern French democracy differs.

The comparison with Switzerland means different things to
different people. A senior officer in the French Army asked
us rhetorically, "But how can you imagine Europe if not as
a large-scale Switzerland?" He was thinking of the way in
which the Swiss have organized an efficient defense force out
of a multilingual people, one, moreover, which, while threat-
ening no one outside the Swiss borders, is capable of giving
an excellent account of itself in their defense. To almost everyone, Switzerland means peace, but few outside the military
think of how peace is to be secured. To a thoroughly pro-Euro-
pean socialist bureaucrat, making Europe into Switzerland
meant being able to engage in reforms on a large scale, and
with a contented population.

In short, it appears that what people expect from a united
Europe in the future is not so very different from what they
expect of their country today.

Summary: Reforms and the Evolution of Modern France

How remarkably similar in tone and content are the views
of democracy we have just seen! Gaullists, to be sure, put
more emphasis on maintaining the state as something greater
than its parts, while the Socialists want to strengthen the
former for the benefit of the latter. To be sure, also, differences
between Socialists and Communists remain, but the old categories of Left and Right no longer help us to understand them.

The alternative approaches to reform we have just examined are primarily attempts to define in word and in deed the meaning of democracy in our time.

Of course, there are vital differences between Gaullists, Communists, Radicals and Socialists; lives lived with preoccupations as different from one another as the glory of France, the interest of constituencies, the welfare of workers, and the will of the infallible Communist Party, cannot help but indelibly mark men and movements. Still, however great the differences between the movements, they do not lie in their understanding of modern democratic society.

Communists, Socialists, Gaullists, Radicals, all agree that the requirements of democracy in our time cannot be fulfilled by what are commonly called representative institutions. These are singularly unfit for democracies because they have shown themselves little suited to building the consent of the people to the exercise of *the* public *Pouvoir.* For all modern democrats, the people of the nation taken as a whole are the only source of power, the only source of authority. For all, the test of any regime's democratic character is its ability to get its acts ratified by the population. Can *this* way of doing things, they ask, engender bonds among citizens sufficient to hold the state and society together? In fact, even as one finds no distinction made between power and authority, one finds no essential distinctions between the state and society in the several theories of modern democracy. Society is not something which pre-existed and will outlast the state: it exists only insofar as cooperation fruitful to each of its members can be successfully organized. The state is effectively the form without which society cannot be said to exist. All problems in society are, therefore, ipso facto political problems.

The most bothersome problem is also the one most peculiar to democracy: how the citizen, part sovereign in theory but wholly subject in fact, can be brought to feel less like the latter and more like the former. The more the sovereignty of the whole with regard to social problems is affirmed, the less can the authority of each member of society be admitted. With only a few exceptions, modern democrats, true to the tradition of the Renaissance, deny any part of the people, any social corporation, *a fortiori* any individual, has any inherent authority to act in a manner disapproved by the whole people, effectively represented by the *Pouvoir.* They do not in fact even conceive the problem in terms of the unity and variety of authority, but rather in terms of the unity and variety of social forces. Evidently the problem of democratic politics is not how to arrange for the political articulation of men and groups equal in their God-given right to be left alone, but rather is to so juxtapose the will to power, the desire of each for gain at the expense of others, that all will be tied together. The complex of juxtapositions, the shape of the mass, is altered by the sovereign will according to the requirements of the moment. Its right or rather its *Pouvoir* to do so is generally recognized. As for the component parts of the social state, their liberty, their interest, their very existence, rest on the ability of each to make itself powerful enough, to arm itself with enough of a potential for nuisance to force the power to take its desires into account. But, significantly, all modern democrats—though each for his own reasons—consider the role of pressure groups in modern society undesirable. Besides the ideological reasons—Communists and Socialists believe the working class is by definition united, though its enemies may not always be; Gaullists think almost the same about the nation—there are facts which every *Pouvoir* must face. There is no pressure group for the common good. In any regime there is not even any particular group with an unshakable interest in supporting the regime. Even the regime's own members can imagine more advantageous arrangements for themselves. In theory there is no limit to the demands groups and individuals can make. In short, modern democrats' views of the state and of democracy imply constant conflict.

Plans for reform in France agree on two ways of overcoming

the problems of democracy: personal participation of citizens in the administration of society, as it were, from below, and what for want of a better term we will call vicarious participation of particular individuals with the purposes of the democratic state.[66] Reformers have found that it is hard work to get large numbers of people to take part even in deliberations which directly affect their interests, never mind institutions concerned with the general welfare such as local government. Participation is not so much a popular desire crying to be satisfied as something the people must be trained to want. Participation means training men to pursue their immediate desires through proper channels and to accept the verdict of the state. Here the Communists diverge from other modern democrats in their conviction that grassroots participation should be so organized as to ensure at all costs that it results in just the desired modes of behavior. They also stress more strongly than Gaullists and Socialists that there should be a clear understanding—one they claim only they can provide—of how grassroots, personal participation in innumerable local enterprises and social committees, can be used to foster vicarious participation in the decisions of the national leadership. Without such an understanding, success in fostering the former kind of participation must redound to the detriment of the latter kind.

The best example of how interest in the component parts of a polity can occur at the expense of allegiance to the whole is provided by the nascent or rather re-nascent regionalism observable not only in France but throughout the Western world. In Italy it is Trentino and Lombardia; in Spain it is the Basque regions and Catalonia; in Canada it is Quebec; in England it is Wales and Scotland; in Belgium it is both the country's halves. Long is the list of parts of modern unitary states—not to speak of heterogeneous empires such as the Soviet Union—in which inhabitants are showing interest in local or regional affairs along with increasing disinterest in the affairs of the state. This is a quite recent phenomenon: the political history of the nineteenth century (and of several centuries before) consists rather largely of the flowering of nation-building movements in substantially all the regions which now make up modern European states. The new regional separatism in Europe was commented on by Jose Ortega Y Gasset as early as 1921.[67] Though his analysis takes its examples from Spain, it is meant to be generally valid. A nation, he says, is not born spontaneously out of a racial community or out of the ties which united separate local communities in the past. Rather it is fashioned by a part of its people—in the case of Spain, Castile, in the case of France the old Ile-de-France—which is possessed of "a suggestive plan for life in common." The groups which form a state "do not live together to *be* together, but to *do* something together,"[68] (emphasis his). Political society should not be thought of as a homogeneous mass, but as a body formed by the articulation of its several parts, each of which retains its identity. As distinguished from a tribe or a race, political society as such is both ecumenical and ever-fragile. When the group or region which has articulated the others for action in history itself ceases to believe in its own *projecto,* why should not the other components seek to lighten themselves of whatever burdens attachment to a dead polity might still impose? People who rally to local government while losing interest in the state do not seek to set up their own nations, but merely to be left alone.

What is true of local collectivities is true, albeit in a different way, of all other groups in which citizens might participate. Therefore, in order to make of participation an instrument for the preservation of the democratic state, it must be structured either through organization, through some sort of appeal made by the state to its component groups, or by a combination of both. The Communist solution, democratic centralism, on one end, depends most heavily on organization, while on the other, the Radicals and Socialists say they would rely most on the good sense of groups, worker-run enterprises and local collectivities to cooperate harmoniously to achieve the good society. Gaullists on this matter have one foot in either camp. State control is very highly valued but, even when one relies on organization, as even Communists well know, one must try to show participants that their actions, that their organizations serve purposes greater than themselves. It follows with even greater force that to the extent that the basic participatory units are not placed in a rigorous hierarchy, it is vital that the state which attempts to integrate them present itself as the representative of a task or of a truth they all share.

Modern democrats are one in proclaiming individual self-fulfillment as the purpose of human existence. Communists promise that in the ultimate socialist commonwealth every man will be able, if he wants, to fish in the morning, make a car in the afternoon, and do literary criticism at night. Socialists, Gaullists, etc., are more vague and their appeals to the ideal of individual self-fulfillment leave the imaginations even freer. The purpose of modern democratic politics, it seems, is a far more comprehensive one than that of former regimes. The purpose of the American union is merely justice, domestic tranquility, common defense, general welfare; that of the French republics has traditionally been broader: liberty, equality, fraternity. Now the end is nothing else than happiness itself. Observers have noted[69] that political men of all parties in recent years have been speaking more and more of a "problem" which, whether called "the quality of life" or "the humanization of modern life" or something else analogous, amounts to nothing but the burden which all theoretically omnicompetent governments, including democratic ones, must bear. They must necessarily be held responsible for the happiness of the governed. But how are human beings made full and happy? In democratic societies the question is necessarily sharpened, for it is the citizens' understanding of themselves which determines the quality of the regime. Thus it becomes what kind of man is most happy? What are the activities, the habits, the mores which make men enduringly happy and why?

Yet democratic politics itself does not seem conducive to the serene search for the answers to the questions it poses, nor to the examination of previous answers to similar questions,[70] for it is engaged in a daily struggle to survive. By definition, one does not discuss mores with social *forces,* one weighs them and harmonizes them accordingly. The politics of the bare minimum aims at assuring the functioning of the democratic state's machinery by manipulating the most immediately available levers on human behavior. The *content* of politics necessarily must take second place. But though it may not answer the questions it poses, though it may not inspire anyone to defend it against enemies foreign or domestic, modern democratic politics contains, in its concern with efficacy and success, a means of survival in the short run and in the long run a principle capable of transforming it.

Notes to Chapter 6

[1]Cf. the Speech at Bayeux, 16 June 1946, in which he outlined his views on the appropriate constitution of French political life. *Le Salut,* p. 499.

[2]Charles de Gaulle, *Le Fil De L'Epée,* Paris, 1944, p. 39. Wholly and *consistently* embraced the idea that the desire for power confers upon leaders and their actions a noble heroic quality. p. 54.

[3]*Ibid.,* pp. 74-75.

[4]Authority here seems to be essentially inseparable from the person who exercises it by virtue of his successes. It is not something existing independent of all, of which now one, now another can partake. It is something made by each for his own use only.

[5]*Le Renouveau,* p. 283.

[6]One of the most revealing passages in the general's war memoirs recounts his reaction to the news that General Koenig's First Light Division, after very valiantly gaining two weeks' time for the British VIIIth Army in a crucial phase of the North African Campaign, had escaped Rommel's siege at Bir Hakeim with the bulk of its men. "Oh heart beating with emotion, sobs of pride, tears of joy!" *L'Appel,* p. 322.

[7]*Ibid.,* p. 302.

[8]Even as the lack of programmatic material in the forefront of Gaullism made it possible for quite diverse political figures to adhere to the general,

it opened the general to the charge of eclecticism. One of the most biting remarks on the subject was made by one of his oldest enemies, General Weygand, discredited by the events of 1940: "De Gaulle is a military man, but not a soldier; a Catholic, but not a Christian."

[9]His views on this matter remained quite constant over the years. Cf. *Le Fil De L'Epée*, pp. 95-97 and *L'Effort*, pp. 115-117.

[10]*L'Appel*, Chapter 1, "La Pente."

[11]*Le Salut*, p. 320.

[12]"It is a sort of will to assure to France, by means of its industrial development, its agricultural modernization, its exporting activities, a capacity of power." *Le Figaro*, 30 Nov., 1970.

[13]*L'Effort*, p. 188.

[14]*Ibid.*

[15]The most innovative parts of the proposal were Article 6 which actually gave the regional administration—still, however, headed by *Monsieur Le Préfet*—full responsibility for public works, and Article 11, which attributed to the region—actually to the council—the authority to dispose of certain taxes heretofore collected by the state, and actually to raise or lower their rates. Although the regional domain would have been very narrow, subject to the prefect's veto, and the council still would not have been directly elected, the regions would have become, like it or not, somewhat political entities.

[16]If a poll be needed to confirm the obvious, we cite the following: 64 percent favorable to "the creation of regions endowed with extensive powers" to 12 percent opposed, 59 percent in favor of having the regional executive officer elected directly to 7 percent for his appointment by the state. SOFRES poll published in *Le Figaro*, 15 December 1970.

[17]*Le Figaro*, 26 April 1972. The debate over the regions has been on and off since 1871. Some other pertinent declarations on the subject by leading Gaullist figures since the 1969 referendum are as follows: Oct. 30 and 31, 1970 and July 29, 1971 in *Le Monde* speeches by G. Pompidou; Jan. 15, 1972 in *Le Monde* declaration by the author of the 1972 regional law, M. Roger Frey; and Feb. 5, 1972 *Le Monde*, statement by Prime Minister Chaban-Delmas. Between 25 and 29 April, 1972, *Le Monde* and *Le Figaro* carried statements by every political group on the subject.

[18]*Le Figaro*, 26 April, 1972.

[19]"If the Regional Council is constituted without the deputies, it will be constituted against them," says a prominent Gaullist.

[20]*Les Dernières Nouvelles D'Alsace*, 30 January 1972, and *Le Figaro*, 5 March 1971, respectively.

[21]*Le Monde*, 20 September 1970.

[22]*L'Effort*, p. 190.

[23]Raymond Aron, *La Révolution Introuvable*, Paris, 1968, p. 126.

[24]*L'Effort*, pp. 122-123. "Doubtless the malaise of the soul which results from a civilization dominated by material things cannot be healed by any

regime whatsoever. At least one day it might be relieved a bit by a change in moral conditions which would make men responsible rather than mere instruments."

[25]*Le Salut,* pp. 261-262. "If the overseas territories were detached from Metropolitan France, or if our forces were to be tied down there, for how much would we count between the North Sea and the Mediterranean? If they remain ours, associated, on the contrary, then the way is open for our action on the continent. Secular destiny of France!"

[26]The following is a partial list of references on the Algerian drama: Dorothy Pickles, *Algeria and France,* London, 1963; William G. Andrews, *French Politics and Algeria,* New York, 1962; Charles de Gaulle, *L'Effort,* Paris, 1970. The Journal *Nef,* special issue of Jan. 1963, "Histoire de la guerre d'Algérie;" from a leftist viewpoint, Jules Roy, *Le Guerre d'Algérie,* Paris, 1960; from a rightist viewpoint, Jacques Soustelle, *L'Espérance d'Algérie,* Paris, 1962; from a combatant's, General (Ret.) Jacques Massu, *La Vraie Bataille d'Alger,* Paris, 1971. But certainly the most evocative books are those by Jean Lartéguy, *Les Centurions,* Paris, 1960, and *Les Prétoriens,* Paris, 1961.

[27]"In this vast and painful operation my responsibility is consequently entire. So be it . . . I will have to proceed not by leaps but step by step, myself executing each stage and then only after having prepared it in events and in the public mind. Constantly I will try to remain master of the hour, never letting either the stirrings of politics nor the bitterness of the press nor the pressures of foreigners nor the troubles of local populations ever sway me from my path." *Le Renouveau,* p. 90.

[28]Jacques Chapsal, *La Vie Politique en France Depuis 1940,* Paris, 1969, pp. 417, 429.

[29]See the series of public opinion polls on Algerian matters in early 1958 *SONDAGES,* No. 3, pp. 39-46.

[30]Jacques Chapsal, *op. cit.,* p. 415.

[31]*Le Renouveau,* p. 64. De Gaulle gives the impression he thought this particular move quite elegant.

[32]*Ibid.,* p. 81.

[33]*Ibid.,* p. 110.

[34]*Ibid.,* p. 130.

[35]*Ibid.,* p. 132. Evian is one of the largest spring-water resort towns in France. The largest is Vichy.

[36]*Le Renouveau,* p. 221.

[37]*Ibid.,* p. 216.

[38]*Ibid.,* p. 201.

[39]*Ibid.,* p. 235-238. For a full description of the Berlin affair, see Robert Kleiman, *Atlantic Crisis,* New York, 1964. Adenauer's gratitude to de Gaulle was without bounds. One can date Germany's search for an alternative to the American alliance from that incident.

[40]*L'Appel*, p. 10-11.

[41]See *Le Fil de L'Epée*, pp. 94-95. This sort of thinking was influenced by a certain interpretation of the thought of Henri Bergson, with which de Gaulle was quite familiar. See especially the former's *The Two Sources of Morality and Religion.*

[42]See Michel Debré, "Les Cinq Commandements du Gaullisme," *Le Figaro,* 30 November 1970.

[43]Reported by *France-Soir,* June 3, 1972.

[44]Daniel Cohn-Bendit, *Obsolete Communism—The Left Wing Alternative,* New York, 1969, p. 135.

[45]*The Spirit of May,* New York, 1968, p. 16.

[46]*Ibid.,* p. 9 and 40 and 64. "The problem is power itself. Power now must be broken up and redistributed. This is the only way we can hold our society together." And "If democracy is to become a vital force, it has to work on a small scale."

[47]Rousseau, *Le Contrat Social,* Chap. 3, Sec. 1.

[48]Jean Larteguy, *Les Centurions,* Paris, 1960, p. 83. Captain Boisfeuras, a man of long experience with communism, is explaining to his French comrade in arms why they were defeated in Indochina in 1954.

[49]At the PCF's Congress of February, 1970, the general secretary, M. Georges Marchais, explained once again the system of democratic centralism and how it worked in the case of the expulsion of Roger Garaudy. His explanation was later taken up by the Soviet journal *Kommunist,* in February, 1972. See *Est et Ouest,* No. 489, May, 1972, pp. 1-10.

[50]The principal European institutions resulting primarily from the Treaty of Rome of 1958, but also from the Council of Europe Statute of 1949, the Coal and Steel Treaty of 1951 and the Euratom Treaty of 1957 are as follows: 1. The European Commission, formerly the EEC or Common Market Commission, but reorganized in 1966 to administer what remained of the Coal and Steel and Euratom Organization. It sits in Brussels where it employs about 5,000 officials. Commission posts have been divided among the nationals of the nine countries and the chairmanship is rotated. The commission has, more than any other European institution, attempted to clothe itself with the appearances of sovereignty, asking that foreign countries accredit ambassadors to it, that its chairman be received with the protocol due a head of government, etc. It is the commission which, since 1958, has been the focus of the debate whether a supranational power should be established. In effect, the commission, though it has vast administrative and coordinative responsibilities, works under the direction of the Council of [Foreign] Ministers from the several states. The latter decides on important matters and its votes must be unanimous whenever any party deems the matter important. The council has its own secretariat; there is in addition a European Court of Justice to decide on disputes arising from the commission's actions. 2. The European

Parliament, a congress of delegates from the national parliaments of the several nations. A similar Parliament of the Council of Europe sits in Strasbourg and promotes action on such matters as local government and environment as well as European unity. Seventeen nations are members. Though it can theoretically force the resignation of the commission, something it never even considers, it does try to resemble a European legislature.

[51]Federico Chabod, *Storia dell' Idea d'Europa,* Bari, 1962.

[52]In the person of Robert Schuman, even within single sentences of his, one finds intermingled concern with Christianity, technical progress and economic growth. Statements concerning Christianity, whether by Schuman or others usually are directed to two points: Christians should no longer war among themselves, and Christian civilization appears to be threatened by communism. See especially Schuman's speech at Harvard, *Vital Speeches,* June, 1954, p. 16, and *Pour L'Europe,* Paris, 1964.

[53]See Adenauer, *World Indivisible,* New York, 1955, especially p. 12 and R. N. Coudenhove-Kalergi, *Crusade for Pan-Europe, Autobiography of a Man and a Movement,* New York, 1943.

[54]See especially de Gaulle's *Le Salut.*

[55]For example, Walter Hallstein, *United Europe,* Cambridge, 1962.

[56]By far the most thoughtful of the dozens of books in this category is Henri Brugmans' *L'Europe à faire,* Bruges, 1972. For an analytic overview of the European Movement, see Angelo M. Codevilla, *Implications of Several Approaches to European Unity,* Notre Dame (Thesis), 1968.

[57]Though economic and monetary integration are essential to the ultimate merger of European economies (one need only recall that France imposed exchange restrictions during and long after the '68 crisis, or the heavy effort which has been long required of the French and German banking systems to sustain the Italian Lira, always in danger of a major crisis), we will restrict for reasons of space our discussion to matters of trade.

[58]For a fuller explanation of the difference between the Common Market's highly structured exchange system and free trade, see Wilhelm Röpke's article "European Economic Integration and its Problems" in *Modern Age,* Summer, 1964.

[59]Sometimes, as in the case of vegetables, the rise has been dramatic. For as long as anyone can remember, the staple of poorer Frenchmen and Italians had been vegetable soups. Today in Europe, unless one produces one's own vegetables, these dishes are among the more expensive ones one can prepare.

[60]Some examples are the pamphlet published jointly by the Crédit Lyonnais, the Commerzbank and the Banco di Roma in 1972 called "La CEE en Chiffres" and the special issues of *Le Monde,* "L'Europe en 1975," February 24, 1972 and *Le Figaro,* 20 April 1972.

[61]For example, when in 1972 Iraq nationalized the Iraq petroleum company

owned equally by American and British and Dutch interests and by the French government, the latter hardly took pains to disguise its eagerness to respond favorably to an Iraqi request that France alone negotiate an agreement for continued cooperation with the new owners. This provided a pattern for French behavior during the 1973 Arab oil boycott. West Germany, for its part, has also long been in violation of the letter of the Treaty of Rome according to which no member nation may conclude economic agreements with nonmember nations except after authorization by the commission. Germany has been buying Soviet oil and generally making every possible deal with the Soviet Union and with the Communist countries of Eastern Europe.

[62]The common issue of *Le Monde, La Stampa, Die Welt* and *The Times,* published on 24 February 1972, on the occasion of the signing of the treaty admitting Britain to the community, published back to back statements by leading statesmen of France (Michel Debré), Italy (Emilio Colombo), Germany (Franz-Josef Strauss) and of England (Alec Douglas-Home), stressing that political Europe would have to be first of all such a single voice. In 1973 these newspapers concluded a long-term agreement on cooperation.

[63]*Ibid.*

[64]*Le Monde,* 11 February 1972. President Georges Pompidou and Chancellor Willy Brandt, meeting for one of the bi-yearly consultations prescribed by the Franco-German treaty of 1963, considered the problem of European defense, taking for granted the absence of American troops.

[65]See especially John Lukacs, *The Decline and Rise of Europe,* New York, 1965 and Walter Laqueur, *The Rebirth of Europe,* New York, 1970.

[66]Almond and Verba, *The Civic Culture,* p. x, define the essential pillars of all modern democracies as "full participation" and "social betterment."

[67]José Ortega Y Gasset, *España Invertebrada,* Madrid, 1964.

[68]*Ibid.,* p. 40. Also see Ernest Renan, *Qu'est ce qu'une Nation?,* Paris, 1882. A nation, says the latter, results not from a community of race, language, religion, interests ("un Zollverein n'est pas une Patrie"), nor from geographic factors. A nation is a spiritual community of men who want to do something together. Its existence is a daily plebiscite.

[69]For example, Pierre Vianson-Ponté, "Les Moeurs en Question," *Le Monde,* 30 October 1970.

[70]The central question of Aristotle's *Nicomachean Ethics* is precisely what kind of man is happiest, while that of his *Politics* is what kind of regime is most conducive to happiness.

Chapter 7
The Political Culture
of Modern Democracy
in France

Modern Democracy Is Not Undemocratic

There is no reason for us to deny the democratic character of French politics today and there are several reasons for affirming it.

First of all, as a political principle, democracy today has—in France and almost everywhere else in the world outside Arabia—the whole field to itself. Outside very few places in the modern world one will look in vain for principles other than democratic ones ruling and explaining the orientation of institutions and of political actors. The mere usage in common discourse of the names of other principles, for example, monarchy, aristocracy, oligarchy, as terms of accusation is an indication. Aristocracy is the principle of union about a right order for the purpose of doing or being good. The very words are out of tone with the political language of our time. A condescending smile is the best such words can hope to draw in polite company. As for the terms "aristocracy or aristocrat" themselves, they denote little more than haughtiness. Oligarchy has lost one of its original meanings, rule of the wealthy, and now means only power of the few. It is the most common accusation hurled at governments, committees, procedures, etc., naturally by those to whom they do not give power. Kingship belongs to a closed chapter of history, and the sort of wartime one-man rule inspired by ardor for national honor is something which not even Charles de Gaulle chose to embrace as a permanent way of life.

But the reigning principle, democracy, is not so easily explained, and its espousal may lead equally logically to several quite distinct ways of life. Democracy means that the people of a nation themselves are considered the only source of power and (or) authority (the two terms being interchangeable in democratic discourse). But although by grounding itself on popular will alone it excludes *a priori* all substantive principles from what it considers the source of political power, democracy can not, any more than any other regime, engage in value-free politics. Politics is conducted by men, and men make choices, each man, each polity willy-nilly systematically showing preferences, revealing habits and character. Thus democracy more than any other type of regime exists in what we might call hyphenated forms: social-democracy, capitalist-democracy, socialist-democracy, liberal-social-democracy, even American democracy, British democracy, and so on. De Tocqueville a century and a half ago pointed out to Frenchmen how the very same principle of popular sovereignty which had wreaked so much harm on the social fabric of France was largely responsible for the happiness of the peoples of the United States of America because there it was animated by different popular concerns, different mores, and channeled through different institutions. The result of political developments in France since the war, we contend, far from being undemocratic, should be considered as one of the principal branches, one of the most eminently logical and legitimate offsprings of the democratic family.

Compatibility of the French experience with democracy

Democracy, the classic texts tell us, is a daily-renewable contract among equals for the aggregate benefit of all. No society is as concerned with contracts as the French. The state and virtually every social organism try to further their own purposes, be they stability, wages, working conditions, production quotas, housing conditions, political support, via "social" collective contracts. All regimes but the most tyrannical recognize the validity of contracts, but only in democracies is public life thought to be built on them. This emphasis on contracts proceeds from the basic understanding of public life as merely an extension of the private lives of particular individuals and corporations. The purpose of each contracting party is to increase the size and comfort of its private sphere.

The social reformist thrust of the French state, involving as it does the change in the way of life of the many by the efforts of the few, is also very much within the tradition of European democracy. De Tocqueville even foresaw that with the majority's consent, though not necessarily with its approval, reforms would increasingly shrink every individual's private sphere. The fact that every Frenchman's sphere of wholly private activity is today incomparably smaller than it was under Louis XIV should not be taken as an indication that recent French governments have been moving away from democracy; quite the contrary.

Nor should the decreasing role of Parliament and of all elected officials but the President be taken as an indication of a waning of democratic spirit. The increase in the prerogatives of the executive and bureaucracy is bemoaned by few other than those who feel personally diminished by any given act of the state. Who bemoans a subsidy, an exclusive franchise, or a job? True, there is very little that can be called positive support for the bureaucratic state, and people are perhaps no more happy with their government today than they ever were, but it would be unrealistic to say that the shift of power from individuals and corporations to the state, and from elected to appointed officials, has been accomplished despite popular opposition. Distrust of popular assemblies, centralization, rigorous affirmation of the general will, are themes which have characterized a certain conception of modern democracy visible as well in the 18th century Frenchmen Rousseau and Buonarroti as in the 20th century Americans James MacGregor Burns and Richard Hofstadter.

The charge that the modern French state is insensitive to popular opinion must also be quickly rejected: it is, especially since May 1968, very sensitive to non-official opinions, providing they represent social forces capable of significantly contributing to a mass denial of the state such as occurred then. It is a regime concerned first of all with survival, and convinced that popular support is essential to it. Of course the legal status of cooperative consultation is uncertain: "representatives" of any interest group have little legal, and according to some older views of democracy, no theoretical standing, for they were not chosen by the whole population on whose behalf they act; furthermore, modern democracy does not recognize "partial" representation. From another standpoint, though, it can be said that any group which succeeds in making itself heard over any other contending to speak for the same social category, or any group which makes itself listened to by the state better than any of its competitors, evidently speaks with a louder voice, and why not the voice of more supporters? But no group in this democratic society has the legal right to do anything for itself which is not approved by the state. Group activity in fact is directed almost exclusively at getting the state to act. In practice, this means that groups will do what they desire to the extent that they can marshal and organize their supporters. The people are the key.

The people, of course, can vote the President out of office and can say no to his referendum proposals. It is even easier for the people to sanction the state in its highest than in its lowest offices, since to do the latter takes work, organization, discipline. To do the former it is but necessary to cast a ballot. They may not have the opportunity to give specific directions to the massive administrative apparatus which is the state, but they do not lack opportunities to deny it.

It may also be objected that modern France is not truly democratic because power is held by an elite. Modern research, however, has shown that the traditional theory of democracy according to which each citizen is possessed of an equal amount of power must take account of the total lack of public ambitions, the unwillingness of a large and growing part of the population to get mixed up in political things. The split between the political and the unpolitical classes is, *mutatis-mutandis,* a worldwide phenomenon in democratic countries, and, therefore, something democratic theory will just have to get used to. But if a whole class of elected leaders on the national and local level is giving up its important role to bureaucrats and leaders of interest groups, the latter appear to be made more in the image of the people they represent than the former. Thus is ever more fulfilled, albeit in a different way, the democratic principle that rulers and ruled be identical.

In an article published in *The New York Times Magazine* (29 August 1971) entitled "A New European Man Runs France," Mr. Keith Botsford tells of his impression upon meeting the President of the French Republic: "He is one of us." By this he meant that the man had risen to the very top in his country strictly by judicious use of "sober skills" largely available to anyone. Because of this, he says, the man is close to his people and to the spirit of modernity. But the article also mentions M. Pompidou's highly abnormal intelligence and his rise to the top of the French educational meritocracy. He is not only in power, but is generally recognized by virtue of his *agrégation* as intrinsically at least a cut above other men. The latter is not in the spirit of modernity, for as we previously mentioned, no principle is more generally under

attack in France today than that of the educational meritocracy. But if the principle of merit, necessarily anchored to
a notion of goodness, goes, nothing but success itself will dis-
tinguish the ruler from the ruled except the power to rule itself.

Modern Democracy rid of old illusions

Outside of the United States, France is the world's oldest
democracy. From their long experience with democracy, its
people and politicians have distilled in their present ways a
profound and internally consistent understanding of democracy; not the only understanding possible (witness the American Republic prior to 1936), but one which is nonetheless
grounded in experience. It is a grown-up democracy which
has shed many of the illusions of its youth.

One will not easily find in France someone who will affirm
with a straight face that the public rules the country by means
of the votes it casts in national elections. The dogma that each
individual forms an equal part of the sovereign and shares
equally in the government of the state is voiced by no one
but a few ultra-leftists and then rather as an epithet against
those who hold power than as a serious statement of belief.
Elections are a means of choosing among rulers, not a means
of self-government. The men who come on television to talk
politics are not primarily the people's delegates, but the men
who run the country, and who decide how much things will
cost, what wages will be paid. Voting is not an exercise of
sovereignty, but a means of dealing with it.

Public affairs even more than private ones are seen as
clashes among interests. Politicians and private men as well
have their own particular interests in mind, are competent
about them, and one can lend a measure of confidence to
someone who lays his cards on the table. But any expression
of what may be good or desirable in itself is simply presumed
to be a disguise or a sublimation of desires. Modern politics
is based not on judgment, but on will. Laws are the expression

of the prevailing resultant (in the mathematical sense) will. Still, it is preferable to submit to the will of the state rather than risk subordination to that of private parties, for the former is faceless and all powerful (Voltaire's well-born lion), and it is therefore no shame to submit to it.

Modern democracy, in accord with democratic theorists of the 17th and 18th centuries, but in opposition to the traditions of the last 150 years, does not believe that government can be limited. Besides, the greatest threat to personal well-being, it is now believed, arises when the state is no longer sufficiently strong to balance its component social forces. Modern democracy believes that it alone keeps the society it has fashioned from destroying itself.

Nonetheless, modern democracy has largely discarded earlier notions of the state as composed of isolated individuals. Modern democracy has recognized the need for social and political corporations or institutions to play a mediating role between the individual and the state. Yet it is unsure of what kind of intermediate corporations to foster, and it fears that by fostering them, it will weaken its own power and risk fragmenting the state. The modern democratic state, somewhat like the Greek polis, but unlike the political units of mediaeval Europe, claims to be that human collectivity which includes all others but is itself included in none. It admits that citizens participate in the life of the national community as members of parties or interest groups far more readily than it is willing to admit that the national community is the sum of local communities or families. Parties and pressure groups are different from local communities and families in at least two essential respects: they are, like the democratic state itself, contractual groups making no claim to inviolability because of "natural" origin, and they are groups which—with some exceptions, notably the Communist Party—engage their members only partially, seek to further but some of their interests, and lay no claim to representing whole persons or other natural beings like families and towns. Modern democratic states are much more wary of local governments, churches, families, in short, of the socio-political corporations which used to be the building blocks of pre-democratic polities, because they dispute the state's claim that it is the sole representative of citizens and because they do so on bases not necessarily contractual and therefore foreign to the spirit of modernity.

Believing strong "intermediary corporations" are necessary, modern democratic statesmen try to avoid fostering the growth of "states within the state." Thus they hope to transform all associations into interest groups, hoping that each citizen will engage parts of his interest in many and himself in none. The interests of all can then be rationally harmonized. But partial, particular (in Rousseau's sense) communities within the whole pose difficulties to the state which are no less great for being in conformity with the spirit of democracy: each group's rapacity is theoretically limited only by its strength, and every one feels the temptation to join in a temporary coalition with others to bring low the common arbiter, the state. How can the latter defend itself? To what can it appeal? Traditionally, democrats have trusted people's knowledge of their own interest. But if this knowledge were farsighted enough and widespread enough, social conflict would be self-adjusting. Personal interest may indeed be a stable point in the human heart, but men, it seems, are at least as likely to mistake its location as any other point's.

Finally, we note that modern democracy differs from earlier forms in that it is committed to provide not the conditions of an equitable pursuit of happiness, but happiness itself. In this it resembles some pre-democratic regimes. But while these had some very definite and complex ideas on what constitutes human happiness, democracy is doctrinally bound to rely on what it considers the only stable point in the human heart. Recent years have seen, in France as elsewhere, some talk by leading politicians and social scientists of the absolute importance of ethical values. In high-level international conferences on the future of defense, youth, growth, and the environment, participants from France, America and the rest of the democratic West, who believe they can personally do very well without religion, vent their fears that democratic society cannot do without a certain kind of man, and a certain kind of civilization, and that these qualities may be indissolubly tied to ways of thinking foreign to modernity. Today as always, fear can be the midwife of wisdom.

Bibliography

Adenauer, Konrad. *World Indivisible.* New York, 1955.

Almond, Gabriel A. and Sidney Verba. *The Civic Culture.* Princeton, 1963.

Andrews, William G. *French Politics and Algeria.* New York, 1962.

Ardagh, John. *The New French Revolution.* New York, 1968.

Arendt, Hannah. *On Revolution.* New York, 1963.

Aron, Raymond. *La Révolution Introuvable.* Paris, 1968.

Avril, Pierre. *Le Régime Politique de la Vème République.* Paris, 1964.

_____. *Politics in France.* Baltimore, 1969.

Banfield, Edward. *The Moral Basis of a Backward Society.* Glencoe, Ill., 1958.

Bauchet, P., *Propriété Publique et Planification.* Paris, 1962.

Beaufre, Général André. *La Défense et la Dissuasion.* Paris, 1964.

_____. *La Stratégie.* Paris, 1963.

Bergson, Henri. *The Two Sources of Morality and Religion.* New York, 1964.

Bodin, Jean. *Six Books of the Commonwealth* (1576). New York, 1955.

Brinton, Crane. *The Americans and the French*. Harvard University Press, 1966.

Brugmans, Henri. *L'Europe à faire*. Bruges, 1972.

Bruhère, Jacquier, (Michel Debré and Emmanuel Monick). *Refaire la France: L'Effort d'une Génération*. Paris, 1945.

Burdeau, Georges. *Droit Constitutionnel et Institutions Politiques*. Paris, 1962.

Burns, James McGregor. *The Deadlock of Democracy*. Englewood Cliffs, 1963.

Chabod, Federico. *Storia dell Idea d'Europa*. Bari, 1963.

Chapsal, Jacques. *La Vie Politique en France Depuis 1940*. Paris, 1969.

Club Jean Moulin. *L'Etat et le Citoyen*. Paris, 1961.

Cohn-Bendit, Daniel. *Obsolete Communism—The Left Wing Alternative*. New York, 1969.

Coudenhove Kalergi, R. N. *Crusade for Pan-Europe, Autobiography of a Man and a Movement*. New York, 1943.

Crozier, Michel. *The Bureaucratic Phenomenon*. Paris, 1967.

de Gaulle, Charles. *La Discorde chez l'ennemi*. Paris, 1924.

———. *Le Fil de L'Epée*. Paris, 1932.

———. *Vers l'Armée de Metier*. Paris, 1934.

———. *La France et Son Armée*. Paris, 1938.

———. Memoires de Guerre; Vol. I, *L'appel 1940-1942*. Paris, 1959; Vol. II, *L'unite 1942-1944*. Paris, 1959; Vol. III, *Le salut 1944-1946*. Paris, 1959.

———. Discours et Messages: *Pendant la Guerre (Juin 1940-Janvier 1946)*, Paris, 1970; *Dans l'Attente (Février 1946-Avril 1958)*, Paris, 1970; *Avec le Renouveau (Mai 1958-Juillet 1962)*, Paris, 1970; *Pour l'Effort (Août 1962-Décembre 1965)*, Paris, 1970; *Vers le Terme (Janvier 1966-Avril 1969)*, Paris, 1970.

———. *Mémoires d'espoir:* Vol. I, *Le Renouveau (1958-1962)*, Paris, 1970; Vol. II., *L'Effort (1962-)*, Paris, 1971.

Debré, Michel. *La Mort de L'Etat Républicain*. Paris, 1947.

_____.*Ces Princes qui nous Gouvernent.* Paris, 1957.

_____.*Refaire une Démocratie, Un Etat, Un Pouvoir.* Paris, 1958.

Detton, Hervé. *L'Administration Régionale et locale en France.* Paris, 1953.

Duverger, M. *Cinquième République.* Paris, 1960.

Erhard, Ludwig. *The Economics of Success.* Princeton, 1963.

Escoubře, Pierre. *Les Grand Corps de L'Etat.* Paris, 1971.

Fortescue, Sir John. *De Laudibus Legum Angliae.* S. B. Chrimes, ed. Cambridge, 1942.

Friedrich, Carl J. *Constitutional Democracy.* Cambridge, 1956.

Goguel, Francois and Alfred Grosser. *La Politique en France.* Paris, 1964.

Graubard, S. *A New Europe?* New York, 1964.

Hackett, A. M. and J. Hackett. *Economic Planning in France.* London, 1963.

Hallstein, Walter. *United Europe.* Cambridge, 1962.

Hermens, Ferdinand A. *The Representative Republic.* Notre Dame, 1958.

Jouvenal, Bertrand de. *L'Art de la Conjecture.* Monaco, 1964.

Kahn, Herman. *On Thermonuclear Warfare.* New York, 1960.

Kendall, Willmoore. *The Conservative Affirmation.* Chicago, 1963.

Kleiman, Robert. *Atlantic Crisis.* New York, 1964.

Kohn, Hans. *Nationalism.* Princeton, 1955.

Laqueur, Walter. *The Rebirth of Europe.* New York, 1970.

Larteguy, Jean. *Les Centurions.* Paris, 1960.

_____. *Les Prétoriens.* Paris, 1961.

Lukacs, John. *The Decline and Rise of Europe.* New York, 1965.

Lutz, Vera. *French Planning.* Washington, 1965.

Macridis and Brown, *The De Gaulle Republic.* Illinois, 1960.

Massu, Général (Ret.) Jacques. *La Vraie Bataille d'Alger.* Paris, 1971.

Michels, Robert. *Political Parties.* New York, 1962.

Montesquieu. *L'Esprit des Lois.* Paris, 1748.

Nolte, Ernst. *Three Faces of Fascism.* New York, 1969.

Ortega Y Gasset, Jose. *España Invertebrada.* Madrid, 1964.

Paranque, Regis. *Le Malaise Français.* Paris, 1967.

Pickles, Dorothy. *Algeria and France.* London, 1963.

———. *The Fifth Republic.* London, 1960.

Postan, M. M. *An Economic History of Western Europe, 1945-1964.* London, 1965.

Publius. *The Federalist Papers.* New York, 1961.

Renan, Ernest. *Qu'est ce qu'une Nation?* Paris, 1882.

Roy, Jules. *La Guerre d'Algérie.* Paris, 1960.

Ruggiero, Guido de. *History of European Liberalism.* Boston, 1959.

Servan-Schreiber, Jean-Jacques. *The American Challenge.* Paris, 1965.

———. *The Spirit of May.* Paris, 1968.

Schuman, Robert. *Pour L'Europe.* Paris, 1964.

Schumpeter, Joseph. *Capitalism, Socialism and Democracy.* New York, 1942.

Shirer, William. *La Chute de la Troisième Republique.* Paris, 1970.

Soustelle, Jacques. *L'Espérance Trahie.* Paris, 1962.

Tocqueville, Alexis de. *De la Democratie en Amérique.*

———. *L'Ancien Régime et la Révolution.*

———. *Oeuvres Completes.* Paris, 1954.

Tournoux, J. R. *Pétain et De Gaulle.* Paris, 1964.

Vedel, Georges. *La Dépolitisation, Mythe ou Réalité?* Paris, 1962.

Voegelin, Eric. *The New Science of Politics.* Chicago, 1952.

Williams, Philip M. *French Politicians and Elections, 1951-1969.* London, 1970.

Wylie, Laurence. *Village in the Vaucluse.* Harvard, 1957.